Excel

Get the Results You

SmartStudy 7

Mathematics

Allyn Jones

PASCAL
PRESS

Copyright © 2013 Allyn Jones

ISBN 978 1 74125 466 2

Pascal Press
PO Box 250 Glebe NSW 2037
(02) 8585 4044
www.pascalpress.com.au

Publisher: Vivienne Joannou
Project editors: May McCool and Rosemary Peers
Edited by May McCool
Proofread by Chris Greef
Answers checked by Peter Little
Cover and page design by DiZign Pty Ltd
Typeset by Post Pre-press
Printed by Green Giant Press

Students
All care has been taken in compiling this book, but please check with your teacher
about the exact requirements of the course as this can change from year to year.

TABLE OF CONTENTS

TAKE THESE REVISION STEPS TO SUCCESS!

Step 1 Study Notes

- This section contains valuable **suggestions**, **tips** and **essential points** about the topic.
- When reading this section, **highlight** the points that are new to you or that you consistently forget. You could also **rewrite** these points so that you are making a summary of the Study Notes. Keep this summary in a prominent place at home—you could stick it on a mirror, wall or door.
- Work carefully through the **checklist** at the end of the section to ensure that you have mastered each of the listed skills.
- If there is something that you are **not sure about**, take time out to read through your class notes, textbooks or another relevant *Excel* book. (Check our website at www.pascalpress.com.au for more titles.)

Step 2 Skills Check

- Check that you know the **basic skills** you need to successfully complete the topic.
- Once you have completed the check, **mark your work** quickly by looking at the answers at the bottom of the page. This is **instant feedback** for you. The **worked solutions** are located at the back of the book if you want to check the working of any answer.
- If you have **scored less than 50%** in this section then you should revise your basic skills.

Step 3 Intermediate Test

- This test has very similar questions to the ones you will get in your **class test** or **exam**.
- Look carefully for the **Hints** which are provided for the trickiest questions—these appear at the bottom of the page.
- **Marks** are allocated for each question. These are similar to the marks in your tests.
- Time yourself—**check** how much **time** you have got to complete the test. Also look at the **total marks** of the test to calculate approximately how much time you should spend on each question. For example, if there are twenty marks in total and twenty minutes have been allocated for completion of the test, then spend about one minute on each mark. If you cannot complete all the questions within the suggested time, you may need to revise the topic.
- Fill in the **Your Feedback** panel once you have marked your work in order to calculate your percentage mark. Then complete the **Test & Exam Results** on page 161 to keep a running total of all your test marks.

Step 4 Advanced Test

- This test features only **extension questions** such as problem–solving questions.
- This test is not like a class test, as all the questions in it are challenging. There are no easier questions in it. Mastery of questions in this test, however, will ensure you gain top marks in your class tests and exams, and will also prepare you for the Mathematics you will learn next year.
- **Marks** are allocated for each question. These are similar to the marks in your tests.
- Time yourself—**check** how much **time** you have to complete the test. Also look at the **total marks** of the test to calculate approximately how much time you should spend on each question. For example, if there are forty marks in total and forty minutes have been allocated for completion of the test, then spend about one minute on each mark.

- Fill in the **Your Feedback** panel once you have marked your work in order to calculate your percentage mark. Then complete the **Test & Exam Results** on page 161 to keep a running total of all your test marks.

Step 5 Check Your Solutions

- **Worked solutions** to all questions are found at the back of the book. Work through the solutions to any questions that you got wrong.
- **Longer questions** are usually worth two or more marks and will involve some working. You should set out all your working, because in Maths you may get some marks for your working even if your answer is wrong.
- The **ticks** that appear in the worked solutions indicate those parts of the working which receive marks. Therefore, even if your answer is wrong, you may be entitled to some marks for what you have written. Compare the worked solution to your own working to find out whether you are entitled to any marks for the question.
- If you still **cannot understand** how the correct answer was obtained, revise that part of the topic and, if necessary, refer to your class notes or ask your teacher for help. It is important to learn from your mistakes.

Step 6 Test & Exam Results

- Go to the **Test & Exam Results** section on page 161 to record your test score as a percentage. When you have completed all topics you will be able to determine your areas of weakness and your areas of strength.
- It is important that you know which **areas need further work**—to 'know what you don't know'. The more you prepare for the topic tests, the more successful you will be and the more you will remember when you sit your end-of-term/semester/year test or exam.

Step 7 Tips for the Sample Exam Papers

- These **useful tips** appear on page 84. Read them before you start one of the Sample Exams (see Step 8 below).

Step 8 Sample Exam Papers

- Three **Sample Exam Papers** are provided at the end of the book. These are of three levels of difficulty: Average, Above Average and Difficult. The Above Average paper will be very similar to your final examination.
- Before attempting the Sample Exam Papers, make sure that you have completed all of the **Tests** and have worked through the solutions to all questions that you answered incorrectly.
- Set aside the **time allowed** for the paper and complete it under **exam conditions**—no sneaking a look at your notes or textbooks! That way you will be better prepared for your final exam.
- **Worked solutions** to the Sample Exam Papers are found at the back of the book. Work through the solutions to any questions that you got wrong. Carefully note the **ticks** in the worked solutions and remember to give yourself marks for correct working. Write down your total marks for each section in the **Your Score** boxes at the end of each part of the paper, then add them up to get a total percentage for each test.

HOW TO USE THIS BOOK TO STUDY FOR A CLASS TEST, HALF-YEARLY OR END-OF-YEAR EXAM

Depending on your teacher or school, you will be given a variety of tests and exams each year. There may be a single-topic test, a test that covers a number of topics, a semester test or exam, or even a half-yearly or yearly exam.

Step 1 | **Find out** which topics will be covered in the class test.

- To do this, look at your class workbook/textbook, laptop/tablet or online study program, and ask your teacher.
- For example, your class test may be on Multiples, Factors, Primes, Numbers and Directed Numbers.

Step 2 | **Match** the topics that your test is on to the topics in this book.

- For example, the first two units in this book cover Multiples, Factors, Primes, Numbers and Directed Numbers.

Step 3 | **Use** this book to study the topics being tested.

- For example, the first two units in this book contain the topics you will study for your class test!

Note:
- When you are using this book to study for a **half-yearly** test, follow the same steps as above—the only difference being that you will have more topics to revise of course!
- When you are using this book to study for an **end-of-year** test, you will more than likely need to study the whole book!

MULTIPLES, FACTORS AND PRIMES
Number and Place Value

1   If a number is multiplied by a second number, then a **multiple** is formed.
For example, the multiples of 7 are 7, 14, 21, 28, 35, 42, 49, etc.

2   When multiples of two or more numbers are listed, **common multiples** can be identified. Often we find the **lowest common multiple (LCM)** of two or more numbers.
For example, the lowest common multiple of 4 and 6 is 12.

3   Any whole number that divides exactly into another number is called a **factor** of that number.
For example, the factors of 12 are 1, 2, 3, 4, 6, 12.

4   When two or more numbers have the same factor, it is said to be the **common factor**. Often we find the **highest common factor (HCF)** of two or more numbers.
For example, the highest common factor of 18 and 24 is 6.

5   A **prime** number has only two factors: 1 and itself. Examples of primes are 2, 3, 5, 7, etc.

6   A **composite** number has more than two factors. Examples of composites are 4, 6, 8, 9, etc.

7   Note that 0 and 1 are **neither prime nor composite**.

8   A **factor tree** is useful for expressing a number as the **product of its prime factors**. These factors can be expressed in index form.
For example, use a factor tree to express 120 as a product of its prime factors, in index form. i.e. $120 = 2 \times 2 \times 2 \times 3 \times 5 = 2^3 \times 3 \times 5$

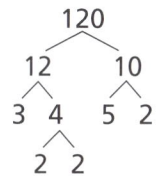

9   These **divisibility tests** are helpful when finding factors of a certain number:
- Divisible by (or multiple of) 2: The last digit is even or zero.
- Divisible by (or multiple of) 3: The sum of the digits in the number is divisible by 3.
- Divisible by (or multiple of) 4: The number formed by the last two digits is divisible by 4.
- Divisible by (or multiple of) 5: The last digit must be 5 or 0.
- Divisible by (or multiple of) 6: The number satisfies the tests for 2 and 3.
- Divisible by (or multiple of) 8: The number formed by the last three digits is divisible by 8.
- Divisible by (or multiple of) 9: The sum of the digits in the number is divisible by 9.
- Divisible by (or multiple of) 10: The last digit must be 0.

For example, is 846 divisible by 3?
We add the digits: $8 + 4 + 6 = 18$, and as 18 is divisible by 3, then 846 is divisible by 3.

Checklist
Can you:

1 *Understand the terms multiple, factor, prime and composite?* ☐
2 *Determine the LCM and HCF of two or more numbers?* ☐
3 *Use a factor tree to find factors?* ☐
4 *Determine and apply divisibility tests to quickly find factors of large numbers?* ☐
5 *Solve word problems including multiples and factors?* ☐

MULTIPLES, FACTORS AND PRIMES

Number and Place Value

SKILLS CHECK

1 Write down the first five multiples of:

  a 7   **b** 11   **c** 13

2 Find the lowest common multiple (LCM) of the following:

  a 3 and 5   **b** 10 and 12   **c** 3, 4 and 6

3 Answer true or false:

  a 48 is a multiple of 3   **b** 120 is a multiple of 2, 3, 4 and 5

4 Write down the factors of:

  a 20   **b** 36   **c** 40

5 Find the highest common factor (HCF) of:

  a 12 and 16   **b** 18 and 24   **c** 10, 20 and 25

6 Write down any prime numbers:

  a less than 10   **b** between 25 and 40

  c greater than 20 but less than 25   **d** between 100 and 110

7 What composite numbers are:

  a less than 12?   **b** between 20 and 30?

  c odd and less than 20?   **d** greater than 40 but less than 50?

8 Answer true or false:

  a 4 is composite

  b 21 is prime

  c 23 is the only prime between 20 and 30

  d there are 5 composites between 10 and 20

9 By the use of a factor tree or otherwise, rewrite the following as products of their prime factors, written in index form:

  a 60   **b** 84   **c** 150

10 Answer true or false:

  a 26 805 is divisible by 5   **b** 129 is divisible by 3

  c 135 is divisible by 4   **d** 24 546 760 is divisible by 10

  e 2 is a factor of 43 983   **f** 9 is a factor of 243

  g 8 is a factor of 3124   **h** 6 is a factor of 246

PAGE 102

Answers 1a 7,14,21,28,35 b 11,22,33,44,55 c 13,26,39,52,65 2a 15 b 60 c 12 3a T b T 4a 1,2,4,5,10,20 b 1,2,3,4,6,9,12,18,36 c 1,2,4,5,8,10,20,40 5a 4 b 6 c 5 6a 2,3,5,7 b 29,31,37 c 23 d 101,103,107,109 7a 4,6,8,9,10 b 21,22,24,25,26,27,28 c 9,15 d 42,44,45,46,48,49 8a T b F c F d T 9a 2²×3×5 b 2²×3×7 c 2×3×5² 10a T b T c F d T e F f T g F h T

Part A   Multiple Choice

1   The lowest common multiple of 4 and 6 is:

A   8   B   12   C   18   D   24   (1 mark)

2   A factor of 78 is:

A   3   B   5   C   7   D   9   (1 mark)

3   Which of the following numbers has a factor of 3?

A   2363   B   4762   C   861   D   3961   (1 mark)

4   The first multiple of 4 greater than 70 is:

A   71   B   72   C   73   D   74   (1 mark)

5   How many primes lie between 80 and 90?

A   2   B   3   C   4   D   5   (1 mark)

6   The only prime between 90 and 100 is:

A   91   B   93   C   95   D   97   (1 mark)

Part B   Short Answer

7   Find all multiples of:

a   4 between 45 and 70   b   6 between 73 and 105   (2 marks each)

8   What is a possible missing digit in: *Hint 1*

a   2387___ , if it is a multiple of 5?   b   476___24 if it is divisible by 6? (1 mark each)

9   Using two different methods, show that 3 is a factor of 375.   (2 marks)

10   Use a factor tree to express the following as a product of its prime factors:

a   180   b   420   (3 marks each)

11   What number am I?

a   I am divisible by 3 and 5. I lie between a prime and a composite.
   I am a multiple of 9, and less than 100.   (2 marks)

b   I am a multiple of 4 and 6. I am greater than 50 but less than 80. I am divisible by 9. (2 marks)

12   Laura and Mitchell are training around a circular track. Starting at the same time,
Laura takes 8 minutes to complete a lap, while Mitchell takes 6 minutes.
How long is it before they meet again at the starting point? *Hint 2*   (2 marks)

13   Two taps are dripping, one every 7 seconds and the other every 12 seconds. They drip
simultaneously at 10 am. At what time will the taps next drip together?   (2 marks)

14   In a bag of jelly beans, there are enough to share equally among four, five or six people.
What is the smallest number of jelly beans in the bag? *Hint 3*   (2 marks)

Hint 1: Use divisibility tests.
Hint 2: Look for the lowest common multiple.
Hint 3: Look for the lowest common multiple of
   the three numbers.

Your Feedback

$\dfrac{}{30} \times 100\% = \boxed{}\%$

PAGE 102

PAGE 161

40 MINUTES

ADVANCED TEST

1 The numbers from 1 to 50 are written on identical cards and placed in a box. What percentage of the cards are:
a prime? (2 marks)
b composite? (2 marks)

2 Find the highest common factor of:
a 32 and 52 (1 mark)
b 120 and 150 (1 mark)
c 75 and 225 (1 mark)

3 Find the lowest common multiple of:
a 16 and 24 (1 mark)
b 15 and 25 (1 mark)
c 25 and 40 (1 mark)

4 At a display booth at a trade show, sample bags are handed to customers. Some of the bags have special items. Every third bag has a pen, every fourth bag has a USB stick and every fifth bag has a calculator. How often will a bag contain all three items? (2 marks)

5 Use a factor tree to express the following as a product of their prime factors, expressed in index notation:
a 400 (2 marks)
b 1089 (2 marks)

6 Two lights are turned on at the same time. One blinks every six seconds and the other every eight seconds. The lights are turned off after five minutes. How many times had the lights blinked at the same time? (2 marks)

7 What is the smallest number that is a multiple of 1, 2, 3 ,4, 5 and 6? (2 marks)

8 Consider the pattern:
$4^1 = 4, 4^2 = 16, 4^3 = 64, ...$
What is the last digit in 4^{2014}? (1 mark)

9 A year seven class and a year eight class are combined for a special lesson. The year seven class has 24 students and the year eight class has 30 students. The students are to divide into groups of the same size. Each small group needs to have the same number of year seven students. How many groups are possible? (2 marks)

10 I am a three-digit number. I am divisible by 9. My middle digit is prime. I am a multiple of 6. I lie between 600 and 700. What number am I? (1 mark)

11 A nursery worker has 72 small trees to be displayed in lines in a rectangular shape. Each horizontal and vertical line must have more than 5 trees. How many different arrangements are possible? (2 marks)

12 Numbers have been represented in the form of a product of prime factors expressed in index notation. What numbers are represented?
a $3^2 \times 7^2$ (2 marks)
b $3^2 \times 2^4 \times 5^2$ (2 marks)

13 Jay bakes 48 choc-chip biscuits and 60 anzac biscuits. He places them in plastic containers to give to his friends. Jay wants every container to have the same number of each biscuit. What is the greatest number of containers he can use? (2 marks)

14 Here is a list of numbers.
76 84 148 224 372 480
How many numbers in the list are
a multiples of 6? (1 mark)
b divisible by 8? (1 mark)

15 The area of a rectangular garden bed is 48 m². If the length of the bed is a whole number, how many different perimeters are possible? (2 marks)

16 Laura picked oranges from her tree to give to her friends. For every 5 oranges she gave to Sam, she gave 8 to Jackie and 12 to Peta. What is the smallest number of oranges that she picked? (2 marks)

17 Sara has 160 white beads, 120 red beads and 75 pink beads. She wants to use all of the beads to make bracelets containing white, red and pink beads. If Sara makes the greatest number of matching bracelets possible, how many red beads are used on each bracelet? (2 marks)

18 The floor of a bathroom measuring 3 metres by 2.4 metres is tiled using the largest square tiles possible. No tiles needed to be cut to complete the job. How many tiles were used? (2 marks)

Your Feedback

$$\frac{\boxed{}}{42} \times 100\% = \boxed{} \%$$

PAGE 103

PAGE 161

1 The language of mathematics:

Addition: sum, total, ... **Subtraction**: difference, exceed, ...

Multiplication: product, times, ... **Division**: quotient, ...

2 Symbols are used in mathematics:

= is **equal to** > is **greater than** < is **less than**

≠ is **not equal to** ≥ is **greater than or equal to** ≤ is **less than or equal to**

≈ is **approximate to**

For example, write in symbols: the sum of six and eight is less than or equal to the product of five and nine. $\therefore 6 + 8 \leq 5 \times 9$

3 **Order of operations**: When evaluating numerical expressions, the important rule is:

Brackets **O**rders **D**ivision or **M**ultiplication then **A**ddition or **S**ubtraction (**BODMAS**)

For example, evaluate (or find the value of):

a $10 - 3 \times 2 = 10 - 6$
$= 4$

b $8 \times 5 - 12 \times 3 = 40 - 36$
$= 4$

c $30 - (4 + 6 \times 3) = 30 - (4 + 18)$
$= 8$

4 A **factor tree** helps to find square and cube roots. For example, to find the square root of 324.

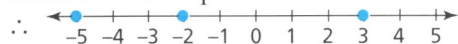

$$\therefore 324 = 2 \times 2 \times 9 \times 9$$
$$= 2 \times 9 \times 2 \times 9$$
$$= 18 \times 18$$
$$\therefore \sqrt{324} = 18$$

5 **Integers** are the **positive** and **negative** counting numbers and zero. i.e. ..., –2, –1, 0, +1, +2, ... They are often referred to as **directed numbers**. Remember that the positive sign is usually ignored, i.e. +4 = 4 or (+4) = 4

6 **Number line:** We extend the number line left of zero to include the negative numbers. The number line helps to order directed numbers.

$\therefore$

$\xleftarrow{} \underset{-5\ -4\ -3\ -2\ -1\ \ 0\ \ 1\ \ 2\ \ 3\ \ 4\ \ 5}{\rule{6cm}{0.4pt}} \xrightarrow{}$

7 **Adding and subtracting integers**: When adding, we can use the number line and move to the right. When subtracting, we can use the number line and move to the left. For example,

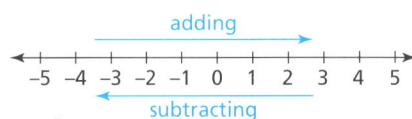

a $4 + -2 = 4 - 2 = 2$ [adding a negative is the same as subtracting]

b $-6 - (-2) = -6 + 2 = -4$ [subtracting a negative is the same as adding]

Summary of **adding and subtracting positives and negatives**:

+ + = + **+ – = –** **– + = –** **– – = +**

8 **Multiplying and dividing integers:** We use the following rules:

+ × + = + **+ × – = –** **– × + = –** **– × – = +**

+ ÷ + = + **+ ÷ – = –** **– ÷ + = –** **– ÷ – = +**

Checklist
Can you:

1 *Apply rules to carry out mental computations?* ☐

2 *Use factor trees to find square and cube roots?* ☐

3 *Compare, order, add, subtract, multiply and divide directed numbers?* ☐

4 *Solve word problems involving directed numbers?* ☐

1. Write in symbols:
   a. The quotient of seventy and ten equals seven.
   b. The sum of five, three and eight is less than eighteen.
   c. Three hundred and sixty five thousand is greater than ten cubed.
   d. Three squared and two cubed is the same as seventeen.
   e. The product of five and the sum of four and two is equal to thirty.
   f. The square of the sum of eight and seven is greater than or equal to one hundred.

2. Evaluate:
   a. $15 - 3 \times 4$
   b. $12 - (3 - 2)$
   c. $40 \div 5 \times 2$
   d. $3 \times 2 + 4 \times 6$
   e. $11(2 + 5 \times 3)$
   f. $21 \div (4 + 3)$

3. Find the value of:
   a. $(4 + 6) \div (2 + 3)$
   b. $(8 \times 7 - 9 \times 6)^2$
   c. $\sqrt{3 \times 4 \times 3 \times 4}$
   d. $\dfrac{12 \times 4}{6 \times 2}$
   e. $\dfrac{42 \div 7 + 3 \times 3}{21 - 3 \times 2}$
   f. $\sqrt{\dfrac{5 \times 7 + 1}{6 \times 3 \div 2}}$

4. Use a factor tree to find the square root of 225.

5. Arrange the following numbers in descending order:
   a. $-6, -10, 5, -3, 8$
   b. $0, -32, -8, 4, -2$

6. Arrange the following numbers in ascending order:
   a. $4, -1, -6, 5, 3$
   b. $-3, 8, -4, 2, -1$

7. On a number line, what number lies 3 units to the left of:
   a. 5
   b. 1
   c. -2

8. On a number line what number lies 6 units to the right of:
   a. 2
   b. -1
   c. -8

9. Insert $>, <$ or $=$ in the following:
   a. -6 ___ -2
   b. 5 ___ -6
   c. -3 ___ 2

10. Evaluate:
    a. $-3 + 5$
    b. $-5 + 2$
    c. $4 - 7$
    d. $-3 - 2$
    e. $-3 + 7$
    f. $-2 + 8$
    g. $2 + (-3)$
    h. $-2 - (-4)$
    i. $3 - (+2)$
    j. $-2 - (-1)$
    k. $9 + (-2)$
    l. $3 + (-5)$

11. Evaluate:
    a. 4×-3
    b. -2×-5
    c. -4×6
    d. -7×-3
    e. 8×-5
    f. $(-2)^2$
    g. $12 \div -3$
    h. $-8 \div -4$
    i. $18 \div -2$
    j. $-21 \div 7$
    k. $22 \div -2$
    l. $-30 \div -5$

PAGE 104

NUMBERS AND DIRECTED NUMBERS
Number and Place Value

INTERMEDIATE TEST

Part A Multiple Choice

1 Evaluate $16 - 4 \times 3$:

   A 36   **B** 12   **C** 8   **D** 4   (1 mark)

2 Which of the following equals 12?

   A $4 - (16 - 12)$ **B** $(8 + 16) \div (3 \times 2)$ **C** $\sqrt{5 \times 5 - 1}$ **D** $20 - 4 \times 2$ (1 mark)

3 Calculate $\dfrac{12 \times 4}{4 \times 3 \times 2}$

   A 72   **B** 12   **C** 4   **D** 2   (1 mark)

4 Evaluate $24 - \{(10 \div [2 + 3] \times 3) + 6\}$

   A 6   **B** 12   **C** 18   **D** 24   (1 mark)

5 The next number in the sequence 18, 11, 4, ___ is:

   A 7   **B** –7   **C** –3   **D** –18   (1 mark)

6 The temperature at 5 am this morning was $-2\,°C$. If by 9 am it had risen by $5°$, the new temperature was:

   A $2\,°C$ **B** $3\,°C$ **C** $5\,°C$ **D** $7\,°C$ (1 mark)

Part B Short Answer

7 Evaluate:

   a $16 - 3 \times (2 + 3)$ **b** $\sqrt{9 + 3 - 4 \times 2}$ (2 marks each)

8 Evaluate $\sqrt{576}$ using a factor tree.   (3 marks)

9 Write the following in symbols:

   a The sum of eighteen and seven is less than the product of four and nine.   (1 mark)

   b The quotient of sixty three and nine is greater than or equal to the difference between forty three and thirty nine.   (1 mark)

10 Insert grouping symbols to make the statement true:

   a $11 - 3 + 12 \div 6 - 2 = 4$ **b** $8 + 2 \times 16 - 3 \times 4 - 5 = 11$ (1 mark each)

11 Cassandra, in answering a word problem, wrote $-6 + 10$.
What might Casandra's word problem be?   (2 marks)

12 Write a number sentence describing the following situation and the final resulting floor.
'I park my car on the 3rd basement level of the underground car park, 3 floors below the ground level. I take the lift up 12 floors and then down 2 floors.' What floor am I on?   (2 marks)

13 Evaluate: *Hint 1*   (1 mark each)

   a $-4 + 2 \times 3$ **b** $5 - 4 \times 3$ **c** $12 \div 4 - 2 \times 5$ **d** $(18 - 7) - (3 + 6)$

   e $5 - 3 \times 7$ **f** $(3 - 5)(4 - 7)$ **g** $(3 - 6)^2$ **h** $(5 - 10) \div (3 - 8)$

Your Feedback

$$\frac{\boxed{}}{29} \times 100\% = \boxed{}\,\%$$

PAGE 105

PAGE 161

Hint 1: Apply the order of operations when evaluating.

1 Express the following in symbols:
- **a** the sum of twelve and sixteen is less than or equal to the product of six and eleven.
- **b** the quotient of eight and the sum of four and two is not equal to ten.
- **c** the product of ten and the sum of four and five is less than the difference between one hundred and two.
- **d** the square of the sum of four and three is greater than the cube of three.
- **e** the square root of the difference between twenty and four is the same as two squared.

(1 mark each)

2 Insert symbols to make the following true:
- **a** $4 + 7 \square 2 - 3 \square 4 = 6$ (1 mark)
- **b** $9 \square 5 - 10 \square 2 \times 2 = 5$ (1 mark)
- **c** $24 \square 4 + 3 \square 8 \square 4 = 12$ (1 mark)

3 Place grouping symbols in the numerical expressions to make true:
- **a** $4 \times 5 - 2 + 6 = 36$ (1 mark)
- **b** $16 - 2 + 3 \times 2 - 4 = 18$ (1 mark)
- **c** $24 \div 2 + 6 \times 6 \div 6 \div 2 = 6$ (1 mark)

4 Evaluate:
- **a** $25 - 4 \times 3 + 10 \div 2$
- **b** $3(11 - 2 \times 4)$
- **c** $(12 + 3 \times 2)(11 - 3^2)$
- **d** $\dfrac{14 + 4}{2 \times 3}$
- **e** $\sqrt{15 - 3 \times 2}$
- **f** $(18 - 4 \times 2)^3$
- **g** $4[2 + 3(15 - 3 \times 4)]$
- **h** $\sqrt{\dfrac{18 + 6 \times 3}{18 - 3 \times 3}}$
- **i** $\dfrac{1}{2}(12 - 2 \times 3)$
- **j** $(2^2 + 2 \times 3)^3 - (2^2 + 2 \times 3)^2$ (2 marks each)

5 On a number plane plot the points $A(-3, 2)$, $B(3, 2)$ and $C(0, -3)$.
Find the area of triangle ABC.   (2 marks)

6 Use a factor tree to write 784 as a product of its prime factors. Use this result to evaluate $\sqrt{784}$.   (2 marks)

7 Complete the sequences:
- **a** $17, 11, 5, \_\_\_, \_\_\_$ (1 mark)
- **b** $-83, -67, -51, \_\_\_, \_\_\_$ (1 mark)

8 The cost of tickets to a soccer match are as follows:

Adults: $62
Students (ages 2 to 16): $48
Seniors (aged 60 or above): $42
Infants (under 2): Free

Write an expression for the total cost for the following people and then calculate:
- **a** Mr and Mrs Smith and their son Adam aged 9   (2 marks)
- **b** Mrs Grace (a senior) and twin grand-daughters Erin and May aged 12   (2 marks)
- **c** Eleven members of the under-10s soccer team with their coach Mr Elms (aged 39) and manager Harry Smith (aged 63)   (2 marks)

9 The cost of a pie is $3 and a bottle of water $2. Bella purchased a pie and two bottles of water. Write an expression for the total cost of her purchase and then calculate it.   (2 marks)

10 Sandy is saving for her trip to Europe. She has already saved $690. For the next six weeks she plans to save $80 each week and then for the following ten weeks she wants to save $100 each week. Write an expression for her total savings and then evaluate the expression.   (2 marks)

11 Evaluate the following:
- **a** $7 - 5 \times 6$
- **b** $4 \times 9 - 10 \times 6$
- **c** $-6 + 4 \times 3 - 16 \div 4$
- **d** $-5 - 5 - 5 - 5$ (1 mark each)

12 On a number plane plot the points $P(-3, -2)$, $Q(-1, 2)$, $R(3, 2)$. What are the co-ordinates of S, where $PQRS$ is a parallelogram?   (2 marks)

13 If $✿ = -3$ and $\square = -5$, then find:
- **a** $\square + ✿$
- **b** $(✿ - \square)^3$ (1 mark each)

14 The temperatures at four ski resorts are recorded in the table below:

Resort	Temperature (°C)
Thredbo	5
Perisher	–1
Mt Hotham	–2
Falls Creek	4

What is the average temperature at the four resorts?   (2 marks)

Your Feedback

$\dfrac{\square}{57} \times 100\% = \square \%$

PAGE 105

PAGE 161

BASIC FRACTION CONCEPTS
Real Numbers

1. The **components** of a fraction are $\dfrac{\text{numerator}}{\text{denominator}}$. The separator line is called the **vinculum**.

2. A fraction with a denominator of 1 is a **whole number.**

    For example, 3 can also be written as $\dfrac{3}{1}$.

3. When the numerator is greater than the denominator, we have an **improper fraction**.

    For example, $\dfrac{13}{4}$ is an improper fraction.

4. An improper fraction is usually rewritten as a **mixed numeral**.

    For example, $\dfrac{13}{4} = 3\dfrac{1}{4}$, as 13 quarters makes 3 wholes with one quarter remaining.

5. To **simplify a fraction**, the numerator and denominator are divided by their **highest common factor**. This process is called **cancelling**.

    For example, $\dfrac{24}{40} = \dfrac{8 \times 3}{8 \times 5} = \dfrac{3}{5}$ $\therefore$ $\dfrac{24}{40}$ and $\dfrac{3}{5}$ are **equivalent fractions**.

6. To express **one quantity as a fraction of another**, we first ensure that there are common units. For example, what fraction is 40 cents of $6?

    First, change $6 to 600 cents, so that units are identical. $\therefore$ $\dfrac{40}{600} = \dfrac{1}{15}$

7. To **compare fractions**, we first make the denominators the same.

    For example, insert > or < to make a true statement for $\dfrac{3}{4}$ ⬚ $\dfrac{2}{3}$.

    $\therefore$ as $\dfrac{3}{4} = \dfrac{9}{12}$ and $\dfrac{2}{3} = \dfrac{8}{12}$ $\therefore$ $\dfrac{3}{4} > \dfrac{2}{3}$

8. To find the **reciprocal** of a fraction, we switch the numerator and denominator. (i.e. we flip the fraction upside down, or we invert the fraction.)

    For example, find the reciprocal of $2\dfrac{3}{4}$. $\therefore$ as $2\dfrac{3}{4} = \dfrac{11}{4}$ then the reciprocal is $\dfrac{4}{11}$.

Checklist
Can you:

1. Recognise the components of a fraction?
2. Convert an improper fraction to a mixed numeral and vice versa?
3. Express one quantity as a fraction of another quantity?
4. Compare fractions by using equivalent fractions?
5. Find the reciprocal of any fraction or mixed numeral?
6. Solve word problems involving fractions?

BASIC FRACTION CONCEPTS
Real Numbers

1 Simplify (or cancel):

a $\dfrac{8}{16}$

b $\dfrac{10}{30}$

c $\dfrac{15}{45}$

d $\dfrac{80}{120}$

e $\dfrac{48}{60}$

f $\dfrac{55}{75}$

2 Find the missing value:

a $\dfrac{2}{3} = \dfrac{\quad}{9}$

b $\dfrac{\quad}{} = \dfrac{20}{36}$ ... $\dfrac{5}{\quad} = \dfrac{20}{36}$

c $\dfrac{2}{5} = \dfrac{\quad}{25}$

d $\dfrac{4}{7} = \dfrac{28}{\quad}$

e $\dfrac{\quad}{8} = \dfrac{35}{56}$

f $\dfrac{4}{\quad} = \dfrac{\quad}{\quad} = \dfrac{16}{100}$

3 Rewrite as a mixed numeral:

a $\dfrac{7}{3}$

b $\dfrac{14}{5}$

c $\dfrac{9}{2}$

4 Change to an improper fraction:

a $2\dfrac{1}{2}$

b $1\dfrac{3}{4}$

c $5\dfrac{1}{3}$

5 What fraction is:

a 4 of 12?

b $3 of $15?

c 50c of $4?

d 20 cm of 2 m?

e 45 seconds of 2 minutes?

f 7 mm of 1 m?

6 Find the reciprocal of:

a 2

b $\dfrac{1}{3}$

c $\dfrac{2}{7}$

d $\dfrac{5}{8}$

e $1\dfrac{1}{4}$

f $3\dfrac{2}{3}$

7 Insert > or < to make a true statement:

a $\dfrac{2}{3} \quad \dfrac{1}{2}$

b $\dfrac{3}{5} \quad \dfrac{2}{3}$

c $\dfrac{7}{10} \quad \dfrac{2}{3}$

8 Rearrange in ascending order:

a $\dfrac{4}{5}, \dfrac{2}{3}, \dfrac{1}{2}$

b $\dfrac{3}{4}, \dfrac{2}{3}, \dfrac{7}{8}$

PAGE 106

BASIC FRACTION CONCEPTS
Real Numbers

INTERMEDIATE TEST

Part A Multiple Choice

1 Which of the following can be simplified to $\frac{2}{3}$?

A $\frac{4}{9}$ 　　　 B $\frac{21}{31}$ 　　　 C $\frac{4+2}{4+3}$ 　　　 D $\frac{24}{36}$ 　　　 (1 mark)

2 On the number line the value of X is:

A 9 　　　 B $\frac{9}{10}$ 　　　 C $\frac{3}{4}$ 　　　 D $\frac{2}{3}$ 　　　 (1 mark)

3 How many tenths in $\frac{45}{90}$?

A 1 　　　 B 5 　　　 C 9 　　　 D 18 　　　 (1 mark)

4 The clock shows the time of 8 o'clock.

What fraction of the clock face is shaded?

A $\frac{1}{3}$ 　　 B $\frac{1}{4}$ 　　 C $\frac{2}{3}$ 　　 D $\frac{3}{4}$ 　　　 (1 mark)

5 What fraction is halfway between $\frac{1}{4}$ and $\frac{1}{2}$?

A $\frac{1}{3}$ 　　　 B $\frac{1}{5}$ 　　　 C $\frac{1}{8}$ 　　　 D $\frac{3}{8}$ 　　　 (1 mark)

Part B Short Answer

6 Rewrite the following in descending order $\frac{41}{50}$, $\frac{3}{4}$, $\frac{4}{5}$, $\frac{17}{20}$ 　　　 (2 marks)

7 Find the value of the missing numeral:

a $\frac{?}{10} = \frac{27}{30}$ 　　　　　　 b $\frac{33}{54} = \frac{?}{18}$ 　　　 (1 mark each)

8 Darren buys a skateboard for \$25 and sells it for \$35.
Find Darren's profit as a fraction of his cost price. *Hint 1* 　　　 (3 marks)

9 Whitebridge High School has 1150 students. A survey shows that 250 catch
buses to school, 500 students use other forms of transport and the remainder
walk to school. What fraction of the total student population walks to school? *Hint 2* 　　　 (2 marks)

10 In a game of cricket, twins Mark and Steve scored 67 and 83 respectively in their
team's total of 350. What fraction of the team's total was scored by the twins? 　　　 (2 marks)

Hint 1: The profit is the selling price minus the
cost price.
Hint 2: Find the number of walkers and then
express as a fraction of the total.

Your Feedback

$\dfrac{\boxed{}}{16} \times 100\% = \boxed{}\%$

PAGE 107

PAGE 161

1 Find the missing numbers:

a $\dfrac{2}{3} = \dfrac{\square}{81}$ (1 mark)

b $\dfrac{\square}{9} = \dfrac{72}{108}$ (1 mark)

c $\dfrac{7}{\square} = \dfrac{56}{96}$ (1 mark)

d $\dfrac{55}{132} = \dfrac{5}{\square}$ (1 mark)

2 Express the following as mixed numerals:

a $\dfrac{53}{7}$ b $\dfrac{94}{5}$

c $\dfrac{403}{4}$ (1 mark each)

3 Rewrite as improper fractions:

a $3\dfrac{7}{9}$ b $5\dfrac{11}{12}$

c $9\dfrac{8}{11}$ (1 mark each)

4 Rearrange the following in ascending order:

a $\dfrac{7}{24}, \dfrac{1}{2}, \dfrac{3}{8}, \dfrac{5}{12}$ (2 marks)

b $\dfrac{3}{5}, \dfrac{13}{20}, \dfrac{3}{4}, \dfrac{27}{40}$ (2 marks)

5 Mia arranged these five fractions in descending order.

$\dfrac{23}{32}, \dfrac{5}{8}, \dfrac{11}{16}, \dfrac{3}{4}, \dfrac{21}{32}$ (2 marks)

What was the middle fraction?

6 Write the reciprocal of the following:

a $1\dfrac{3}{4}$ b $3\dfrac{5}{6}$

c $\dfrac{3}{a}$ d x (1 mark each)

7 A book contains 200 pages and Jack has read 120 pages. What fraction of the book remains to be read? (1 mark)

8 Find the reciprocal of the reciprocal of $\dfrac{5}{8}$. (1 mark)

9 In a class of 30 students, 5 boys and 3 girls had attended the same primary school. What fraction of the class had not attended the particular primary school? (1 mark)

10 a How many tenths are in $4\dfrac{3}{5}$? (1 mark)

b How many quarters are in $45\dfrac{1}{2}$? (1 mark)

c How many twelfths are in $2\dfrac{2}{3}$? (1 mark)

11 A survey was conducted to find the number of people in a group who were university graduates. The results are shown in the table below.

	Male	Female
Graduate	12	14
Non-graduate	8	6

a What fraction of those surveyed had graduated? (1 mark)

b What fraction of males had not graduated? (1 mark)

c What fraction of graduates were female? (1 mark)

12 A bag contains 10 balls numbered from one to 10. What fraction of the balls in the bag are:

a even? (1 mark)

b multiples of 4? (1 mark)

c prime? (1 mark)

13 What fraction is:

a 20 cents of $3? (1 mark)

b 50 millimetres of 1 kilometre? (1 mark)

c 2 litres of 2 megalitres? (1 mark)

d 40 seconds of 4 hours? (1 mark)

14 Aaron was travelling from Donnybrook to Perth and passed this sign.

60 Perth   **Donnybrook 150**

What fraction of the journey has he already completed? (1 mark)

Your Feedback

$\dfrac{\square}{37} \times 100\% = \boxed{}\%$

PAGE 107

PAGE 161

1 **To add/subtract fractions when their denominators are the same**, just add/subtract the numerators.

For example, a $\dfrac{2}{5} + \dfrac{1}{5} = \dfrac{3}{5}$ b $1 - \dfrac{5}{8} = \dfrac{8}{8} - \dfrac{5}{8} = \dfrac{3}{8}$

2 **To add/subtract fractions when their denominators are different**, first find equivalent fractions using lowest common denominator, then add/subtract the numerators.

For example, a $\dfrac{2}{5} + \dfrac{2}{3} = \dfrac{6+10}{15}$ b $\dfrac{9}{10} - \dfrac{3}{4} = \dfrac{18-15}{20}$

$\qquad\qquad\qquad = \dfrac{16}{15} = 1\dfrac{1}{15}$ $\qquad\qquad = \dfrac{3}{20}$

3 To **multiply fractions**, cancel if possible, and then multiply numerators and multiply denominators. When we are finding a fraction 'of' a quantity, we multiply.

For example, a Find $\dfrac{2}{5}$ of $\dfrac{5}{12} = \dfrac{2}{5} \times \dfrac{5}{12}$ b $\left(\dfrac{3}{5}\right)^2 = \dfrac{3}{5} \times \dfrac{3}{5}$

$\qquad\qquad\qquad\qquad = \dfrac{1}{6}$ $\qquad\qquad\qquad = \dfrac{9}{25}$

4 To **divide fractions**, we multiply by the reciprocal of the second fraction.

For example, a $\dfrac{3}{8} \div \dfrac{9}{10} = \dfrac{3}{8} \times \dfrac{10}{9}$ b $\dfrac{2}{3} \div 4 = \dfrac{2}{3} \times \dfrac{1}{4}$

$\qquad\qquad\qquad = \dfrac{5}{12}$ $\qquad\qquad = \dfrac{1}{6}$

5 When **mixed numerals** are involved, express the mixed numerals as improper fractions and then use methods outlined above. However, for addition and subtraction, the whole numbers and fractions can be added/subtracted separately.

For example,

a $3\dfrac{3}{8} + 2\dfrac{1}{10} = 5 + \dfrac{3}{8} + \dfrac{1}{10}$ b $5\dfrac{7}{10} - 3\dfrac{3}{5} = 2 + \dfrac{7}{10} - \dfrac{3}{5}$ c $2\dfrac{7}{10} \times 1\dfrac{2}{3} = \dfrac{27}{10} \times \dfrac{5}{3}$ d $1\dfrac{4}{5} \div \dfrac{3}{10} = \dfrac{9}{5} \times \dfrac{10}{3}$

$\qquad\quad = 5 + \dfrac{15+4}{40}$ $\qquad\quad = 2 + \dfrac{7-6}{10}$ $\qquad\quad = \dfrac{9}{2}$ $\qquad\quad = \dfrac{6}{1}$

$\qquad\quad = 5\dfrac{19}{40}$ $\qquad\quad = 2\dfrac{1}{10}$ $\qquad\quad = 4\dfrac{1}{2}$ $\qquad\quad = 6$

Checklist
Can you:

✔

1 *Perform all operations (addition, subtraction, multiplication, division) with fractions?* ☐

2 *Perform operations with mixed numerals?* ☐

3 *Solve word problems involving fractions?* ☐

1 Simplify:

a $\dfrac{3}{5} + \dfrac{1}{5}$

b $\dfrac{3}{10} + \dfrac{7}{10}$

c $\dfrac{3}{8} + \dfrac{7}{8}$

2 Simplify:

a $\dfrac{3}{10} + \dfrac{1}{3}$

b $\dfrac{4}{5} + \dfrac{3}{4}$

c $\dfrac{3}{4} + \dfrac{5}{8}$

3 Simplify:

a $1 - \dfrac{2}{3}$

b $2 - \dfrac{3}{4}$

c $5 - \dfrac{1}{6}$

4 Simplify:

a $\dfrac{7}{10} - \dfrac{2}{10}$

b $\dfrac{9}{10} - \dfrac{2}{3}$

c $\dfrac{3}{4} - \dfrac{3}{8}$

5 Simplify:

a $\dfrac{4}{5} \times \dfrac{3}{4}$

b $\dfrac{1}{2}$ of $\dfrac{4}{5}$

c $\dfrac{2}{5} \times \dfrac{5}{6} \times \dfrac{1}{3}$

d $\dfrac{3}{4}$ of 12

e $\left(\dfrac{3}{4}\right)^2$

f $\dfrac{7}{10}$ of 35

6 Simplify:

a $\dfrac{3}{4} \div \dfrac{1}{2}$

b $\dfrac{4}{5} \div 2$

c $12 \div \dfrac{1}{2}$

7 a What is the product of $\dfrac{4}{5}$ and $\dfrac{3}{4}$?

b What is the quotient of $\dfrac{7}{10} \div \dfrac{4}{5}$?

8 Simplify:

a $\dfrac{3}{5} \times \dfrac{5}{6} + \dfrac{1}{2}$ of $\dfrac{4}{5}$

b $\dfrac{\frac{1}{2} + \frac{1}{3}}{\frac{1}{2} - \frac{1}{3}}$

9 Simplify:

a $2\dfrac{1}{2} + 3\dfrac{1}{3}$

b $4\dfrac{1}{2} - 2\dfrac{1}{4}$

c $1\dfrac{1}{4} \times 3\dfrac{1}{3}$

d $4\dfrac{1}{3} \div 3\dfrac{1}{2}$

e $\left(2\dfrac{1}{2}\right)^2$

f $\dfrac{2}{3\frac{1}{2}}$

PAGE 108

USING FRACTIONS
Real Numbers

INTERMEDIATE TEST

Part A Multiple Choice

1 Simplify $\dfrac{2}{5} + \dfrac{1}{3} \times \dfrac{3}{5}$

A $\dfrac{4}{5}$ B $\dfrac{7}{15}$ C $\dfrac{3}{5}$ D $\dfrac{13}{15}$ (1 mark)

2 A recipe to serve 4 people requires $\dfrac{3}{4}$ cup of sugar. If 12 people will be present at the meal, how many cups will Daniel need to add?

A $2\dfrac{1}{4}$ B 4 C 6 D 9 (1 mark)

3 Which of the following is not equal to 6?

A $2\dfrac{2}{3} + 3\dfrac{1}{3}$ B $3 \div \dfrac{1}{2}$ C $36 \div \dfrac{1}{6}$ D $\dfrac{3}{4}$ of 8 (1 mark)

4 Fiona leaves Kearsley to travel to Minmi. When she passes this sign, what fraction of the journey does she still have to travel?

35 Kearsley • Minmi 25

A $\dfrac{3}{5}$ B $\dfrac{2}{5}$ C $\dfrac{5}{12}$ D $\dfrac{7}{12}$ (1 mark)

Part B Short Answer

5 Draw a diagram to illustrate: *Hint 1*

a $\dfrac{1}{4} + \dfrac{1}{2}$ b $\dfrac{1}{2} \times \dfrac{3}{4}$ (1 mark each)

6 Tom's 49 hectare farm is to be subdivided into small lots of $3\dfrac{1}{2}$ hectares each. How many lots are there? (2 marks)

7 Simplify:

a $5\dfrac{3}{5} - 3\dfrac{2}{3}$ b $2\dfrac{1}{4} \times 2\dfrac{2}{3}$ (3 marks each)

8 In a race Mike covers $\dfrac{3}{5}$ of the distance in the first hour and $\dfrac{1}{3}$ of the distance in the second hour. If the race was 45 kilometres, how far does Mike still need to travel? *Hint 2* (2 marks)

9 Aditi's weekly allowance is $12 and she saves $\dfrac{3}{8}$. How much does she spend? (1 mark)

10 A water tank holds 5000 litres when full. At present it is only $\dfrac{3}{4}$ full.

a How much water is presently in the tank? (1 mark)

b After heavy rain, the tank reached $\dfrac{9}{10}$ full. How much water has been added? (2 marks)

Your Feedback

$\dfrac{\boxed{}}{20} \times 100\% = \boxed{}\%$

PAGE 109

PAGE 161

Hint 1: Use a rectangle divided into equal units.
Hint 2: Find the fraction of the race yet to complete.

USING FRACTIONS
Real Numbers

1 Evaluate:

a $\dfrac{2}{5}+\dfrac{1}{2}+\dfrac{3}{10}$ b $\dfrac{7}{8}+\dfrac{3}{4}+\dfrac{1}{2}$

c $1\dfrac{2}{3}+\dfrac{3}{4}$ d $2\dfrac{4}{5}+1\dfrac{1}{2}$

e $5\dfrac{3}{4}+3\dfrac{7}{10}$ (2 marks each)

2 Evaluate:

a $\dfrac{9}{10}-\dfrac{2}{5}-\dfrac{1}{2}$ b $6-3\dfrac{2}{5}$

c $3\dfrac{4}{5}-1\dfrac{2}{3}$ d $3\dfrac{2}{5}-2\dfrac{7}{10}$

e $4\dfrac{1}{3}-1\dfrac{5}{6}$ (2 marks each)

3 Evaluate:

a $2\dfrac{3}{5}\times 5$ (2 marks)

b $1\dfrac{2}{3}\times 2\dfrac{1}{5}$ (2 marks)

c $3\dfrac{1}{4}\times 3\dfrac{1}{3}$ (2 marks)

d $\left(2\dfrac{2}{3}\right)^{2}$ (1 mark)

e $\left(5\dfrac{1}{2}\right)^{2}$ (1 mark)

4 Evaluate:

a $1\dfrac{2}{3}\div 5$ b $8\div 1\dfrac{3}{5}$

c $\dfrac{5}{8}\div 4\dfrac{1}{6}$ d $3\dfrac{1}{2}\div 1\dfrac{3}{4}$

e $\dfrac{1\dfrac{2}{3}}{2\dfrac{1}{2}}$ (2 marks each)

5 Evaluate:

a $\dfrac{\dfrac{2}{3}+\dfrac{1}{2}}{\dfrac{2}{3}-\dfrac{1}{2}}$ b $\dfrac{4}{5}\times 1\dfrac{2}{3}-\dfrac{5}{6}\div\dfrac{2}{3}$

(2 marks each)

6 A tank is five-eighths full of water. A storm adds 300 litres of water and the tank is at two-thirds full. How much more water is required for the tank to be completely full? (2 marks)

7 On his farm, Bill has planted $14\dfrac{2}{3}$ hectares of wheat and $25\dfrac{1}{4}$ hectares of barley. What is the total area? (2 marks)

8 Lily studied for $1\dfrac{3}{4}$ hours each night for a week. Find the total time studied? (2 marks)

9 Jacob has decided to give part of his stamp collection away. He gives $\dfrac{1}{4}$ of the stamps to his brother, and then $\dfrac{2}{3}$ of the remaining to his sister. If he has 48 stamps remaining, how many more stamps did he give his sister than his brother? (2 marks)

10 Sophie had saved $\dfrac{3}{5}$ as much money as her brother Ethan. Ethan had saved $120 more than Sophie. What was their total savings? (2 marks)

11 A mooring pole for a boat has one-third of its length in the sea-bed and one-sixth of its length in the water at low tide. At high tide the top of the pole is 1 metre out of the water. If there is a 2 metre difference between the levels of low and high tides, how long is the mooring pole? (2 marks)

12 One-third of Ned's weekly wage is used to pay for the rent, while he spends one-fifth of the remainder on food. He saves one-quarter of the rest of the money. If he still has $360 left, how much was Ned originally paid? (2 marks)

Your Feedback

$\dfrac{\boxed{}}{56}\times 100\% = \boxed{}$ %

PAGE 109

PAGE 161

1 Place value

The values of each place in a number, on either side of the decimal point, are:

... hundreds | tens | units | . | tenths | hundredths | thousandths | ten thousandths ...

For example, what is the place value of 4 in 25.7451? $\therefore$ 4 hundredths

Note: 25.7451 has 4 decimal places.

2 Rounding off

Let's look at some examples.

a   Round off 5.2417 to the nearest tenth (or one decimal place).

$\therefore$ 5.2417 = 5.2 [to nearest tenth], as '4' in second decimal place < 5 (round down).

b   Correct 32.798 to two decimal places.

$\therefore$ 32.798 = 32.80 [correct to 2 dec. pl.], as '8' in third decimal place $\geq$ 5 (round up).

3 Converting a fraction to a decimal

Use division to rewrite a fraction as a decimal.

For example, rewrite $\frac{7}{8}$ as decimal. $\therefore$ $\frac{7}{8}$ = 0.875 $8 \overline{\smash{)}\ 7.000}$ (0.875)

4 Converting a decimal to a fraction

Note the link between the number of decimal places with the zeros in the denominator.

For example, $0.3 = \frac{3}{10}$, $0.77 = \frac{77}{100}$, $0.407 = \frac{407}{1000}$, $0.09 = \frac{9}{100}$

5 Repeating/recurring decimals

Most decimals terminate, such as 0.4, 0.023, and so on. Others repeat, or recur, and a repeating symbol is used.

For example, rewrite $\frac{7}{11}$ as a decimal. $\therefore$ $\frac{7}{11} = 0.\dot{6}\dot{3}$ $11 \overline{\smash{)}\ 7.000...}$ (0.636 ...)

6 Fraction-decimal equivalents to memorise

$\frac{1}{2} = 0.5$, $\frac{1}{3} = 0.\dot{3}$, $\frac{1}{4} = 0.25$, $\frac{1}{5} = 0.2$, $\frac{1}{8} = 0.125$, $\frac{1}{9} = 0.\dot{1}$, $\frac{1}{10} = 0.1$, $\frac{1}{20} = 0.05$

For example, express $\frac{7}{20}$ as decimal. $\therefore$ as $\frac{7}{20} = 7 \times \frac{1}{20}$

$= 7 \times 0.05$

$= 0.35$ $\therefore \frac{7}{20} = 0.35$

Checklist
Can you:

1 *Correct, or round off, decimals to particular decimal places?* ☐
2 *Convert decimals to fractions?* ☐
3 *Solve word problems involving fractions and mixed numerals?* ☐

1 Find the place value of 5 in:

    a 24.453   **b** 302.5876   **c** 0.000051

2 Round off to the nearest hundredth:

    a 0.643   **b** 0.4865   **c** 0.185754

3 How many decimal places in:

    a 0.2314   **b** 0.6003   **c** 186.5

4 Correct to 3 decimal places:

    a 6.9815   **b** 21.8901   **c** 0.000911

5 Write in decimal form:

    a $\dfrac{78}{100}$ **b** $\dfrac{1}{10} + \dfrac{5}{100}$ **c** $\dfrac{2}{100} + \dfrac{3}{1000}$

6 Write in expanded form:

    a 2.53   **b** 0.035   **c** 0.00309

7 Rewrite in ascending order:

    a 2.4, 2.041, 2.41, 2.104   **b** 6.402, 6.024, 6.24, 6.04

8 Write the decimal represented by the points on the number lines:

    a

    b

9 Convert to decimals:

    a $\dfrac{3}{4}$ **b** $\dfrac{12}{25}$ **c** $\dfrac{19}{50}$

    d $\dfrac{7}{8}$ **e** $\dfrac{4}{9}$ **f** $\dfrac{3}{11}$

10 Convert to fractions:

    a 0.8   **b** 0.08   **c** 0.071

    d 0.105   **e** 0.880   **f** 0.1001

11 Find the reciprocal of:

    a 0.125   **b** 1.25   **c** 3.2

PAGE 111

Answers **1a** 5 hundredths **b** 5 tenths **c** 5 hundred thousandths **2a** 0.64 **b** 0.49 **c** 0.19 **3a** 4 **b** 4 **c** 1 **4a** 6.982 **b** 21.890 **c** 0.001 **5a** 0.78 **b** 0.15 **c** 0.023 **6a** 2 + 0.5 + 0.03 **b** 0.03 + 0.005 **c** 0.003 + 0.000 09 **7a** 2.041, 2.104, 2.4, 2.41 **b** 6.024, 6.04, 6.24, 6.402 **8a** 2.75 **b** 4.24 **9a** 0.75 **b** 0.48 **c** 0.38 **d** 0.875 **e** 0.4 **f** 0.27 **10a** $\frac{4}{5}$ **b** $\frac{2}{25}$ **c** $\frac{71}{1000}$ **d** $\frac{21}{200}$ **e** $\frac{22}{25}$ **f** $\frac{1001}{10000}$ **11a** 8 **b** $\frac{4}{5}$ **c** $\frac{5}{16}$

BASIC DECIMAL CONCEPTS
Real Numbers

20 MINUTES

INTERMEDIATE TEST

Part A Multiple Choice

1 Which one of the following decimals lies between $\frac{1}{2}$ and $\frac{3}{4}$?

    A 0.4   **B** 0.43   **C** 0.6   **D** 0.07   (1 mark)

2 When 8.___57 is rounded to 1 decimal place, the answer is 8.7
What number must have been written in the space?

    A 4   **B** 5   **C** 6   **D** 7   (1 mark)

3 Which decimal is closest to 7.25?

    A 7.2   **B** 7.26   **C** 7.248   **D** 7.253   (1 mark)

4 The value of $\frac{3}{10} + \frac{61}{100}$ is:

    A 0.91   **B** 0.361   **C** 0.34   **D** 0.3061   (1 mark)

5 As a decimal $\frac{2}{3}$ correct to 2 decimal places, is:

    A 0.66   **B** 0.67   **C** 0.23   **D** 0.24   (1 mark)

6 0.065 =

    A $\frac{6}{10} + \frac{5}{100}$ **B** $\frac{6}{10} + \frac{5}{1000}$ **C** $\frac{6}{100} + \frac{5}{1000}$ **D** $\frac{6}{1000} + \frac{5}{10\,000}$ (1 mark)

7 Correct to the nearest thousandth, 0.027 658 is:

    A 0.028   **B** 0.027   **C** 0.0276   **D** 0.0277   (1 mark)

Part B Short Answer

8 Place $\frac{5}{8}$ on the number line: *Hint 1*   0   0.5   1   (2 marks)

9 Arrange the following in ascending order:

    a 0.68, $\frac{3}{5}$, $0.\dot{6}$, $\frac{62}{100}$ **b** 1.34, $1\frac{19}{50}$, $1\frac{1}{3}$, 1.3   (2 marks each)

10 Look at this pattern: $\frac{1}{11} = 0.\dot{0}\dot{9}$, $\frac{2}{11} = 0.\dot{1}\dot{8}$, ... Write $\frac{6}{11}$ as a decimal.   (1 mark)

11 a What do you notice about these fractions: $\frac{1}{13} = 0.\dot{0}76\,92\dot{3}$ and $\frac{12}{13} = 0.\dot{9}23\,07\dot{6}$?   (1 mark)

    b Using your answer in part **a**, if $\frac{5}{13} = 0.\dot{3}84\,61\dot{5}$, what is $\frac{8}{13}$?   (1 mark)

    c Now, write down two characteristics of the decimal form of fractions with a denominator of 13.   (2 marks)

Your Feedback

$\dfrac{\boxed{}}{18} \times 100\% = \boxed{}\,\%$

PAGE 112

PAGE 161

BASIC DECIMAL CONCEPTS
Real Numbers

1 Rewrite the following as decimals:

a $\dfrac{5}{10}+\dfrac{3}{100}+\dfrac{9}{10000}$ (1 mark)

b $\dfrac{7}{100}+\dfrac{9}{1000}+\dfrac{1}{10000}$ (1 mark)

2 Round off the following to the nearest hundredth:

a 24.9818   (1 mark)
b 0.025 08   (1 mark)
c 1.9898   (1 mark)
d 2.0999   (1 mark)
e 149.4049   (1 mark)

3 Round off the following to the nearest thousandth:

a 209.7932   (1 mark)
b 0.006 78   (1 mark)
c 0.666 66   (1 mark)
d 8671.9006   (1 mark)
e 11.372 499   (1 mark)

4 How many times greater is the first **5** than the second **5** in the following decimals:

a **54.5**   (1 mark)
b **259.75**   (1 mark)
c **514.0356**   (1 mark)

5 Find the reciprocal of:

a 0.7   b 0.4
c 0.81   d 2.6
e 1.001   (1 mark each)

6 Change the following to decimals:

a $\dfrac{5}{12}$ b $\dfrac{17}{40}$

c $\dfrac{7}{11}$ d $\dfrac{6}{7}$ (2 marks each)

7 Arrange the following in ascending order:

a $\dfrac{7}{8}$, 0.85, 0.9, $\dfrac{4}{5}$ (2 marks)

b $\dfrac{34}{50}$, 0.66, $\dfrac{2}{3}$, 0.67   (2 marks)

8 A nanosecond is one-billionth of a second. Write this as a decimal.   (1 mark)

9 Insert either < or > to make a true statement:

a $\dfrac{5}{8}$ ☐ 0.635   (1 mark)

b 0.78 ☐ $\dfrac{7}{9}$ (1 mark)

10 The following decimals are to be arranged in order. What will be the third decimal in the list?

a 2.42, 2.403, 2.4, 2.03, 2.43   (1 mark)
b 4.5, 4.054, 4.405, 4.045, 4.04   (1 mark)

11 Locate the following decimals on the number line provided:

a 0.8   (1 mark)

b 0.3   (1 mark)

c 2.7   (1 mark)

12 The table shows the times for a 200-metre race.

Lane	Athlete	Time
1	Rose	22.91
2	Hollie	22.89
3	Suzy	22.05
4	Elle	22.87
5	Jasmine	22.3
6	Christie	22.59
7	Michelle	22.28
8	Kim	22.53

Which athlete finished:

a first?   (1 mark)
b third?   (1 mark)
c last?   (1 mark)

13 Express the largest fraction as a decimal:

a $\dfrac{3}{10}, \dfrac{34}{100}, \dfrac{304}{1000}, \dfrac{3024}{10000}$ (1 mark)

b $\dfrac{65}{1000}, \dfrac{64}{100}, \dfrac{6}{10}, \dfrac{604}{1000}$ (1 mark)

Your Feedback

$\dfrac{}{45} \times 100\% = \boxed{}\%$

PAGE 112

PAGE 161

USING DECIMALS
Real Numbers

1 **Adding/subtracting decimals**: take care with the place value—adding zeros on the end of decimals so that all have the same number of decimal places may help.
For example, simplify:

a $\quad$ 13 + 2.63 = 13.00 + 2.63
$\qquad\qquad\qquad = 15.63$

b $\quad$ 21.06 – 6.321 = 21.060 – 6.321
$\qquad\qquad\qquad\quad = 14.739$

2 **Multiplying decimals**: take note of the number of decimal places in the question—it is the same for your answer? i.e. as 32.5 × 0.5 has 2 decimal places, the answer has 2 decimal places.
For example, simplify:

a $\quad$ 12.4 × 6
$\qquad$ as $\;$ 124 × 6 = 744
$\qquad$ ∴ 12.4 × 6 = 74.4

b $\quad$ 32.5 × 0.5
$\qquad$ as $\quad$ 325 × 5 = 1625
$\qquad$ ∴ $\quad$ 32.5 × 0.5 = 16.25

3 **Dividing decimals**: ensure that the **divisor** (what is being divided by) is a **whole number**. This may mean multiplying both numbers by a **power of ten** (10, 100, 1000, etc). [see Key Point **5**]
For example, simplify:

a $\quad$ 10.45 ÷ 5 = 2.09

b $\quad$ 3.64 ÷ 0.4 = 36.4 ÷ 4 $\quad$ [multiply both by 10]
$\qquad\qquad\qquad\quad = 9.1$

4 **Large numbers** can be written as **powers of ten**, such as $10 = 10^1$, $100 = 10^2$, $1000 = 10^3$.
A **googol** is written as 1 followed by 100 zeros $\quad$ ∴ a googol = 10^{100}
For example, rewrite the following as a power of ten:

a $\quad$ one million $\quad$ (1 000 000)
$\qquad$ ∴ 1 000 000 = 10^6

b $\quad$ one trillion $\quad$ (1 000 000 000 000)
$\qquad$ ∴ 1 000 000 000 000 = 10^{12}

5 When a decimal is **multiplied** by a power of ten, the decimal point moves to the **right** a number of decimal places equal to the number of zeros (or the power of ten).
When a decimal is **divided** by a power of ten, the decimal point moves to the **left** a number of decimal places equal to the number of zeros (or the power of ten).
For example, evaluate:

a $\quad$ 4.743 × 100
$\qquad$ As 100 has 2 zeros $\quad$ (or $100 = 10^2$)
$\qquad$ the dec. point moves 2 pl. to the right
$\qquad$ ∴ 4.743 × 100 = 474.3

b $\quad$ 76.438 ÷ 1000
$\qquad$ As 1000 has 3 zeros $\quad$ (or $1000 = 10^3$)
$\qquad$ the dec. point moves 3 pl. to the left
$\qquad$ ∴ 76.438 ÷ 1000 = 0.076 438

Checklist
Can you:

1 *Perform all operations (addition, subtraction, multiplication, division) with decimals?* ☐

2 *Express large numbers as powers of ten?* ☐

3 *Multiply and divide decimals by powers of ten?* ☐

4 *Solve word problems involving decimals?* ☐

1 Simplify:

a 5.2 + 0.34

b 0.03 + 0.012

c 12 + 2.1 + 5.03

d −4.1 + 5

e 14 + 7.06

f $10 + $3.13

2 Simplify:

a 1 − 0.23

b 14 − 1.3

c 0.6 − 0.4 − 0.1

d 0.3 − 0.5

e −3.2 − 1.4

f $1 − $0.95

3 Simplify:

a 0.3 × 5

b 1.6 × 4

c 1.3 × 0.4

d 4.5 × 0.3

e $(0.7)^2$

f $(0.04)^2$

4 Simplify:

a 1.5 ÷ 5

b 3.8 ÷ 4

c 0.55 ÷ 0.5

d 10 ÷ 0.1

e 24 ÷ 0.04

f 1.08 ÷ 0.9

5 Find the value of:

a 1.5 × 100

b 7.345 × 1000

c $16.038 × 10^4$

d 16.78 ÷ 10

e 24 ÷ 100

f $0.0563 ÷ 10^3$

6 Evaluate:

a 0.4 × 3 + 1.6

b $(3.2 ÷ 4)^2$

c $\dfrac{2.3 + 1.7}{0.4}$

7 Find the:

a sum of 0.65 and 1.344

b difference between 1.85 and 0.6

c product of 1.76 and 0.04

d quotient of 5.5 and 0.05

e average of 0.3, 0.6, 0.2 and 0.1

f square root of 0.36

8 Complete:

a 4.5 + ____ = 7.876

b 3 − ____ = 1.056

c ____ × 1.1 = 2.97

d 4.5 ÷ ____ = 900

9 A new bathroom requires 32 square metres of tiles. The tiles come in boxes each containing 1.2 square metres. How many boxes are needed to tile the bathroom.

10 A local fish and chips shop purchases 45 kg of potatoes at $0.80 per kg. Find the total cost of the potatoes.

PAGE 113

Answers 1a 5.54 b 0.042 c 19.13 d 0.9 e 21.06 f $13.13 2a 0.77 b 12.7 c 0.1 d −0.2 e −4.6 f $0.05 3a 1.5
b 6.4 c 0.52 d 1.35 e 0.49 f 0.0016 4a 0.3 b 0.95 c 1.1 d 100 e 600 f 1.2 5a 150 b 7345 c 160380 d 1.678 e 0.24
f 0.0000563 6a 2.8 b 0.64 c 10 7a 1.994 b 1.25 c 0.0704 d 110 e 0.3 f 0.6 8a 3.376 b 1.944 c 2.7 d 0.005 9 27
10 $36

USING DECIMALS
Real Numbers

Part A Multiple Choice

1 Simplify 4.5 ÷ 0.5

   A 3   **B** 9   **C** 0.3   **D** 0.9   (1 mark)

2 Simplify 0.24 × 3

   A 0.72   **B** 7.2   **C** 72   **D** 720   (1 mark)

3 Which of the following does not equal 0.4?

   A $\dfrac{0.24}{0.6}$ **B** $(0.2)^2$ **C** 12.1 − 11.7   **D** 2(0.7 − 0.5)   (1 mark)

4 Half of 4.75 is: *Hint 1*

   A 2.37   **B** 2.375   **C** 2.725   **D** 2.325   (1 mark)

5 The next term of the sequence 48, 12, 3, 0.75, ... is:

   A 0.046875   **B** 0.2875   **C** 0.2415   **D** 0.1875   (1 mark)

6 Simplify 1.4 × 0.5 + $(0.6)^2$ *Hint 2*

   A 0.736   **B** 1.36   **C** 1.06   **D** 4.3   (1 mark)

7 Noel is planning an overseas trip and exchanges his Australian currency at the rate of A\$1 = US\$0.942   This means that for every \$1 Australian, Noel receives 94.2 cents US. How much in US currency will Noel receive for \$2000 Australian? *Hint 3*

   A US\$1884   **B** US\$2123   **C** US\$1940   **D** US\$212 300   (1 mark)

Part B Short Answer

8 A student in answering a word problem wrote 0.25 × 0.5
What might the word problem have been?   (2 marks)

9 The average weight of 4 watermelons was 3.6 kg. When one watermelon is sold, the average weight of the remaining watermelons was 4 kg. How heavy was the watermelon that was sold? *Hint 4*   (3 marks)

10 Salena purchased 40 litres of petrol at 158.9 cents per litre.

   a How much did she pay for the petrol? *Hint 5*   (2 marks)

   b Salena's car averages 12.3 km/L. How far will it travel on the 40 litres?   (2 marks)

11 A 4 litre can of paint covers an area of 60 square metres.
Bruce needs to cover an area of 250 square metres.

   a How many cans of paint will Bruce need to purchase?   (2 marks)

   b What is the cost of the paint if the cans cost \$62.50 each?   (2 marks)

Hint 1: Finding half is the same as dividing by two.
Hint 2: Use the rules for order of operations.
Hint 3: Estimate your answer before finding the answer.
Hint 4: Find the total weight of the four watermelons first.
Hint 5: Take care when using cents—express your answer in dollars.

Your Feedback

$$\frac{\boxed{}}{20} \times 100\% = \boxed{}\%$$

PAGE 114

PAGE 161

1 Evaluate:
a   12.3 + 3.45
b   2.08 + 17 + 0.092
c   12 − 3.5
d   5.09 − 3.8
e   5 − 2.9817
(1 mark each)

2 Evaluate:
a   3.4 × 4
b   1.08 × 5
c   19.002 × 400
d   5.2 × 0.08
e   (0.09)²
(1 mark each)

3 Find the value of :
a   4.6 ÷ 5
b   16.18 ÷ 4
c   45.81 ÷ 0.03
d $\dfrac{123}{0.6}$
e $\dfrac{0.8545}{0.05}$
(1 mark each)

4 Find the value of:
a   87.3 × 2.3   (2 marks)
b   37.6 × 0.078   (2 marks)

5 Evaluate:
a   1.7 − 12.2
b   −0.4 − (−4.2)
c   −3.2 + (−1.04)
(1 mark each)

6 What is the value of:
a   4.2 − (2.3 + 1.002)?   (2 marks)
b   5 − 2.3 × 0.8?   (2 marks)
c   1.64 ÷ 0.2 − (0.5)²?   (2 marks)
d $\dfrac{1.6 + 1.1}{1.6 - 1.1}$?   (2 marks)
e   (0.5 + 2.4 ÷ 4)²?   (2 marks)

7 Lee exchanged his Australian dollars for euros at the rate of $1 = €0.789276. How many euros did he receive for $600?   (1 mark)

8 Tessa rides a distance of 43.85 kilometres each Saturday for six weeks. Find the total distance.   (1 mark)

9 A gym has a special membership offer of annual membership of $798 or a monthly price of $74.50. How much is saved when taking the annual membership?   (1 mark)

10 Vivienne's car uses petrol at the rate of 11.3 L/100 km. How much will it use to travel 450 km?   (2 marks)

11 Brad, Penny and Liam share equally the cost of their restaurant meal. If the total cost was $217.20, how much did each pay?   (1 mark)

12 On his second birthday, Otis's parents measured his height as 0.83 metres. Sixteen years later Otis's height was 1.7 metres. How much did he grow?   (1 mark)

13 The table shows the distances Sam threw in five rounds of discus.

Round	Distance (m)
1	11.3
2	10.2
3	9.5
4	10.4
5	11.1

What was the average of his five throws?   (2 marks)

14 Mitch has a digital thermometer in his house which records both interior and exterior temperatures.

19.7°
23.5°

What is the difference in the two temperatures?   (1 mark)

15 A DVD case is 1.5 cm thick. Kayden's stack of DVDs is 94.5 cm high. How many DVDs are in his stack?   (2 marks)

16 The table shows the approximate mass of water, petrol and diesel fuel at 4°C.

Liquid	Quantity (L)	Mass (kg)
Tap Water	1	1
Petrol	1	0.72
Diesel	1	0.82
Sea Water	1	1.02

a   What is the mass of 32.4 L of petrol?   (2 marks)
b   How many litres of diesel has a mass of 16.4 kg?   (2 marks)
c   Mickaela put $30 worth of petrol into her car. The cost of petrol was $1.50 per litre. What was the additional mass of her car?   (2 marks)
d   Keeley is comparing the mass of tap water and sea water. How much heavier is 20 litres of sea water than tap water?   (2 marks)

Your Feedback

$\dfrac{\boxed{}}{52}$ × 100% = $\boxed{}$ %

PAGE 114

PAGE 161

1 A fraction with a denominator of 100 can be written as a **percentage**.

2 **One whole** is written as **100%**.

3 Conversions involving percentages:

- **fraction to a percentage: multiply by 100%**

  For example, convert to a percentage: **a** $\dfrac{17}{100}$ **b** $\dfrac{3}{25}$

  $$\dfrac{17}{100} \times \dfrac{100}{1}\% = 17\% \qquad\qquad \dfrac{3}{25} \times \dfrac{100}{1}\% = 12\%$$

- **decimal to a percentage: multiply by 100%**

  For example, convert to a percentage: **a** 0.09   **b** 1.6

  $$0.09 \times 100\% = 9\% \qquad\qquad 1.6 \times 100\% = 160\%$$

- **percentage to a fraction: divide number by 100**

  For example, convert to a fraction: **a** 12%   **b** $7\tfrac{1}{2}\%$

  $$12\% = \dfrac{12}{100} = \dfrac{3}{25} \qquad\qquad \dfrac{7\tfrac{1}{2}}{100} = \dfrac{15}{200} = \dfrac{3}{40}$$

- **percentage to a decimal: divide by 100**

  For example, convert to a decimal: **a** 28%   **b** $14\tfrac{1}{2}\%$

  $$28 \div 100 = 0.28 \qquad\qquad 14.5 \div 100 = 0.145$$

4 To find **a percentage of a quantity**, we write the percentage as a decimal (or fraction) and multiply by the quantity.

For example, find: **a** 8% of $4000   **b** 27% of $300

$$\text{As } 0.08 \times 4000 = 320 \qquad \text{As } \dfrac{27}{100} \times \dfrac{300}{1} = 81$$

$$\therefore \ \$320 \qquad\qquad\qquad\qquad \therefore \ \$81$$

5 Writing **one quantity as a percentage of another**, we first check that both are of the same units, then write as a fraction before converting to a percentage. For example,

a Rewrite 14 out of 20 as a percentage.   **b** Express $2.40 as a percentage of $4.

$$\dfrac{14}{20} \times \dfrac{100}{1}\% = 70\% \qquad\qquad \dfrac{240}{400} \times \dfrac{100}{1}\% = 60\%$$

Checklist
Can you:

1 *Convert between fractions, decimals and percentages?* ☐

2 *Find a percentage of a quantity?* ☐

3 *Express one quantity as a percentage of another?* ☐

4 *Solve word problems involving percentages?* ☐

1 Convert to a percentage:

   a $\dfrac{71}{100}$ **b** $\dfrac{3}{100}$ **c** $\dfrac{7}{25}$

   d $\dfrac{3}{5}$ **e** $\dfrac{17}{20}$ **f** $\dfrac{3}{8}$

   g $\dfrac{2}{3}$ **h** $1\dfrac{1}{4}$ **i** $\dfrac{7}{1000}$

2 Express as a fraction:

   a 16%   **b** 6%   **c** 95%

   d $12\dfrac{1}{2}\%$ **e** $5\dfrac{1}{4}\%$ **f** $\dfrac{3}{5}\%$

3 Express as a mixed numeral:

   a 111%   **b** 186%   **c** 550%

4 Express as a percentage:

   a 0.4   **b** 0.07   **c** 0.019

   d 1.6   **e** 1.05   **f** 0.125

5 Write as a decimal:

   a 32%   **b** 6%   **c** 120%

   d 8.5%   **e** 12.5%   **f** 7.25%

6 Find:

   a 16% of $700   **b** 8% of $72   **c** 101% of $280

   d 125% of $4000   **e** $3\dfrac{1}{2}\%$ of $2000   **f** $5\dfrac{3}{4}\%$ of $600

7 Find:

   a 6% of 3 metres   **b** 30% of 2 minutes   **c** 108% of 12 mm

   d 21% of 12 kg   **e** 135% of 40 km   **f** $4\dfrac{1}{2}\%$ of 2 L

8 Express the first quantity as a percentage of the second quantity:

   a $14, $56   **b** 20 minutes, 2 hours

9 What percentage is:

   a $4.20 of $21?   **b** 15 seconds of 2 minutes?

PAGE 116

BASIC PERCENTAGE CONCEPTS
Real Numbers

INTERMEDIATE TEST

Part A — Multiple Choice

1 1.06 written as a percentage is:

A 106%   B 10.6%   C 1.06%   D 0.0106%   (1 mark)

2 18% of $50 equals:

A $9   B $32   C $68   D $90   (1 mark)

3 What percentage of a revolution is 120°?

A 3%   B 30%   C $33\frac{1}{3}\%$ D 40%   (1 mark)

4 42% is closest to:

A $\frac{2}{5}$ B $\frac{43}{100}$ C 0.042   D 4.2   (1 mark)

5

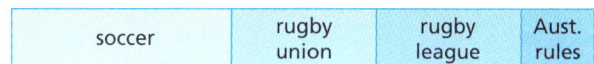

Part of the rectangle has been shaded. The percentage shaded is: *Hint 1*

A 32%   B 60%   C 64%   D 83%   (1 mark)

6 A bus is carrying 50 passengers of which 24 are females. The percentage that is male is:

A 12%   B 24%   C 48%   D 52%   (1 mark)

Part B — Short Answer

7 An election was held and the results put into a table at right. If there were 200 votes, then:

Students	Votes
Brown	64
Black	
Green	48
White	70

a how many votes did Black receive?   (1 mark)

b who received the most votes?   (1 mark)

c what percentage of the voters selected Green?   (1 mark)

8 One hundred and sixty boys who play Saturday sport were surveyed and the results were displayed in the horizontal bar graph at right.

soccer	rugby union	rugby league	Aust. rules

a How many boys play Australian Rules?   (2 marks)

b What percentage of the boys played soccer?   (2 marks)

9 Ninety students were asked for their favourite school subjects and the results recorded in a sector graph (at right).

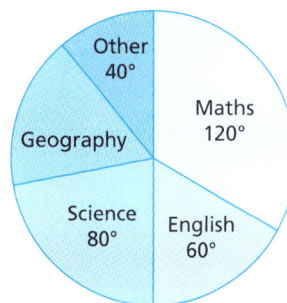

a What angle is represented by geography?   (2 marks)

b What percentage of students selected:

   i mathematics?   (2 marks)

   ii science?   (2 marks)

Your Feedback

$$\frac{\boxed{}}{19} \times 100\% = \boxed{}\%$$

PAGE 116

PAGE 161

Hint 1: Measure the bar graph and find percentage.

BASIC PERCENTAGE CONCEPTS
Real Numbers

45 MINUTES

ADVANCED TEST

1 Change the following to percentages:

a $\dfrac{37}{40}$ b $2\dfrac{21}{25}$

c $\dfrac{17}{1000}$ d $\dfrac{3}{500}$

e 1.003 f 0.0009 **(1 mark each)**

2 Rewrite as a simplified fraction:

a $\dfrac{3}{4}\%$ b $7\dfrac{4}{5}\%$

c 15.5% **(1 mark each)**

3 Rewrite as a decimal:

a 270% b 0.03%

c 5.05% d $7\dfrac{4}{5}\%$

e $20\dfrac{17}{20}\%$ **(1 mark each)**

4 What percentage is:

a 20 cents of $1.60? **(1 mark)**

b 3 litres of 1 kilolitre? **(1 mark)**

c 15 marks out of a possible 40? **(1 mark)**

d $\dfrac{1}{2}$ of 2? **(1 mark)**

e $2\dfrac{1}{4}$ of 10? **(1 mark)**

f 15 months of 2 years? **(1 mark)**

g a millimetre of a kilometre? **(1 mark)**

h half a dozen of 10 dozen? **(1 mark)**

5 Find:

a 23% of $400 **(1 mark)**

b $12\dfrac{1}{4}\%$ of $800 **(1 mark)**

c 120% of 60 **(1 mark)**

d 95% of 200 **(1 mark)**

e 16% of 3 mg **(1 mark)**

6 A bronze alloy contains 75% copper, 16% tin and the remainder zinc. The alloy is used to make a statue with a total mass of 65 kg. What is the mass of zinc in the statue? **(2 marks)**

7 Charlotte is paid $960 per week. If her pay increases by 4%, what is the increase in her pay? How much per week is she then paid? **(2 marks)**

8 Ming scored 80% in a maths test. If the test had 40 questions, all of equal value, how many questions did he get incorrect? **(2 marks)**

9 Sixty percent of the players in a mixed netball club were females. If there were 24 males at the club, what was the total membership? **(2 marks)**

10 A hockey team played 20 games in a season. They won 11 games, lost 5 games and drew the remainder.

a In what percentage of the games did the team draw? **(2 marks)**

b Of the games the team drew, three were nil-all results. In what percentage of the drawn games did the team score? **(2 marks)**

11 Each week a group of runners increases the distance they run by 20%.

a If last week Isaac ran 2.4 km, how far will he run this week? **(2 marks)**

b If Mim runs 4.8 km this week, how far did she run last week? **(2 marks)**

c If next week Liam increases the distance by 1.6 km, how far will he run the week after. **(2 marks)**

12 A school has 120 students in year 12. If this represents 15% of the school's population, how many students are not in year 12? **(2 marks)**

13 The table shows the votes received by five candidates in a recent election.

Candidate	Votes
King	350
Pickering	500
Strickland	800
Turton	250
Whiteford	100

What percentage of the total votes did King receive? **(2 marks)**

14 Seth has a coin collection. Jo has three times as many coins in her collection as Seth. Ryan has twice as many coins in his collection than Jolene. What percentage of the total coins are in Ryan's collection? **(2 marks)**

Your Feedback

$\dfrac{\boxed{}}{51} \times 100\% = \boxed{}\%$

PAGE 117

PAGE 161

RATIOS
Real Numbers

1 A **ratio** is a comparison between quantities of the same units. The ratio of 'a to b' is written as $a:b$, but can also be written as a fraction, $\frac{a}{b}$.

For example, in a class there are 17 girls and 13 boys. What is the ratio of:
- a girls to boys $17:13$
- b boys to girls $13:17$
- c boys to total students $13:30$

2 Ratios can be **simplified** in a similar manner to fractions.
For example, simplify:

- a $12:16$ As each has a highest common factor of 4, we divide through by 4:
$$12:16 = 3:4$$

- b $30:120$ We can first cross out a zero at the end of each number (this is dividing by 10), then we divide through by 3:
$$30:120 = 3:12$$
$$= 1:4$$

- c $\$3.50:\$5$ Change both to cents, ignore common units and then divide by 50:
$$\$3.50:\$5 = 350c:500c$$
$$= 7:10$$

- d $1\frac{1}{2}:\frac{3}{4}$ Rewrite with the same denominator, ignore denominators and simplify:
$$1\frac{1}{2}:\frac{3}{4} = \frac{3}{2}:\frac{3}{4} = \frac{6}{4}:\frac{3}{4} = 6:3 = 2:1$$

3 Quantities can be **divided in a given ratio**. For example,
- a Share \$400 in the ratio of $3:5$.

  The ratio is 3 parts to 5 parts which means there is a total of 8 parts.

  The smaller amount is $\frac{3}{8}$ of the total and the larger amount is $\frac{5}{8}$ of the total.

  $$\frac{3}{8} \times 400 = 150 \text{ and } \frac{5}{8} \times 400 = 250$$

  ∴ the amounts are \$150 and \$250

- b Twin brothers Bobby and Bennie shared an inheritance of \$64 000 in the ratio of $3:2$. What was Bennie's share?

  In the question, Bennie is named second, which means his share is 2 out of a total of 5.

  $$\text{Bennie's share } = \frac{2}{5} \times 64\,000$$
  $$= 25\,600$$

  ∴ Bennie's share is \$25 600

Checklist
Can you:

1 *Simplify ratios?* ☐

2 *Divide a quantity in a given ratio?* ☐

3 *Solve word problems involving simple ratios?* ☐

Excel SMARTSTUDY YEAR 7 MATHEMATICS   29

RATIOS
Real Numbers

1 A class of 30 students has 12 boys and the remainder girls. Writing in simplest form, what is the ratio of:

    a boys : girls?   **b** girls : boys?   **c** total students : boys?

2 On a bus there are 5 men, 8 women, 15 boys and 12 girls. Writing in simplest form, what is the ratio of:

    a men : women?   **b** women : men?   **c** boys : girls ?

    d women : girls?   **e** men : total?   **f** males : females?

3 Simplify:

    a 12 : 16   **b** 40 : 400   **c** 25 : 15

    d 30 : 5   **e** 100 : 10 000   **f** 557 : 557

4 Simplify:

    a $\dfrac{1}{5} : \dfrac{3}{5}$ **b** $1 : \dfrac{1}{3}$ **c** $1 : \dfrac{4}{7}$

    d $\dfrac{1}{2} : \dfrac{1}{4}$ **e** $\dfrac{3}{5} : \dfrac{7}{10}$ **f** $2 : 1\dfrac{1}{2}$

5 Simplify:

    a $1 : 40c$ **b** $2 : $1.50   **c** 1 m : 20 cm

    d 2 minutes : 40 seconds   **e** 2 kg : 500 g   **f** 40 mL : 2 L

6 Complete:

    a 2 : 3 = 8 : ____   **b** 4 : ____ = 16 : 20   **c** 3 : ____ = 24 : 40

7 **a** Divide 40 in the ratio 2 : 3

    b Share $64 in the ratio 3 : 5

    c Split up $350 such that for every $2 that Pam gets, Jen gets $5.

8 At a concert, the ratio of adults to children was 3 : 7. If the total number in the audience was 540, how many were children?

9 A length of timber is to be cut into two parts in the ratio of 3 : 5. If the timber was originally 2.4 metres, how long is the longer piece?

PAGE 118

RATIOS
Real Numbers

Part A Multiple Choice

1 Simplify $25:35$

  A $2:3$ **B** $5:7$ **C** $1:1$ **D** $5:6$ (1 mark)

2 Simplify $3:\dfrac{2}{3}$ *Hint 1*

  A $3:2$ **B** $3:1$ **C** $9:2$ **D** $6:1$ (1 mark)

3 The ratio of 4 kilometres to 200 metres is:

  A $1:50$ **B** $50:1$ **C** $20:1$ **D** $2:1$ (1 mark)

4 What is the missing number if $4:?=12:27$?

  A 19   **B** 5   **C** 9   **D** 12   (1 mark)

5 The ratio $4:6$ is equivalent to:

  A $2:1$ **B** $8:16$ **C** $4:9$ **D** $2:3$ (1 mark)

6 The ratio of male passengers to female passengers on a bus is $4:7$. This means that the bus could be carrying:

  A 18 males   **B** 2 males   **C** 35 females   **D** 28 passengers (1 mark)

Part B Short Answer

7 Simplify: (1 mark each)

  a $\$2.40:\$6$ **b** $\dfrac{2}{3}:\dfrac{1}{6}$ **c** 2 hours : 20 minutes

8 Robert has 60 books on a bookshelf. He has read 24 books. What is the ratio of read books to unread books?   (1 mark)

9 Bob's Books had a one-day sale. By closing time he had sold 140 fiction and 180 non-fiction books. What was the ratio of fiction to the total books sold? Write the answer in simplest form.   (2 marks)

10 Zhang surveyed the 28 students in her class. Four students had green eyes, eight students had blue eyes and the remainder had brown eyes. What is the ratio of brown eyes to blue eyes?   (2 marks)

11 Divide: **a** 20 metres in the ratio $3:1$ **b** $\$560$ in the ratio $3:4$ (2 marks each)

12 The ratio of present students to absent students in a class on a certain day is $9:1$. If there are 30 students in the class how many students are present?   (2 marks)

13 A fruit bowl contains oranges and apples in the ratio of $3:2$. There is a total of 10 pieces of fruit in the bowl.

  a How many oranges are in the bowl?   (2 marks)

  b If Bernie takes an apple and orange for lunch find the new ratio. *Hint 2*   (1 mark)

Your Feedback

$$\dfrac{\boxed{}}{23} \times 100\% = \boxed{}\%$$

PAGE 118

PAGE 161

Hint 1: Express both with the same denominator.
Hint 2: Use the answer in part **a**.

1 Simplify :
   a   0.7 : 0.007
   b   3.2 : 0.004
   c $\frac{21}{25} : \frac{47}{50}$
   d $1\frac{2}{3} : \frac{7}{12}$
   e $1 : 1\frac{5}{9}$
   f $\frac{2}{3} : \frac{8}{27}$
   g $\frac{3}{4} : \frac{4}{5} : \frac{5}{6}$
   h $0.6 : \frac{6}{25}$ (1 mark each)

2 Simplify :
   a   25c : $25.25   (1 mark)
   b   120 cm : 1 m   (1 mark)
   c   3 days : 6 hours   (1 mark)
   d   20 centuries : 10 millennia   (1 mark)
   e   10 mm : 1 km   (1 mark)
   f $1 cm^2 : 1 m^2$ (1 mark)
   g   1 year : 1 leap year   (1 mark)
   h   1 mL : 1ML   (1 mark)

3 Terry makes two cubes. The first has a side length of 4 cm. For the second cube, Terry doubles the length of each side. Find the ratio of the cubes':
   a   sides
   b   front face area
   c   volume   (1 mark each)

4 An art dealer purchased a painting for $60 000 and later sold it for $100 000. Express, in simplest form, the ratio of :
   a   profit : selling price   (1 mark)
   b   cost price : selling price : profit   (1 mark)

5 James spent 25% of his salary on rent and saved a third of the remainder. Find the ratio of savings to rent.   (2 marks)

6 Rita's quarterly electricity bill rose from $640 to $720. What is the ratio of the increase to the original cost?   (2 marks)

7 In a parking lot the ratio of cars to vans to trucks is in the ratio of 9 : 2 : 1. If there was a total of 240 vehicles, how many were vans?   (2 marks)

8 In Bronte's stamp collection the ratio of Australian stamps to European stamps is 5 : 3 and the ratio of European stamps to African stamps is 4 : 1.
   a   What is the ratio of Australian stamps to African stamps?   (2 marks)
   b   If the total number of Australian, European and African stamps was 210, how many Australian stamps are in Bronte's collection?   (2 marks)

9 In a rectangle, the ratio of length to breadth is 5 : 2. If the perimeter is 56 cm, what is the area of the rectangle?   (2 marks)

10 A 7.4 metre length of rope is cut into three pieces. The ratio of piece A to piece B is 2 : 3, while the ratio of piece B to piece C is 5 : 4.
   a   What is the ratio of piece A to piece B to piece C?   (2 marks)
   b   How long is piece C?   (2 marks)
   c   What is the length of the shortest piece?   (2 marks)

11 The ratio of 20 cent coins to 50 cent coins in Ryan's money jar was 3 : 5. If he had 160 coins, what was the total value of the money?   (2 marks)

12 A bag contains red, blue and white balls. For every two red balls there is a blue ball. For every three red balls there is a white ball.
   a   What is the ratio of blue balls to red balls to white balls?   (2 marks)
   b   If there were 55 balls in the bag, how many are white?   (2 marks)
   c   What is the smallest possible number of red balls in the bag?   (1 mark)

13 A bag has twice as many red jelly beans as black jelly beans and twice as many pink jelly beans as red jelly beans.
   a   What is the ratio of black jelly beans to red jelly beans to pink jelly beans?   (1 mark)
   b   If there are 28 jelly beans in the bag, how many are black?   (2 marks)

14 1200 mL of juice is poured into three jugs in the ratio of 3 : 4 : 5. The juice from the first jug is then poured into the second. How much more juice is now in the second jug than the third?   (2 marks)

Your Feedback

$\frac{\boxed{}}{51} \times 100\% = \boxed{}\%$

PAGE 119

PAGE 161

DISCOUNTS AND BEST BUYS
Money and Financial Mathematics

1 **Discount** is the amount that a price of an object has been reduced by.

2 The discount could be expressed as an **amount** that the price has been reduced by.
For example, a dress was originally priced at $80 and is reduced by $15. What is the new price?
New price = $80 – $15
$\qquad\quad$ = $65 $\qquad$ ∴ the new price is $65

3 The discount could be expressed as a **percentage** of the original price.
For example, an electric drill is priced at $80. If it is discounted by 10%, what is the new price?
Discount = 10% of $80
$\qquad\quad$ = 0.1 × 80
$\qquad\quad$ = 8
New price = 80 – 8
$\qquad\quad$ = 72 $\qquad$ ∴ the new price is $72

4 The **percentage discount** can be calculated by writing the discount as a percentage of the original price. For example, a DVD is originally priced at $25. It is reduced in price to $20. What is the percentage discount?
Discount = $25 – $20
$\qquad\quad$ = $5
Discount as percentage $= \dfrac{5}{25} \times 100\%$
$\qquad\qquad\qquad\qquad\quad = \dfrac{5}{25} \times \dfrac{100}{1}$
$\qquad\qquad\qquad\qquad\quad = 20\% \qquad$ ∴ the discount is 20%

5 Stores can offer **other discounts** such as 'buy-two, get-the-next-free' deals.
For example, a restaurant offers a 'the second meal half-price' deal. This means that the cheaper meal will be half-price. Mr and Mrs Jacob's meals cost $38 and $36. What will they pay for their meals?
Total cost = $38 + half of $36
$\qquad\quad$ = $38 + $18
$\qquad\quad$ = $56 $\qquad$ ∴ the cost is $56

6 When a product is available in different sized packaging, we can find the **best buy** by finding the cost of each package per unit, e.g. cost for 100 grams. For example, peanut butter is available in three different jars: 200 g at $2.70, 400 g at $5.00 and 500 g at $6.50.
200 g jar: $2.70 ÷ 2 = $1.35 per 100 g
400 g jar: $5.00 ÷ 4 = $1.25 per 100 g
500 g jar: $6.50 ÷ 5 = $1.30 per 100 g $\qquad$ ∴ the best buy is the 400 g jar

Checklist
Can you:
1 Calculate a discount?
2 Express a discount as a percentage?
3 Solve word problems involving discounts?
4 Determine the best buy from a range of products?

DISCOUNTS AND BEST BUYS
Money and Financial Mathematics

1   What is the new price, if a:
   a   bike priced at $120 is discounted by $45?
   b   watch priced at $165 is discounted by $55?
   c   console game priced at $89 is discounted by $11.50?

2   After a hailstorm the price of a car is discounted by $1500. If the new price is $18 500, what was the original price?

3   Complete the table:

	Original price	Discount	New price
a	$540	$54	
b	$19.90		$15.60
c		$6	$11.70

4   What is the new price of a pair of shoes marked at $80, if it is discounted by:
   a   10%?   b   15%?   c   30%?

5   Find the new price of a pair of speakers which originally cost $60 but were discounted by:
   a   20%   b   25%   c   40%

6   A shop held a 25%-off-everything discount sale. What is the new price of a:
   a   bike marked at $300?   b   helmet marked at $50?

7   What is the percentage discount, if:
   a   a loaf of bread originally priced at $4 is sold for $3?
   b   a book originally priced at $15 is sold for $12?
   c   a tennis racket originally priced at $120 is sold for $84?

8   Toby bought two pairs of shoes. The store had a 'buy-one, get-the-second-half-price' offer. If the shoes cost $89 a pair, what will Toby pay?

9   A loyalty program at a coffee shop gives the fifth coffee free. If each coffee costs, $4.50, how much will Kylie spend before she receives her free coffee?

10   Which of these is the better buy:
   a   A—300 mL juice for $2.40   or   B—500 mL juice for $4.20?
   b   A—200 g rice for $1.80   or   B—700 g rice for $5.60?

PAGE 120

Money and Financial Mathematics

15 MINUTES

INTERMEDIATE TEST

Part A Multiple Choice

1 The marked price of a hockey stick was $32. If it was discounted by $4.50, the price paid is:

   A $28.50   **B** $27.50   **C** $36.50   **D** $77   (1 mark)

2 In a sale the price of a microwave oven is marked down to $389. If this is a discount of $35, the original price was:

   A $424   **B** $434   **C** $426   **D** $354   (1 mark)

3 Lenore bought a pair of jeans at a sale. The original price of the jeans was $80, but she received a discount of 20%. The price she paid for the jeans was:

   A $60   **B** $64   **C** $74   **D** $100   (1 mark)

4 Which of these is the best buy for a jar of coffee? *Hint 1*

   A 100 g for $3.10   **B** 200 g for $6.30

   C 300 g for $9.60   **D** 400 g for $12.20   (1 mark)

5 A television set was originally priced at $1000. At a discount sale, Tenealle paid $800 for the set. The price was discounted by:

   A 8%   **B** 20%   **C** 25%   **D** 80%   (1 mark)

6 A shop offered a variety of discounts on a lawnmower. If the original price was $360, which of these offers gives the greatest discount?

   A '$50 off'   **B** '$60 voucher'   **C** 'you pay $320'   **D** '10% saving' (1 mark)

Part B Short Answer

7 Complete the table.   (4 marks)

Original price	Percentage discount	Discount amount
$10	20%	
$20	10%	
$80		$20
$50		$15

8 Three people went out to a restaurant that offered a '25% off the most expensive main course' deal. If their main meals cost $40, $37 and $35.40, what will they pay for their meals?   (2 marks)

9 A store sells toilet paper in different sized packs. A six-roll pack sells for $4.55, an eight-roll pack for $6.20, a twelve-roll pack for $9.60 and a sixteen-roll pack for $11.84. Which pack gives the best value? *Hint 2*   (2 marks)

10 Alec buys 3 CDs at $12 each and 4 DVDs at $16 each. If he is given a 10% discount on his purchases, what amount will he pay?   (2 marks)

11 At a sale the price of a dishwasher drops from $1200 to $900. Find the percentage discount. (2 marks)

Hint 1: Find the cost of 100 g of coffee for each jar.

Hint 2: Find the cost of 1 toilet roll for each packet.

Your Feedback

$$\frac{\boxed{}}{18} \times 100\% = \boxed{}\%$$

PAGE 121

PAGE 161

1 A shop held a 15% sale on all its lounges and sofas. Find the new price of a:
  a lounge originally priced at $1200 (2 marks)
  b sofa originally priced at $800 (2 marks)

2 A rice cooker drops in price from $40 to $35. Express this reduction in price as a discount. (2 marks)

3 An electrical shop held a store-wide discount sale on **all** items. The price of a set of headphones dropped from $70 to $63.
  a Find the store-wide discount percentage. (2 marks)
  b Find the discount on a vacuum cleaner originally priced at $560. (1 mark)
  c What does Amanda save on an electric blanket priced at $68. (1 mark)
  d What will Lee pay for a toaster originally priced at $36? (2 marks)
  e A washing machine is marked at $1340. What will Sarah pay after her discount? (2 marks)

4 Sam has two vouchers for a restaurant. One voucher is 20% off the entire bill, while the other is for 'Buy one meal and get the next at half-price'. Sam and her friend each order a curry priced at $12. Explain which voucher should be used to save the most money? (2 marks)

5 A hardware store has a 20% sale on all power tools. What does Keith save on a hammer drill priced at $80, if he can also use his 10% Senior's discount card? (2 marks)

6 Due to the hot weather a fruit shop manager is dropping the price of fruit he sells. On Tuesday, cases of mangoes were priced at $15. Each day he discounts the price by 20%. What is the price on
  a Wednesday? **b** Thursday? (2 marks each)

7 A bee-keeper sells honey in four sized jars:
  200 g for $4.80 300 g for $7.50 400 g for $9.50
  500 g for $11.50
  What is the best buy? (2 marks)

8 Leon's electricity bill has been discounted from $650 to $520. Find the percentage discount. (2 marks)

9 The price of a handbag was dropped by 20%. If this meant a discount of $16, find:
  a the old price (2 marks)
  b the discounted price (1 mark)

10 A butcher offers meat packs for sale for $100. Any school making a purchase at the shop is given a 15% discount. The manager offers a further 10% discount because his daughter attends the school.
  a How much will be paid for the meat pack?
  b Find the total discount as a percentage? (2 marks each)

11 A pub offers the following deals:
  Cheap Tuesday: 25% off bill
  Wednesday Mega Deal: $10 schnitzels
  Thursday Savings: 2nd meal half price
  The normal price of a schnitzel is $14. Jack and Jill go to the pub each night and order a schnitzel each. On which night will they pay the least for their meal? (2 marks)

12 A bookshop offered a 10% discount on all study guides. Tenille paid $18 for a maths study guide.
  a What was the original price? (2 marks)
  b What was the discount? (1 mark)

13 On Tuesday, a store manager raised all prices by 20%. On the following Sunday she discounted all products by 25%. Before the price changes, a pair of shoes was priced at $100.
  a What is the new price of the shoes? (2 marks)
  b By comparing the original and the final price, find the percentage discount. (1 mark)

14 This sign was displayed in a supermarket.

> **Peanut Butter**
> **Was $4.50**
> **Now $4.00**
> **SAVE 10%**

Comment on the accuracy of the calculations. (2 marks)

15 A store buys a shirt from the manufacturer for $16. It increases the price to make a profit of $64.
  a What will be the profit as a percentage of the cost price? (2 marks)
  b The shirt does not sell, and a month later the price is discounted by 40%. What will be the amount of profit and percentage profit made by the store if the shirt sells? (2 marks)
  c Two months later the shirt still has not sold and the store reduces the price by a further 50%. If the shirt finally sells, find the percentage profit made by the store on the shirt. (2 marks)

Your Feedback

$$\frac{}{49} \times 100\% = \boxed{} \%$$

PAGE 121

PAGE 161

1. Symbols such as letters, called **pronumerals**, are used to take the place of numbers. They are often referred to as **variables** because the numbers they replace may vary.

2. Statements involving pronumerals are often referred to as **algebraic expressions**.

3. There are a number of **conventions** used when working with pronumerals.

   $1a = a$ $\qquad$ $2 \times a \times b = 2ab$ $\qquad$ $a^1 = a$ $\qquad$ $a \times a = a^2$ $\qquad$ $a \div b = \dfrac{a}{b}$

4. Algebra is often used to describe **number patterns**.
   For example, a number of matches are used to make a series of squares.

    and so on.

   If s = number of squares and m = number of matches used, the information can be summarised in the **table** at right.

s	1	2	3	4
m	4	7	10	13

   A '**rule**' is found linking the number of matchsticks (m) to the number of squares (s).
   $\therefore$ matchsticks = 3 × squares + 1
   $\qquad$ i.e. $m = 3s + 1$

   This 'rule' can now be used to predict the number of matches to make 12 squares.
   Using $m = 3s + 1$
   $\qquad \therefore m = 3 \times 12 + 1$
   $\qquad \qquad = 37$ $\qquad \qquad \therefore$ 37 matches

5. Numbers can **replace pronumerals** in algebraic expressions.
   For example, if $a = 3$, $b = 4$, find $2a + 5b$
   $\therefore 2a + 5b = 2 \times 3 + 5 \times 4$
   $\qquad \qquad = 6 + 20$
   $\qquad \qquad = 26$

Checklist
Can you:

1 *Understand what is meant by the terms pronumeral, variable and algebraic expression?* ☐
2 *Translate between words and algebraic symbols?* ☐
3 *Complete a table using a pattern relationship?* ☐
4 *Find the 'rule' from information contained in a table?* ☐
5 *Substitute numbers for pronumerals in an expression?* ☐

1 Write in simplified form:

   a $3 \times a \times b$ **b** $2 \times y \times y$ **c** $1x^1$

   d $2 \times 3 \times b \times a$ **e** $a \times a \times a$ **f** $2a \times a \times b \times b$

2 Write in expanded form:

   a $5ab$ **b** $3x^2$ **c** $7x^3y^2$

3 Write an expression for the:

   a product of a and 3

   b sum of x, y and 8

   c average of a, $2b$ and c

   d number 5 more than k

   e difference between a and b, if $a > b$

   f product of 5 and the sum of x and 4

4 **a** What is the next consecutive whole number after x?

   b If y is an odd number, find the next two consecutive odd numbers.

5 Write the rule for:

   a

x	1	2	3	4	5
y	4	7	10	13	16

   b

a	2	4	6	8	10
b	0	4	8	12	16

6 If $a = 4$, $b = 3$, $c = 2$, find:

   a $ab + c$ **b** $(2b)^2 - 2b^2$ **c** $\dfrac{ab}{c}$

   d $cb - a$ **e** $\dfrac{a-b}{c-1}$ **f** $(a-c)^2$

7 If $x = -3$ and $y = -4$ find:

   a $x + y$ **b** $x - y$ **c** $y - x$

   d $6 + y$ **e** $5 - (y + x)$ **f** $x - (3 - y)$

8 To find the area of a rectangle we use the formula $A = lb$. Find A if:

   a $l = 18$ and $b = 11$

   b $l = 4.2$ and $b = 0.8$

PAGE 123

Answers 1a $3ab$ b $2y^2$ c x d $6ab$ e a^3 f $2a^2b^2$ 2a $5 \times a \times b$ b $3 \times x \times x$ c $7 \times x \times x \times x \times y \times y$ 3a $3a$ b $x + y + 8$
c $(a + 2b + c) \div 3$ d $k + 5$ e $a - b$ f $5(x + 4)$ 4a $x + 1$ b $y + 2$, $y + 4$ 5a $y = 3x + 1$ b $b = 2a - 4$ 6a 14 b 18 c 6 d 2 e 1
f 4 7a -7 b 1 c -1 d 2 e 12 f -10 8a 198 b 3.36

BASIC ALGEBRA CONCEPTS
Patterns and Algebra

INTERMEDIATE TEST

Part A Multiple Choice

1 Lee buys 3 pies at p cents each and 2 cans at c cents each. If total cost $= T$, this can be summarised as:

    A $T = 3p + 2c$ **B** $T = 3p \times 2c$ **C** $p = 2c + 3T$ **D** $c = 3p + 2T$ (1 mark)

2 Write the rule for the table.

    A $y = x^2 + 1$ **B** $y = 3x + 1$

    C $y = 4x - 2$ **D** $y = x^2 + 3$

x	2	3	4	5	6
y	5	10	17	26	37

(1 mark)

3 If a is an even number, the next consecutive even number is: *Hint 1*

    A $2a$ **B** c **C** $a + 1$ **D** $a + 2$ (1 mark)

4 How many centimetres in p metres?

    A p **B** $10p$ **C** $100p$ **D** $1000p$ (1 mark)

5 If $a = -4$ and $b = -6$, the value of $\dfrac{a - b}{2}$ is: *Hint 2*

    A -1 **B** -2 **C** 2 **D** 1 (1 mark)

Part B Short Answer

6 A series of octagons is made from matches.

    a Complete the table linking the number of octagons(o) with matches(m).

o	1	2	3	4
m				

(2 marks)

    b Write a formula linking o and m.   (1 mark)

    c Use your formula to find the number of matches used to make 20 octagons.   (2 marks)

7 When $a = 0.3$ and $b = 0.5$, find the value of:

    a $6a - 3b$ **b** $\dfrac{10a}{b}$ **c** a^2b

    d $2a^2$ **e** $3b - a$ **f** $(0.2 - ab)^2$ (2 marks each)

Your Feedback

$\dfrac{\boxed{}}{22} \times 100\% = \boxed{}\%$

PAGE 123

PAGE 161

Hint 1: The difference between consecutive even numbers is two.
Hint 2: Use the order of operations rules.

1 Find the number rule linking x and y:

a (1 mark)

x	0	1	2	3
y	–2	1	4	7

b (1 mark)

x	0	1	2	3
y	3	1	–1	–3

c (1 mark)

x	2	4	8	16
y	0.5	1	2	4

d (1 mark)

x	0	1	2	3
y	0	–1	0	3

e (1 mark)

x	–2	–1	0	1
y	–8	1	4	1

2 Squares are used to form a pattern:

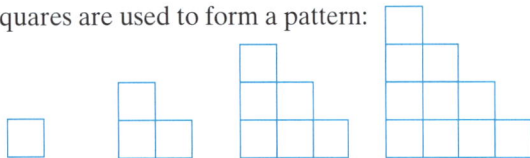

Figure 1   Figure 2   Figure 3   Figure 4

a Complete the table using f = figure and s = squares. (1 mark)

f	1	2	3	4
s	1	3		

b How many squares are used in figure 6? (1 mark)

c The rule linking f and s is $s = \dfrac{f^2 + f}{2}$

Use the rule to find the number of squares used in figure 12. (2 marks)

3 Margot babysits and uses a table to record the amount she charges for lengths of babysitting.

n (hours)	2	3	4	5
c ($)	40	50	60	70

a How much does she charge for 6 hours? (1 mark)

b How many hours of babysitting will earn her $100? (2 marks)

c Write the rule linking n and c:

$c =$ _____ (1 mark)

d Use the rule in part **c** to find the amount she would receive for 9 hours of babysitting. (1 mark)

4 If $a = 3, b = 5, c = 2$, find the value of:

a $\dfrac{ab - 1}{c}$ (2 marks)

b $(b - c)(a + c)$ (2 marks)

5 Rhiannon's car needs to be fixed. The mechanic charges $80 per hour plus $210 parts. Write an expression for the cost (c) in dollars, if the mechanic takes n hours. (1 mark)

6 Rahul starts to save for a new bike. He plans to save $75 every week from his part-time job and is given $100 by his parents as a birthday present. Write an expression to represent the total amount (A) in dollars he has after working t weeks. (1 mark)

7 Evaluate T, where $T = p^2 - qr$, when:

a $p = 3, q = 4$ and $r = 2$ (2 marks)

b $p = -4, q = 2$ and $r = -3$ (2 marks)

8 Write an algebraic expression for the following by letting the number be x:

a The sum of a number and three is less than sixteen. (1 mark)

b The product of two whole consecutive numbers is twenty. (1 mark)

c The product of two consecutive odd numbers is subtracted from seven times the smaller odd number is equal to six. (1 mark)

9 Let the width of a rectangle be x cm. If the length is 5 cm longer than the width, write an algebraic expression for the:

a perimeter (P) (1 mark)

b area (A) (1 mark)

10 Write an algebraic expression for the selling price (P) in dollars, if a painting originally purchased for $700 is sold for a profit of x%. (1 mark)

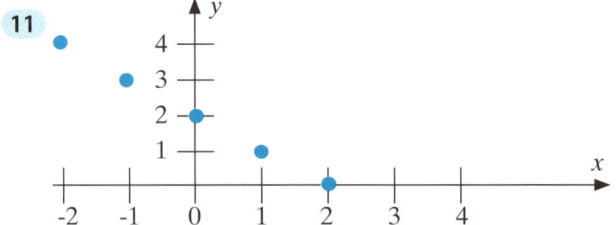

11

a Use the points to complete the table: (1 mark)

x				
y				

b Write the rule that is used to plot the points. (1 mark)

Your Feedback

$\dfrac{\boxed{}}{32} \times 100\% = \boxed{}\%$

PAGE 124

PAGE 161

USING ALGEBRA
Patterns and Algebra

1   Terms are separated by '+' and '–' signs. To find an answer we reduce the number of terms, that is, we **simplify** the algebraic expression.

2   Expressions in **expanded form** can be written using **index form**.
    For example, rewrite $a \times a \times a \times a$ in index form. This means $a \times a \times a \times a = a^4$

3   **Like terms** have identical algebraic parts. For example, $4a, 3a, -6a, a$, etc. are like terms.

4   **Unlike terms** have different algebraic parts. For example, $3a, 6a^2, -2ab, -7y$, etc. are unlike terms.

5   We can **only add like terms**. If terms are not like terms, we cannot add them.
    For example, simplify:
    a $4a + 7a = 11a$
    b $6x + 2y = 6x + 2y$
    c $-p + 8p = 7p$
    d $-3a^2b + 3a^2b = 0$

6   We can **only subtract like terms**. If terms are not like terms, we cannot subtract them.
    For example, simplify:
    a $4xy - 2yx = 2xy$
    b $4a^2 - 3a = 4a^2 - 3a$
    c $-7a - 3a = -10a$
    d $-7mn - mn = -8mn$

7   We can **multiply like and unlike terms**.
    For example, simplify:
    a $4a \times 2a = 8a^2$
    b $3a \times 2b \times 4c = 24abc$

8   We can **divide like and unlike terms**.
    For example, simplify:
    a $15xy \div 5x = 3y$
    b $7a \div a = 7$
    c $\dfrac{12a}{6} = 2a$
    d $\dfrac{25b}{5b} = 5$

9   **Algebraic expressions** can involve a variety of terms.
    For example, simplify:
    a $12x + 3y + 2x + 7y = 14x + 10y$
    b $5ab - 2b + 3ba - 6b = 8ab - 8b$

10 **Order of operation rules** apply to algebraic expressions. That is, multiplication and division take priority over addition and subtraction.
    For example, simplify:
    a $5a \times 2b - 3 \times 7ab = 10ab - 21ab$
                                  $= -11ab$
    b $12a - 10a \div 5 = 12a - 2a$
                         $= 10a$

Checklist
Can you:

1   *Understand what is meant by the term simplify?*
2   *Identify like and unlike terms from a list of algebraic expressions?*
3   *Add, subtract, multiply and divide algebraic expressions?*
4   *Simplify algebraic expressions using order of operation rules?*

USING ALGEBRA
Patterns and Algebra

1 Identify the like terms:

   a $4a, 7a, 3b, ab$ **b** $xy, 4y, 3xy, x^2y^2, -yx$

2 Simplify:

   a $4x + 7x + 2x + x$ **b** $a + a + a + a$ **c** $4xy + yx + 3xy$

   d $4x^2 + 2x^2$ **e** $-6y + 3y + y$ **f** $-a^3 + a^3$

   g $-2x^3 + 2x^3 + 2x^3$ **h** $ab + 2ab + 3ab$ **i** $-4g + g$

3 Simplify:

   a $3a - 2a$ **b** $7b - b$ **c** $15a^2b - 20ab$

   d $-12y^2 - 2y^2$ **e** $8ab - 9ab$ **f** $4r - 3r - 2r - r$

   g $7a - 8b$ **h** $-7k - 2k$ **i** $2aa - a^2$

4 Simplify:

   a $4z - 3x + 2z - 5z$ **b** $12a - 4ab + a - ab$ **c** $3 - 2a + 7 + a$

   d $2y^2 + 3y - 6y + y^2$ **e** $-4s - 5st + s + ts$ **f** $7a^2 - 3a + 8a - a^2$

   g $6y + 2a - 3a - 5y$ **h** $12a - a^2 + a - 12a^2$ **i** $32 - 5w + 3w - 30$

5 Simplify:

   a $a \times a \times a \times a$ **b** $b \times c \times b \times c$ **c** $4 \times y \times y \times y \times y$

6 Write in expanded form:

   a a^3 **b** b^6 **c** $5x^2 y^3$

7 Simplify:

   a $8x \div 4$ **b** $3y \div y$ **c** $15a \div 5a$

   d $90cd \div 10c$ **e** $16x^2 \div 4x$ **f** $12abd \div 3ad$

   g $\dfrac{18d}{9d}$ **h** $\dfrac{6x^2}{3x}$ **i** $\dfrac{24bg^2}{6g}$

8 Simplify:

   a $3 \times 6y - 5y \times 2$ **b** $3a \times 5b - 10ab$ **c** $20d \div 4d + 3$

   d $12x - (14x - 2x)$ **e** $32a \div 16 \times 2$ **f** $(4a)^2 - 4a^2$

9 Find the missing algebraic expression:

   a $10a - \underline{\hspace{1cm}} = 6a$ **b** $3y \times \underline{\hspace{1cm}} = 21xy$ **c** $\underline{\hspace{1cm}} \div 4z = 3$

   d $\underline{\hspace{1cm}} + 4g = 3g$ **e** $8ab \div \underline{\hspace{1cm}} = 4$ **f** $\underline{\hspace{1cm}} \times 5w = 30w^2$

PAGE 124

Part A   Multiple Choice

1   Which expression is not equal to $3m$?

   A $5m - 2m$ **B** $m \times m \times m$ **C** $m + m + m$ **D** $\dfrac{6m}{2}$ (1 mark)

2   Simplify $5a - 4 + 3a - 2$

   A $8a - 6$ **B** $8a + 6$ **C** $8a + 2$ **D** $8a - 2$ (1 mark)

3   Which of the following lists contain only like terms?

   A $-2a, 2, 2a$ **B** $3b^2, b^2, ab^2$ **C** $2r^3, 5^3, 2r^3$ **D** $-m^2, mm, 5m^2$ (1 mark)

4   The sum of $4b$ and the product of 6 and $2b$ is:

   A $16b$ **B** $8b + 6$ **C** $50b$ **D** $48b^2$ (1 mark)

5   Simplify $(3a)^2 - 3a^2$

   A 0 **B** $3a^2$ **C** $6a^2$ **D** $9a^2$ (1 mark)

Part B   Short Answer

6   Write down the perimeter of the triangle.   (2 marks)

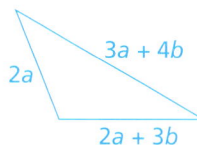

7   The first of three consecutive whole numbers is x. What is the average of the three numbers? *Hint 1*
(2 marks)

8   Find the area of the following shapes:

   a   (2 marks)

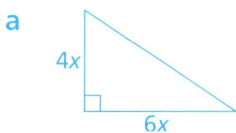

   b   (3 marks)

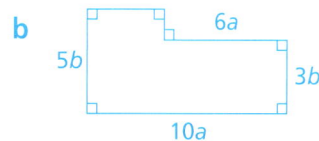

9   Simplify:

   a $3a - 2b - 5a + 6b$ **b** $8x - 3xy + x$ (1 mark each)

10   Each packet of biscuits contains m biscuits. If Sarah bought 3 packets and Con bought 2 packets, how many biscuits are there altogether?   (2 marks)

11   Simplify:

   a $40y \div 10 + 3 \times 2y$ **b** $\dfrac{12x}{6} + 3x$ (2 marks each)

12   Darren is paid $\$p$ per hour for his part time job. If he works for 2 hours each day from Monday to Friday, how much will he be paid for his 5-day week?   (2 marks)

Your Feedback

$\dfrac{\boxed{}}{24} \times 100\% = \boxed{}\%$

PAGE 125

PAGE 161

Hint 1: Let the numbers be $x, x + 1, x + 2$

1 Simplify:

  a $3x - 2y - 4x + 5y$ **b** $4a - 3 - 9 - 7a$

  c $2x^2 - 2xy - 6x^2 - yx$ **d** $-2w - q - w + q$

                            (1 mark each)

2 Simplify:

  a $3^x \times 3^y$ **b** $3^x \div 3^y$

  c $(3^x)^y$ (1 mark each)

3 Simplify:

  a $5y \times (-3y)$ **b** $(-4a)^2$

  c $16d^2 \div 4d$ **d** $\dfrac{16g}{4g^2}$

  e $\dfrac{-20w^2}{5w}$ (1 mark each)

4 A gardener plants n tomato seedlings. He also plants twice as many lettuces as tomato seedlings and six fewer pumpkin plants as lettuces. What was the total planted? (2 marks)

5 Find the perimeter of an equilateral triangle with side length $7y$ cm. (1 mark)

6 A square has an area of $25x^2$ cm². What is the perimeter of the square? (2 marks)

7 Simplify:

  a $12y \div 4 - 2 \times 5y$ **b** $(10a - 6a \times 3)^2$

  c $\dfrac{3a - 4a \times 2}{5a}$ **d** $r(3 - 4 \times 2) - 3r$

  e $(2a - 7a)(6b - 8b)$ (2 marks each)

8 Konrad wrote four consecutive odd numbers starting with n.

  a   What is the sum of the four numbers. (1 mark)

  b   What is the difference between the largest and the smallest number? (1 mark)

  c   Find the average of the numbers. (1 mark)

9 The width of a rectangle is x cm. The length is three less than four times the width. In terms of x, write an algebraic expression for:

  a   length   (1 mark)

  b   perimeter   (1 mark)

  c   area   (1 mark)

10 Write the following as algebraic expressions by letting the number be x:

  a   The sum of a number and twelve is forty.

  b   The difference between a number and six is forty.

  c   The product of a number and five is thirty.

  d   The quotient of a number and four is seven.

                            (1 mark each)

11 Three university friends earn money picking grapes. Raj earns $\$p$. Toni earns $\$40$ more than Raj, while Simon earns $\$80$ less than Raj. Find the total amount earned by the three friends. (2 marks)

12 Adrianna swims b laps this week and plans to double the number of laps each week over each of the next four weeks. What will be the total number of laps swam in the five weeks? (2 marks)

13 Find the next term of the sequence:

  a $2, 4c, 8c^2,$ _____   (1 mark)

  b $27p, -9p, 3p,$ _____   (1 mark)

  c $3x + 7y, 5x + 4y, 7x + y,$ _____ (1 mark)

  d $4a - 3b, 3a - 2b, 2a - b,$ _____ (1 mark)

  e $125x^3, 25x^2, 5x,$ _____   (1 mark)

  f $3x - y, -6x + 2y, 12x - 4y,$ _____ (1 mark)

14 What exceeds $3x - 7y$ by $2x + 3y$?   (1 mark)

15 Cameron is y years old and is 6 years older than his sister Emilie. Their father Jack is three times Cameron's age. There are 28 years between Jack and his father. What is the difference in age between Jack's father and Emilie? (2 marks)

16 Rewrite the following in symbols:

  a   The product of x and 4 more than x is equal to twenty-eight. (1 mark)

  b x is multiplied by 5, and 7 is added to that product, the answer is 22. (1 mark)

  c   If 8 is subtracted from the product of 3 and x, the answer is 34. (1 mark)

  d x is divided by 3 and 11 is added to the result, the result is 17. (1 mark)

  e   The product of 8 and x is subtracted from 40, the answer is 16. (1 mark)

17 One number is six more than another number. The sum of the two numbers is twenty-seven. By letting the smaller number be x, express the information in an equation. (2 marks)

Your Feedback

$\dfrac{\boxed{}}{57} \times 100\% = \boxed{} \%$

PAGE 125

PAGE 161

SIMPLE EQUATIONS AND GRAPHS
Linear and Non-linear Relationships

1 An **equation** is an algebraic statement involving an equal sign.

2 Points can be located on a **number plane** in a pattern determined by a **number rule** (or **equation**). The pattern of points is often in the shape of a line (called **linear relationship**) or as a curve (called **non-linear relationship**). For example, complete the table, using the rule $y = 2x - 1$, to graph the result on a number plane:

$y = 2x - 1$

x	0	1	2	3
y	−1	1	3	5

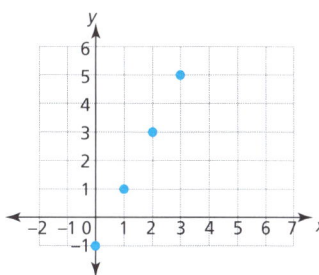

3 Equations are solved and the answer is called the **solution**. Simple equations can be solved '**by inspection**' which means that we look for the value of the pronumeral that makes the equation have the same values on both sides of the equal sign. One way is to replace the pronumeral with the phrase 'what number'.
For example, $x + 3 = 7$ can be solved if we say 'what number' plus 3 is 7.
The answer is 4. We can check that this is the correct solution by substitution: $4 + 3 = 7$.

4 We need to learn a more formal approach. When we solve an equation, we must remember the important rule: **what we do to one side of the equation we must do to the other side**. The final line will have the pronumeral on the left of the equal sign and a number on the right.
For example, solve:

a $x + 2 = 6$

$x + 2 - 2 = 6 - 2$

$x = 4$

b $x - 2 = 6$

$x - 2 + 2 = 6 + 2$

$x = 8$

c $2x = 6$

$\dfrac{2x}{2} = \dfrac{6}{2}$

$x = 3$

d $\dfrac{x}{2} = 6$

$2 \times \dfrac{x}{2} = 6 \times 2$

$x = 12$

5 A **travel graph** graphs time (t) and distance (d) together. When a section of the graph is horizontal, we know the traveller has stopped. The steeper the section of the graph, the faster the traveller is moving. For example, the graph shows Peter leaving home, travelling to his uncle's home and back again.

a What time did Peter arrive home? 2 pm

b How many times did he stop? 2 (10 to 11am and 12:30 to 1 pm)

c Between what two times did he travel the fastest? Between 1 pm and 2 pm

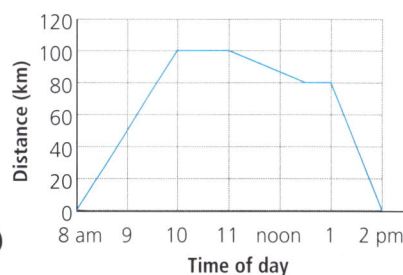

Checklist
Can you:

1 Use a number rule to graph a linear relationship on a number plane? ☐

2 Solve basic equations? ☐

3 Interpret the features of a travel graph? ☐

SIMPLE EQUATIONS AND GRAPHS
Linear and Non-linear Relationships

1 Complete the table and graph your results on a number plane:

a $y = x + 3$

x	0	1	2	3
y				

b $y = 2x + 1$

x	0	1	2	3
y				

c $y = 3 - x$

x	0	1	2	3
y				

2 Solve:

a $x + 4 = 7$ **b** $a + 3 = 2$ **c** $k + 6 = -1$

3 Solve:

a $r - 3 = 2$ **b** $s - 7 = 10$ **c** $w - 4 = -2$

4 Solve:

a $4y = 12$ **b** $3w = 18$ **c** $2a = 11$

5 Solve:

a $\dfrac{x}{2} = 5$ **b** $\dfrac{a}{3} = 2$ **c** $\dfrac{x}{5} = 4$

6 Solve:

a $2a - 3 = 5$ **b** $1 + 2y = 3$ **c** $\dfrac{t - 1}{4} = 2$

7 True or false? $x = 2$ is a solution of:

a $x + 5 = 7$ **b** $4x + 1 = 9$ **c** $3 - x = 5$

8 The travel graph represents a cyclist's journey.

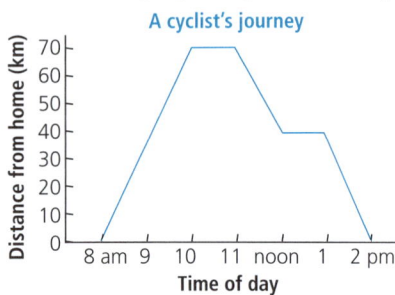

A cyclist's journey

a How many rest stops did he have?

b Between 11:00 and 12:00, how far did he travel?

c What total distance did he cycle during the day?

d When did the cyclist travel the fastest?

PAGE 126

Answers **1a** 3,4,5,6 **b** 1,3,5,7 **c** 3,2,1,0 see solutions for the graphs **2a** $x = 3$ **b** $a = -1$ **c** $k = -7$ **3a** $r = 5$ **b** $s = 17$ **c** $w = 2$ **4a** $y = 3$ **b** $w = 6$ **c** $a = 5.5$ **5a** $x = 10$ **b** $a = 6$ **c** $x = 20$ **6a** $a = 4$ **b** $y = 1$ **c** $t = 9$ **7a** T **b** T **c** F **8a** 2 **b** 30 km **c** 140 km **d** between 1 pm and 2 pm

SIMPLE EQUATIONS AND GRAPHS
Linear and Non-linear Relationships

INTERMEDIATE TEST

Part A Multiple Choice

1 For the rule $y = 2x + 1$, Jason completed a table of values. The missing value is:

x	0	1	2	3
y	1	3		7

   A 3   **B** 4   **C** 5   **D** 6   *(1 mark)*

2 The value of x in the equation, $x + 3 = 5$, is:

   A $x = 4$ **B** $x = 2$ **C** $x = -2$ **D** $x = -4$ *(1 mark)*

3 $x = 2$ is the solution to the equation: *Hint 1*

   A $x - 2 = 8$ **B** $2x = 6$ **C** $4 - x = 2$ **D** $x - 8 = 6$ *(1 mark)*

4 $b = -1$ is NOT the solution to the equation:

   A $b - 3 = -4$ **B** $2 - b = 3$ **C** $b + 2 = 1$ **D** $3b = 3$ *(1 mark)*

Part B Short Answer

5 Solve the following equations:

   a $2x - 1 = 9$ **b** $\dfrac{t - 1}{4} = 3$ **c** $2 + 3a = 4$ *(2 marks each)*

6 For the rule $y = 3x - 1$, complete the table and then plot the points on the number plane.

x	0	1	2
y	-1	2	

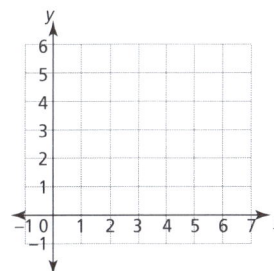

(2 marks)

7 Fong used a number rule to graph points on this number plane. What is his number rule? *Hint 2*

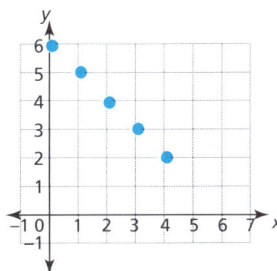

(2 marks)

8 The travel graph represents Jack's journey.

   a What was the total time Jack stopped?   *(1 mark)*

   b What was his average speed between noon and 1 pm?   *(1 mark)*

   c How far did Jack travel?   *(1 mark)*

   d What was the fastest average speed Jack travelled?   *(1 mark)*

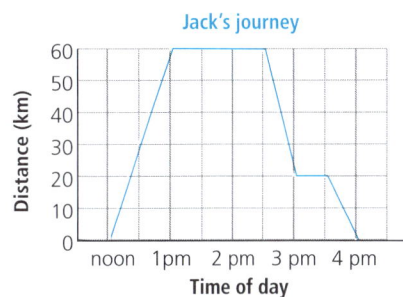

Jack's journey

Your Feedback

$$\frac{\boxed{}}{18} \times 100\% = \boxed{}\%$$

PAGE 127

PAGE 161

Hint 1: Substitute $x = 2$ into each of the options.

Hint 2: Consider the points: what do we do to the x-value to give the y-value?

1 Solve for the pronumeral:

   a $3x - 2 = 2x + 1$ (2 marks)

   b $4t - 3 = t - 9$ (2 marks)

   c $8p = 28 - 6p$ (2 marks)

   d $\dfrac{2t - 1}{3} = 5$ (2 marks)

2 In the following let the number be x, write an equation and solve:

   a   The sum of a number and 3 more than the number is 21. What is the number?   (2 marks)

   b   If 6 is subtracted from the product of a number and 4, the answer is 14. What is the number?   (2 marks)

   c   The product of a number and 6 is added to 20 and the answer is 32. What is the number?   (2 marks)

   d   The sum of a number and 3 is divided by 2 and the answer is 7. What is the number?   (2 marks)

3 Nicole collects teapots and has x teapots in her collection. She is given 12 more teapots for her birthday.

   a   Write an expression to represent the total number of teapots.   (1 mark)

   b   If she has now got a total of 54 teapots, write an equation to represent this.   (1 mark)

   c   Solve the equation to find the number of teapots she had before her birthday.   (2 marks)

4 The length of a rectangle is 4 cm longer than its width. The perimeter of the rectangle is 40 cm. By solving an equation find the dimensions of the rectangle.   (2 marks)

5 The sides of a regular pentagon are $(x + 2)$ cm. If the perimeter is 45 cm, what is the value of x?   (2 marks)

6 The sum of three consecutive odd numbers is 27. By letting the smallest number be p, and solving an equation, find the three numbers.   (2 marks)

7 The ages of three friends are added together and the total is 49. Phoebe is two years older than Penelope and three years younger than Ingrid. Solve an equation to find the age of each girl?   (2 marks)

8 Aiden is sixteen years old. He is twice as old as his sister Ava plus six years. Let Ava be x years old. Write an equation and solve to find Ava's age.   (2 marks)

9 Dylan paid a $290 bill for the repair of his washing machine. This included $80 for parts and $70 per hour for labour. Solve an equation to find the number of hours it took to repair the machine.   (2 marks)

10 Chi sold an antique ornament online for $96. This was $10 more than twice the amount that he paid for the ornament. Write an equation and solve it to find the cost price.   (2 marks)

11 In a maths test the highest mark was 6 marks more than twice the lowest mark. The sum of the two marks was 120. Solve an equation to find the highest mark?   (2 marks)

12 A survey was held to find the gender of people at a concert. The number of females at the concert was 40 more than three times the number of males. If there were 760 people at the concert, solve an equation to find the number of men at the concert.   (2 marks)

13 Gai earned $80 less than three times the amount that John earned. If the total amount earned by the two people was $2100, solve an equation to find the amount of money earned by Gai.   (2 marks)

14 Emily spent a total of $158 on a pair of shoes and a skirt. The price of the skirt was $22 less than twice what she paid for the shoes. Solve an equation to find the cost of the skirt.   (2 marks)

15 $170 is shared among three people so that the first will have $50 more than the second and $10 less than the third. Use an equation to find the amount each received.   (2 marks)

16 A group of 384 people consists of women, men and children. There are four times as many women as children, and twenty more than twice as many men as children. Use an equation to find the number of each in the group.   (2 marks)

Your Feedback

$\dfrac{\boxed{}}{46} \times 100\% = \boxed{}\%$

PAGE 128

PAGE 161

AREA AND VOLUME
Using Units of Measurement

1 The **area** is a measure of space contained within a plane figure.

2 Area is usually measured in **square units** (written as units²), such as cm², m², and so on.

3 **Area of a square** = side length × side length

$$A = s \times s$$
$$\therefore A = s^2$$

For example, find the area of a square with side 9 cm.

$$A = 9^2$$
$$= 81 \qquad \therefore \text{ area is } 81 \text{ cm}^2$$

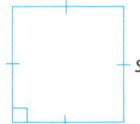

4 **Area of a rectangle** = length × breadth

$$A = l \times b$$
$$= lb$$

For example, find the area of a rectangle measuring 8.2 mm by 3 mm.

$$A = 8.2 \times 3$$
$$= 24.6 \qquad \therefore \text{ area is } 24.6 \text{ mm}^2$$

5 **Area of a triangle** = half of the base × perpendicular height

$$A = \frac{1}{2} \times b \times h \qquad \therefore A = \frac{1}{2}bh$$

For example, find the area of a triangle with base 12 cm and height 10 cm.

$$A = \frac{1}{2} \times 12 \times 10 = 60 \qquad \therefore \text{ area is } 60 \text{ cm}^2$$

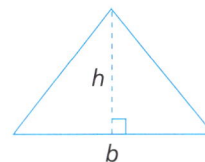

6 **Area of a parallelogram** = base × perpendicular height

$$A = b \times h$$
$$= bh$$

For example, find the area of a parallelogram with base of 12 cm and perpendicular height of 7 cm.

$$A = 12 \times 7$$
$$= 84 \qquad \therefore \text{ area is } 84 \text{ cm}^2$$

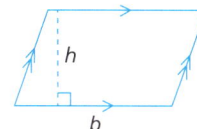

7 The **volume** is a measure of space contained within a solid shape.

8 Volume is measured in **cubic units** (written as units³), such as cm³, m³, and so on.

9 **Volume of a rectangular prism** = length × breadth × perpendicular height

$$V = l \times b \times h$$
$$= lbh$$

For example, find the volume of a rectangle prism measuring 9 m by 6 m by 4 m.

$$V = 9 \times 6 \times 4$$
$$= 216 \qquad \therefore \text{ volume is } 216 \text{ m}^3$$

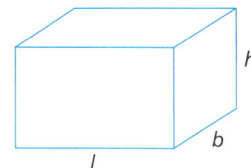

Checklist
Can you:

1 Use the formulae for the areas of a square, rectangle, triangle and parallelogram? ☐

2 Apply area formulae to solve problems? ☐

3 Use the formula for volume of a rectangular prism? ☐

AREA AND VOLUME
Using Units of Measurement

1 Find the area of the following:

a
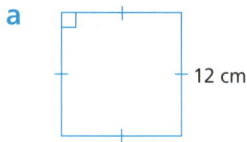
12 cm

b
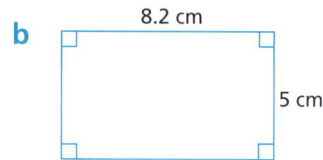
8.2 cm
5 cm

c
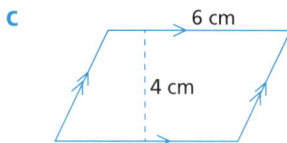
6 cm
4 cm

d
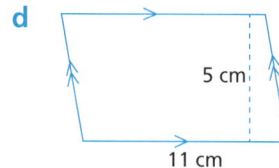
5 cm
11 cm

2 Find the area of the following triangles:

a
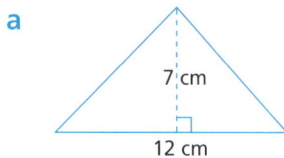
7 cm
12 cm

b
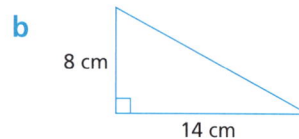
8 cm
14 cm

c
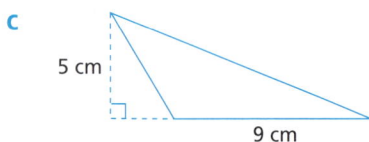
5 cm
9 cm

d
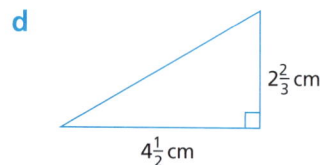
$2\frac{2}{3}$ cm
$4\frac{1}{2}$ cm

3 Find the area of the following composite shapes.

a
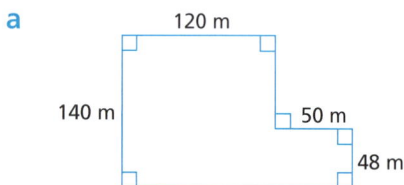
120 m
140 m
50 m
48 m

b
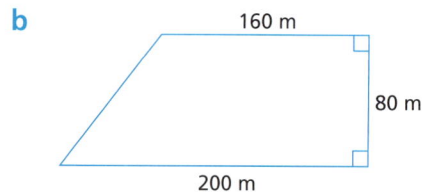
160 m
80 m
200 m

4 Find the cost of fertilising a rectangular paddock with dimensions 140 metres by 80 metres if the cost of fertiliser is 4 cents per m².

5 Find the volume of the rectangular prisms.

a
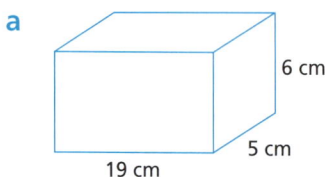
6 cm
5 cm
19 cm

b
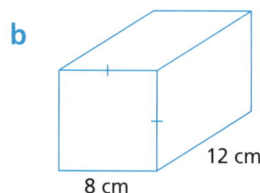
12 cm
8 cm

 PAGE 129

AREA AND VOLUME
Using Units of Measurement

INTERMEDIATE TEST

Part A Multiple Choice

1 A rectangle and a triangle have the same area. The triangle has a base of 8 cm and a perpendicular height of 5 cm. The rectangle could have dimensions of:
   A 10 cm by 4 cm **B** 8 cm by 2 cm **C** 4 cm by 6 cm **D** 10 cm by 2 cm (1 mark)

2 How many squares with side 2 cm can fit into the rectangle measuring 12 cm by 8 cm?
   A 20 **B** 24
   C 36 **D** 48 (1 mark)

3 The perimeter of a rectangle is 20 cm. If the length is 6 cm, its area is:
   A 24 cm^2 **B** 32 cm^2 **C** 48 cm^2 **D** 64 cm^2 (1 mark)

4 The area of a parallelogram is 72 cm^2. If the length of its base is 18 cm, its perpendicular height is:
   A 4 cm **B** 8 cm **C** 12 cm **D** 36 cm (1 mark)

5 The volume of a rectangular prism measuring 8 cm by 6 cm by 4 cm is:
   A 36 cm^3 **B** 48 cm^3 **C** 96 cm^3 **D** 192 cm^3 (1 mark)

6 A cube has a volume of 64 cm^3. The length of each side is:
   A 4 cm **B** 8 cm **C** 16 cm **D** 32 cm (1 mark)

7 The volume of the solid with the at right net is:
   A 24 cm^3 **B** 48 cm^3
   C 96 cm^3 **D** 120 cm^3 (1 mark)

Part B Short Answer

8 Find the area of the shapes: **a** *34 cm* **b** *2 cm* (2 marks each)
   20 cm *6 cm*
   50 cm *8 cm*

9 Find the area of the shaded regions: *Hint 1*
   a *12 m* **b** *20 m* (3 marks each)
   5 m *2 m*
   2 m *7 m* *10 m*

10 Turf is required to cover a rectangular area measuring 8 m by 6 m.
    a Find the area of the rectangle. (1 mark)
    b Rolls of turf are 40 cm wide by 2 m in length. How many rolls are required? (2 marks)
    c Each roll costs $3.60. Find the cost of the turf. (2 marks)
    d Jo rolls out 2 rolls/minute. How long will it take Jo to complete the job? (1 mark)

Your Feedback

$\dfrac{}{23} \times 100\% = \%$

PAGE 130

PAGE 161

Hint 1: Find both areas and then subtract.

1. Find the area of a rectangle with:
   a length 16 cm and width 9 cm   (1 mark)
   b length 3.4 cm and width 0.8 cm   (1 mark)
   c length $2\frac{3}{4}$ cm and width $\frac{4}{5}$ cm   (2 marks)

2. Find the area of a square with:
   a side 30 cm   (1 mark)
   b side 0.07 cm   (1 mark)
   c side $1\frac{2}{3}$ cm   (2 marks)

3. Find the area of a parallelogram with:
   a base 15 cm and perpendicular height 12 cm   (1 mark)
   b base 4.8 cm and perpendicular height 3 cm   (1 mark)
   c base $2\frac{1}{2}$ cm and perpendicular height $1\frac{1}{5}$ cm   (2 marks)

4. Find the area of a triangle with:
   a base of 20 cm and perpendicular height of 11.4 cm   (2 marks)
   b base of 6.4 cm and perpendicular height of 8 cm   (2 marks)
   c base of $1\frac{3}{5}$ cm and perpendicular height of $\frac{5}{8}$ cm   (2 marks)

5. If the area of a:
   a rectangle is 12.09 cm², find the length if the width is 3 cm.   (2 marks)
   b square is $12\frac{1}{4}$ cm², find the length of each side.   (2 marks)
   c parallelogram is $1\frac{3}{4}$ cm², find the perpendicular height if the base is $\frac{3}{8}$ cm.   (2 marks)
   d triangle is 16.5 cm², find the length of the base if the perpendicular height is 3 cm.   (2 marks)

6. A dentist's waiting room is rectangular, measuring 8 m by 5 m. The floor is to be covered with tiles costing \$35/m². Find the cost of the tiles.   (2 marks)

7. Jason's lawn is in the shape of a parallelogram with base length of 25.6 metres and perpendicular height of 10 metres. Bottles of weed killer cost \$4.80 each and cover an area of 64 m². How many bottles are required and what will be the total cost of spraying the entire lawn?   (2 marks)

8. Simone has a pergola in the shape of a rectangle measuring 8 metres by 5 metres. She uses square tiles with side length of 50 cm to cover the floor area. If the tiles each cost \$4, what will be the total cost of the tiles needed?   (2 marks)

9. Jack buys fencing material at a cost of \$5/metre to fence a rectangular paddock. If he spends a total of \$400, what is the largest area that he can fence?   (2 marks)

10. A cereal box has a base measuring 24 cm by 7 cm and a height of 30 cm. The box is two-thirds filled with cereal. What is the volume of cereal inside the box?   (2 marks)

11. Larry's Lawns supply rolls of turf 40 cm and 2 m long for \$5 each. What will be the cost of the turf needed to cover a lawn measuring 16 m by 12 m?   (2 marks)

12. A park has a rectangular garden 36 metres by 5 metres. How many kilograms of fertiliser is required to fertilise the garden at the rate of 100 grams per square metre?   (2 marks)

13. A photograph is to be mounted on a rectangular sheet of cardboard leaving a 4 cm border around the outside. The photograph is 30 cm wide by 22 cm high. What is the area of the border?   (2 marks)

14. One of the faces of a cube has an area of 400 cm². As 1000 cm³ = 1 L, find the capacity of the cube in litres.   (2 marks)

15. The shape of an iceberg approximates a rectangular prism. The iceberg is 16 km long by 4 km wide. The height of the iceberg above water level is 80 m. If one-ninth of the iceberg is above water level, what is the total volume of ice in the iceberg?   (2 marks)

Your Feedback

$$\frac{\boxed{}}{46} \times 100\% = \boxed{}\%$$

PAGE 131

PAGE 161

1. Shapes with width, depth and height are **3-dimensional solids**, and include polyhedra, cylinders, cones and spheres.

2. **Convex polyhedra** are solids with four or more **flat faces** and include prisms and pyramids.

3. A **prism** is a solid with identical flat ends, joined by rectangular faces. They are named according to the shape of the **cross-section** found by the 'slicing' of the prism. For example, if the cross-section is hexagonal, the prism is called an hexagonal prism.

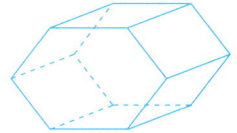

4. A **pyramid** is a solid with a polygon as base, and joined by triangular faces. For example, if the base is octagonal, the pyramid is an octagonal pyramid.

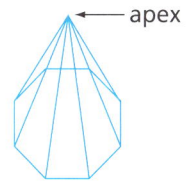
← apex

5. A **platonic solid** is made up of identical regular polygons. For example, a dodecahedron is a solid with every face a regular pentagon.

6. The **net** of a solid is a **plane shape** that can be folded to form a solid. For example, draw the net of a triangular prism.

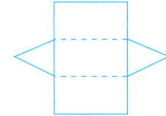

7. Solids can be **viewed** from different directions. For example, draw the top, front and side view of the prism.

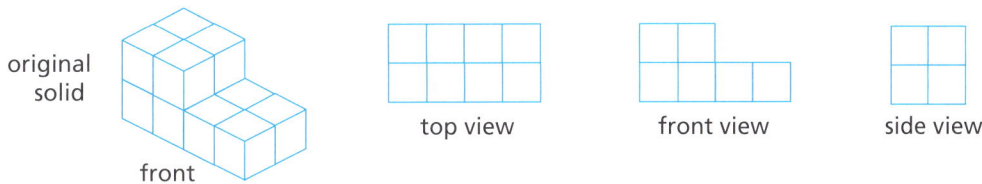

original solid

front

top view   front view   side view

8. A shape has **line symmetry** if it can be divided by a straight line (**axis of symmetry**) into 2 identical mirror images. For example, how many lines of symmetry have the following polygons?

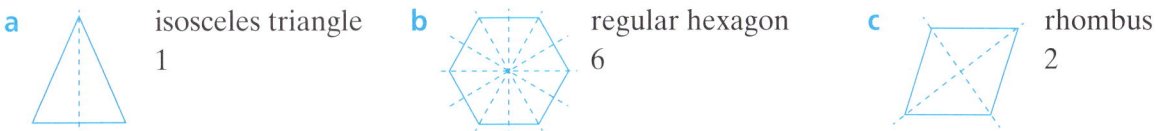

   a   isosceles triangle   b   regular hexagon   c   rhombus
        1   6   2

9. **Rotational symmetry** occurs when a shape is rotated about a point (**centre of symmetry**) and fits over its shape again. If a rotation of 180° (half a turn) is needed, then the shape has **point symmetry**, and the **order of rotational symmetry** is 2 (as 360° ÷ 180° = 2). For example, give the order of rotational symmetry of the following:

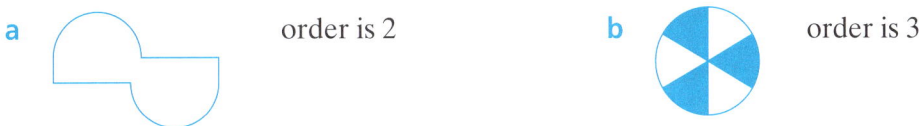

   a   order is 2   b   order is 3

Checklist
Can you:

1 *Draw different views of solids?* ☐

2 *Identify the cross-section of a prism?* ☐

3 *Identify line and rotational symmetries of shapes?* ☐

1 Name the following:

a 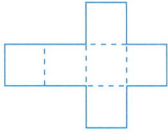   b 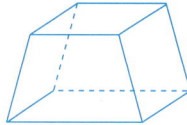   c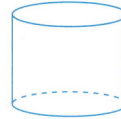

2 The following solids are cut along the line shown. Draw the shape of the cross-sections:

a 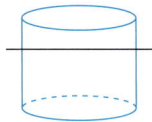   b 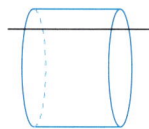   c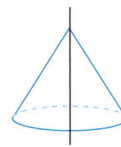

3 For the solid, draw the:
  a   top view
  b   front view
  c   right view

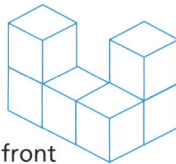
front

4 A solid is built from cubes. If the views are detailed below, draw a possible solid.

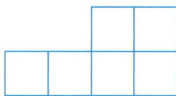

front view   side view   top view

5 On the diagrams, mark in all axes of symmetry.

a 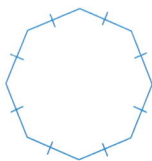   b 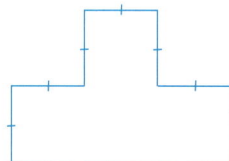   c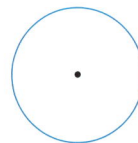

6 What is the order of rotational symmetry around the point X.

a 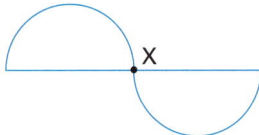   b 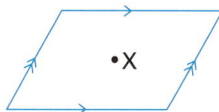   c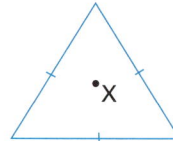

7 Find the order of rotation of the following:

a   b   c

PAGE 132

SOLIDS, TRANSFORMATIONS AND SYMMETRY
Shapes

INTERMEDIATE TEST

Part A   Multiple Choice

1   A solid has the following views. The solid could be a: top view   front view   side view
   A triangular prism   **B** triangular pyramid
   C square pyramid   **D** rectangular pyramid   (1 mark)

2   A plane shape has line symmetry and an order of rotational symmetry of 2. The shape is a:
   A square   **B** rhombus   **C** parallelogram   **D** rectangle   (1 mark)

3   What is the order of rotational symmetry of the shape?
   A 1   **B** 2
   C 3   **D** 4   (1 mark)

4   Which of the following shapes has only one line of symmetry?
   A parallelogram   **B** kite
   C equilateral triangle   **D** scalene triangle   (1 mark)

5   Lauren has shaded some of the grid. She needs to shade more squares
   so that the shape will have two lines of symmetry. What is the fewest
   number of squares she will have to shade? *Hint 1*
   A 3   **B** 4   **C** 5   **D** 7   (1 mark)

Part B   Short Answer

6   Draw the lines of symmetry on the following shapes: (1 mark each)
   a equalateral triangle   **b** semicircle   **c** ellipse

7   Nerida has started to draw a shape which has rotational symmetry of
   order 4 about the point *X*. Complete her shape.   (2 marks)

   X

8   Thao has commenced drawing on some grid paper. Complete
   the shading so that the finished drawing will have four lines of
   symmetry and rotational symmetry of order four. *Hint 2*   (2 marks)

9   If *AB* is the axis of symmetry, complete the diagram.   (2 marks)

   A

   B

Your Feedback

PAGE 132

PAGE 161

$$\frac{}{14} \times 100\% = \boxed{} \%$$

Hint 1: First locate the 2 lines of symmetry.
Hint 2: Rotate your book 90° to help you.

1 Determine which of the following has rotational symmetry and if so, give its order: (13 marks)

a square   b rectangle   c parallelogram

d rhombus   e trapezium   f circle

g ellipse   h scalene triangle   i isosceles triangle

j equilateral triangle   k regular pentagon   l regular hexagon

m regular octagon

2 How many of these cards have a rotational symmetry of order 2? (2 marks)

3 What is the order of rotational symmetry of the following? (6 marks)

a   b   c

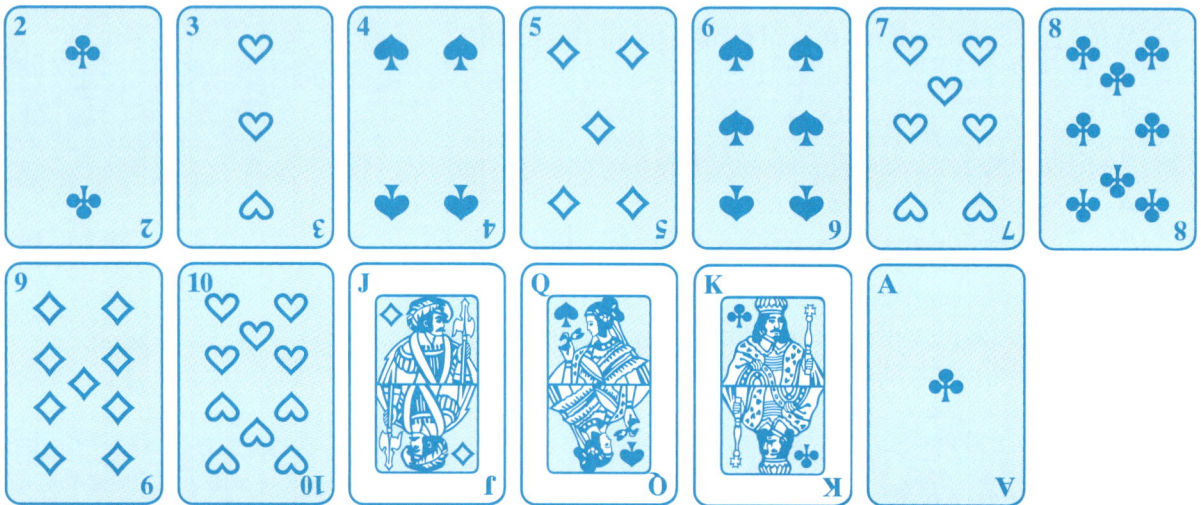

d   e   f

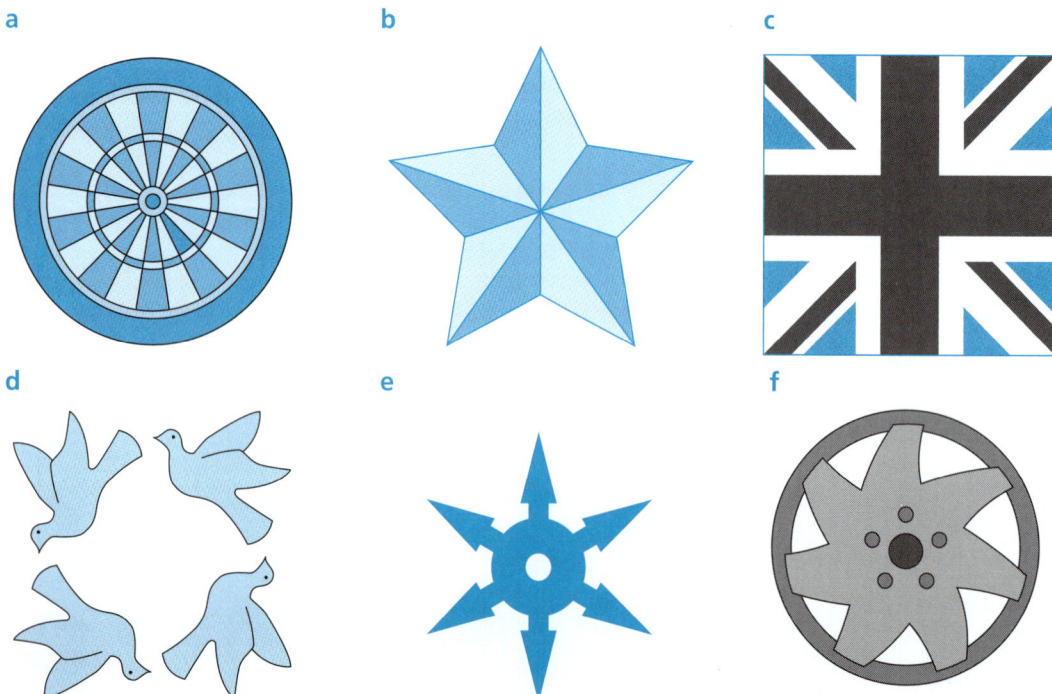

4 Draw the front, top and right views of the following: (18 marks)

a
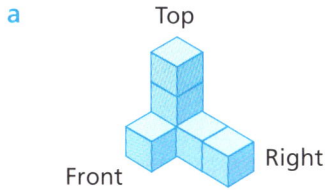

b
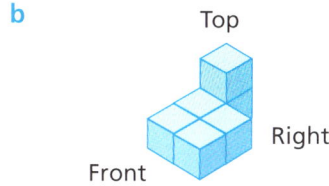

c
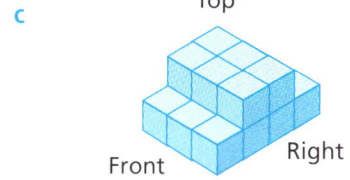

d
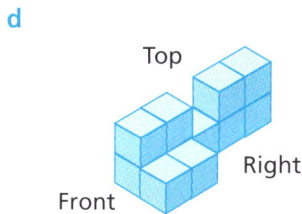

e
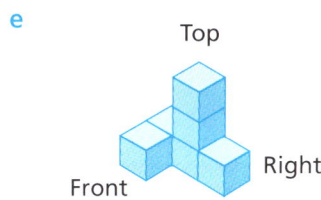

f
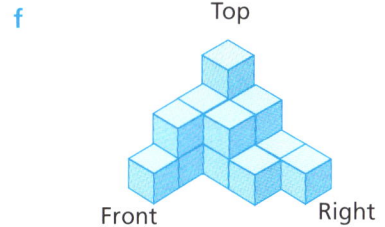

5 Draw the front, top and right views of this shape: (3 marks)

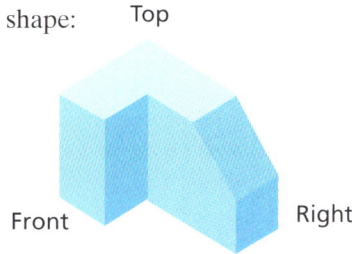

6 Draw the shape with the following views: (4 marks)

a

Front view   Top view    Right view

b
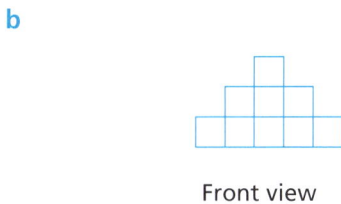

Front view   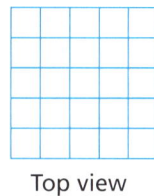 Top view   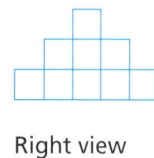 Right view

7
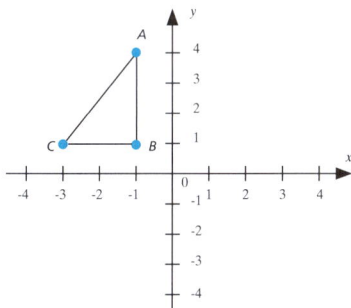

a If $\triangle ABC$ is translated 4 units to the right to form image $\triangle A'B'C'$, what are the co-ordinates of B'? (1 mark)

b If $\triangle ABC$ is reflected about the y-axis to form image $\triangle A'B'C'$, what are the co-ordinates of A'? (1 mark)

c If $\triangle ABC$ is rotated 180° about the origin to form image $\triangle A'B'C'$, what are the co-ordinates of C'? (1 mark)

Your Feedback

$\dfrac{\boxed{}}{49} \times 100\% = \boxed{} \%$

PAGE 133

PAGE 161

ANGLES AND LINES
Geometric Reasoning

1. An **angle** is made up of two arms (**rays**) meeting at a **vertex**.
   For example, the angle shown is named ABC, or CBA, or B.

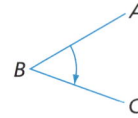

2. Angles ($\angle$s) can be classified according to their size:
   - **acute angle:** less than $90°$
   - **obtuse angle:** between $90°$ and $180°$
   - **reflex angle:** between $180°$ and $360°$
   - **right angle:** equal to $90°$
   - **straight angle:** equal to $180°$
   - **revolution:** equal to $360°$

   For example, what type of angle is $\angle DEF$? It is between $180°$ and $360°$
   $\therefore$ reflex angle

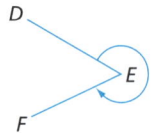

3. Special angles include:

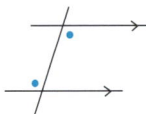

adjacent	complementary	supplementary	vertically opposite
share a common arm and vertex	two or more angles adding to $90°$	two or more angles adding to $180°$	opposite angles are equal

   For example: Find the supplement of $50°$.
   As supplementary angles add $180°$, then the supplement of $50°$ is $130°$ $(50 + ? = 180)$

4. **Markings** are used to show equal size and length.
   For example, in the diagram, $\angle ACB = \angle DCE$ and $BC = DC$

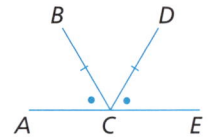

5. **Parallel** lines have the same direction. AB parallel to CD is written $AB \parallel CD$.
   When a third line, called a **transversal**, cuts parallel lines, the angles formed have special relationships.

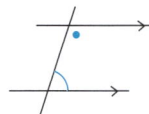

corresponding	alternate	co-interior
angles are equal	angles are equal	angles are supplementary

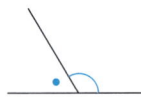

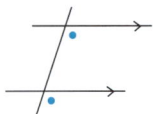

6. **Perpendicular** lines meet at right angles.
   AB perpendicular to CD is written $AB \perp CD$.

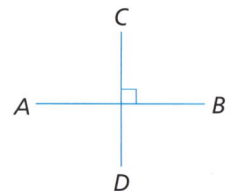

Checklist
Can you:

1. Name and classify angles? ☐
2. Recognise adjacent, complementary, supplementary and vertically opposite angles? ☐
3. Identify corresponding, alternate and co-interior angles? ☐
4. Use symbols to represent equal angles, equal sides, parallel lines and perpendicular lines? ☐

1 Name the angles marked with an asterisk (*).

a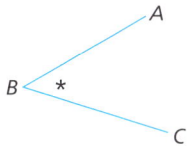

b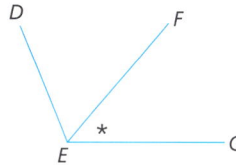

2 What type of angle is each of the following?

a $62°$ **b** $355°$ **c** $151°$

3 From the diagram, where $ADEC$ is a rectangle, name:

a a right angle

b an acute angle

c a pair of adjacent angles.

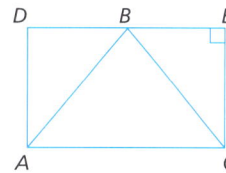

4 Find the:

a complement of $72°$

b supplement of $100°$

c complement of $x°$

d supplement of $y°$

5 Find the value of each pronumeral.

a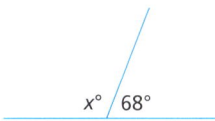

b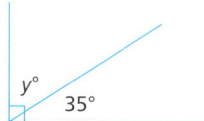

c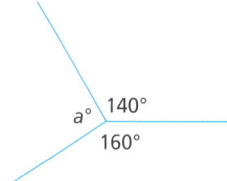

6 Find the value of each pronumeral.

a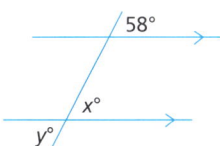

b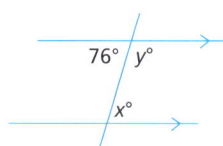

c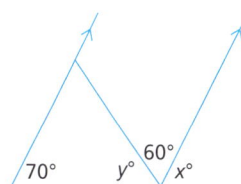

7 Find the value of x, giving reasons.

a

b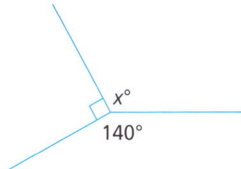

c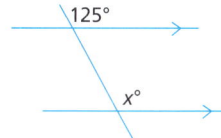

PAGE 134

ANGLES AND LINES
Geometric Reasoning

INTERMEDIATE TEST

Part A Multiple Choice

1 The values of *x* and *y* are:
   A *x* = 120, *y* = 60   **B** *x* = 120, *y* = 120
   C *x* = 60, *y* = 120   **D** *x* = 60, *y* = 60

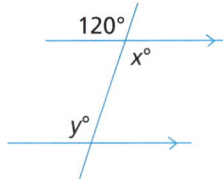

(1 mark)

2 The complement of 75° is:
   A 5°   **B** 15°
   C 105°   **D** 125°

(1 mark)

3 Which of the following angles are supplementary?
   A ∠ABC and ∠CBD   **B** ∠BAC and ∠BDC
   C ∠ACB and ∠DCB   **D** ∠CBA and ∠CDB

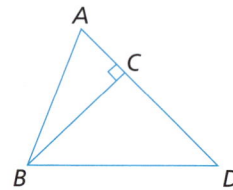

(1 mark)

4 Which of the following is true?
   A *x* = 75 (corresponding ∠s, *AB* ∥ *CD*)
   B *x* = 75 (alternate ∠s, *AB* ∥ *CD*)
   C *x* = 105 (vertically opposite ∠s)
   D *x* = 105 (co-interior ∠s, *AB* ∥ *CD*)

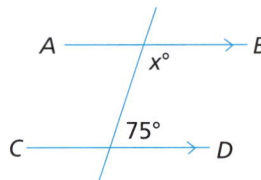

(1 mark)

5 Which of the following is **not** true?
   A *a* = 115   **B** *b* = 60
   C *c* = 120   **D** *d* = 135

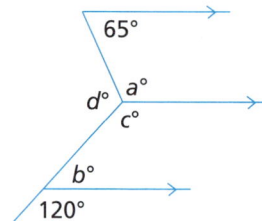

(1 mark)

Part B Short Answer

6 Find the value of each pronumeral: *Hint 1*

a
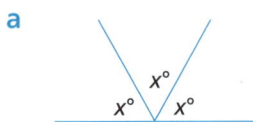

b
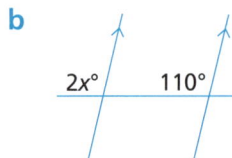

c
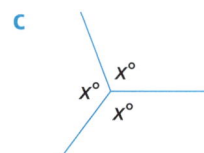

(2 marks each)

7 Complete with reason: *Hint 2*
   ∠BDE = _____ (_____)
   ∠CBE = _____ (_____)
   ∠DBE = _____ (_____)

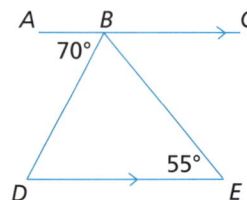

(6 marks)

PAGE 135

PAGE 161

Your Feedback

$\dfrac{\boxed{}}{17} \times 100\% = \boxed{}$ %

Hint 1: Form a simple equation to solve.
Hint 2: Keep your reason concise.

ANGLES AND LINES
Geometric Reasoning

ADVANCED TEST

1 Find the value of the pronumerals:

a   **b**   **c**   (1 mark each)

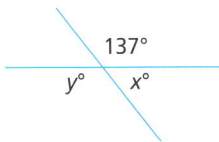 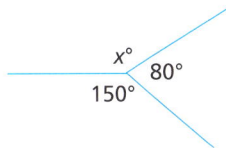 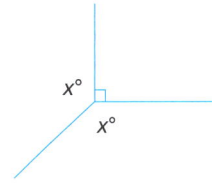

2 Find the value of x:

a   **b**   **c**   (2 marks each)

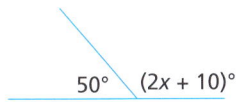 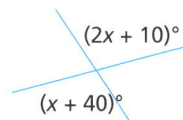 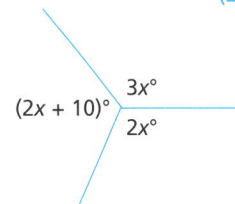

3 Find the complement of $y°$ (1 mark)

4 Find the supplement of $p°$ (1 mark)

5 Find the pronumeral:

a   **b**   **c**   (1 mark each)

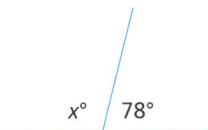 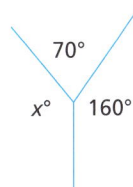 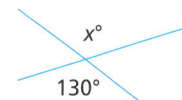

6 Write the value of the pronumerals:

a (1 mark)   **b** (1 mark)   **c** (1 mark)

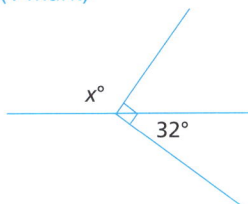 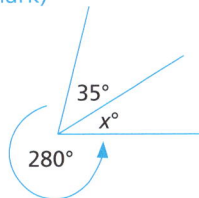 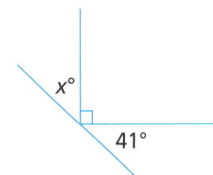

d (3 marks)   **e** (1 mark)   **f** (1 mark)

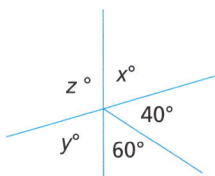 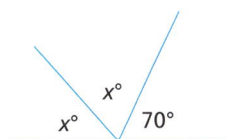 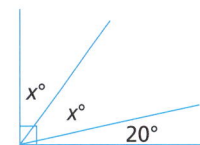

7 Find the value of the pronumerals:

a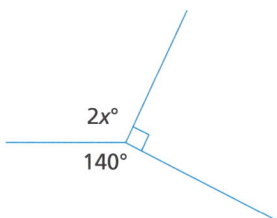

b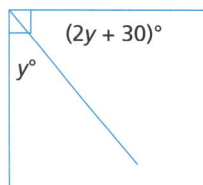

c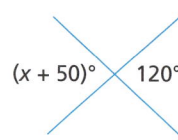

d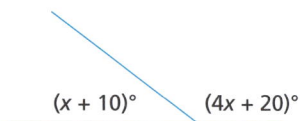

e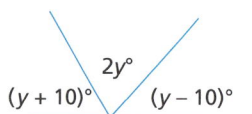

f (2 marks each)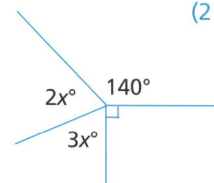

8 Two complementary angles are $(2x + 20)°$ and $(x + 10)°$.
Find the value of x. (2 marks)

9 The vertically opposite angles are $(4x + 20)°$ and $(2x + 60)°$.
Find the value of x. (2 marks)

10 Supplementary angles are $2x°$, $(x + 40)°$ and $20°$.
Find the value of x. (2 marks)

11 Find the value of the pronumerals:

a (3 marks)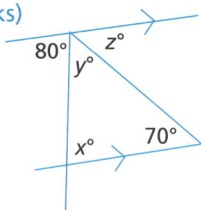

b (1 mark)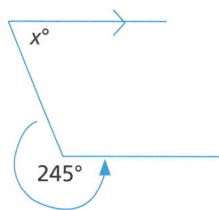

c (3 marks)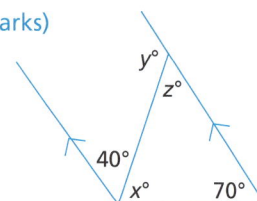

d (1 mark)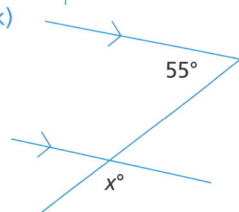

e (1 mark)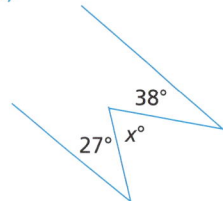

f (2 marks)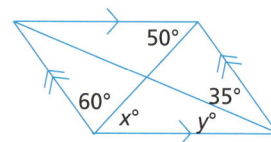

12 Find the value of the pronumeral:

a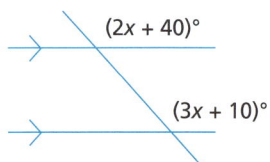

b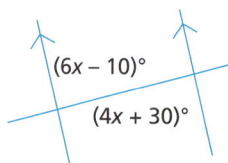

c (2 marks each)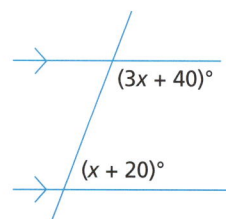

Your Feedback

$\dfrac{}{57} \times 100\% = \%$

PAGE 135

PAGE 161

1 A **triangle** (Δ) has an angle (∠) sum of 180°, and can be categorised according to:
- Sides: **equilateral**—3 sides equal; **isosceles**—2 sides equal; **scalene**—0 sides equal
- Angles: **acute-angled**—all angles less than 90°; **right-angled**—90°; **obtuse-angled**—between 90° and 180°.

For example, find the value of x, giving reasons:

a

$x = 50$ [base ∠s of isos. Δ equal]

b

$x = 110$ [ext. ∠ of Δ equal to sum of 2 int. opp. ∠s]

2 A **quadrilateral** has four sides, and includes:

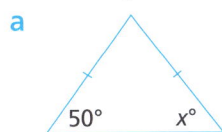
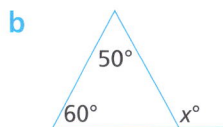

square   rectangle   parallelogram   rhombus   trapezium   kite

3 A **convex quadrilateral** is a four-sided polygon wih diagonals inside the figure.

4 The **angle sum** of a quadrilateral is 360°. For example, find the value of the pronumerals:

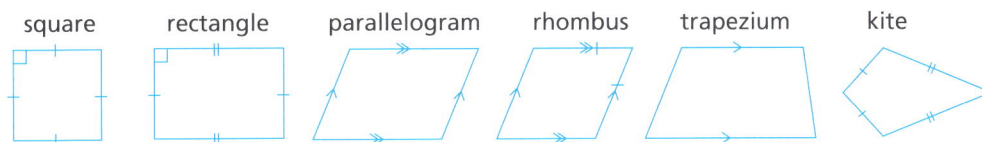

a $x = 360 - 260$

      $= 100$

b $7x + 80 = 360$

      $\dfrac{7x}{7} = \dfrac{280}{7}$

      $x = 40$

5

Special quadrilateral properties	Parallelogram	Rhombus	Rectangle	Square	Trapezium	Kite
Opposite sides equal	✓	✓	✓	✓		
Opposite sides parallel	✓	✓	✓	✓	one pair	
Adjacent sides equal		✓		✓		some are
Adjacent sides perpendicular			✓	✓		
Opposite angles equal	✓	✓	✓	✓		one pair
Diagonals equal in length			✓	✓		
Diagonals bisect each other	✓	✓	✓	✓		one is bisected
Diagonals cross each other at 90°		✓		✓		✓
Diagonals bisect angles of quad.		✓		✓		two bisected

For example, find the value of the pronumerals:

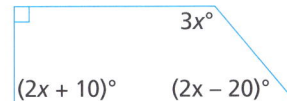

a $\dfrac{3x}{3} = \dfrac{75}{3}$

     $x = 25$

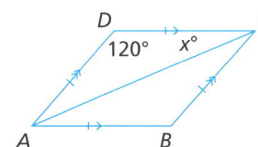

b $\angle BCD = 60°$

     $x = 30$

Checklist
Can you:

1 *Find the value of unknown pronumerals in triangles and quadrilaterals?*

2 *Give adequate reasons when finding the size of angles in triangles and quadrilaterals?*

1 Find the value of each pronumeral:

a

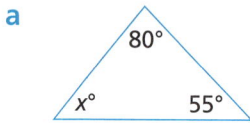

b

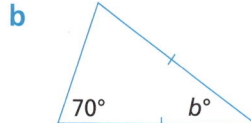

c

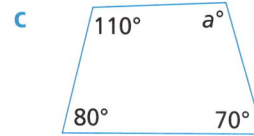

d

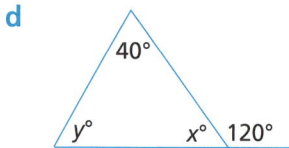

e

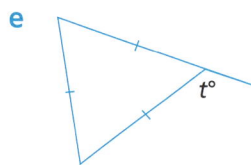

f

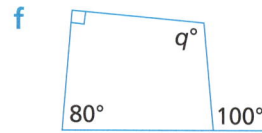

2 Find the value of the pronumerals:

a

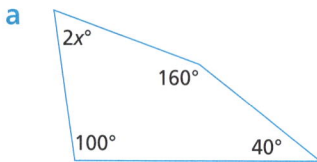

b

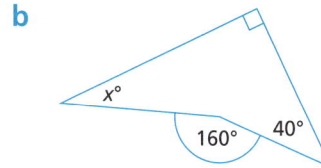

c

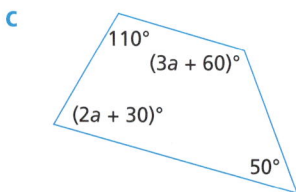

d

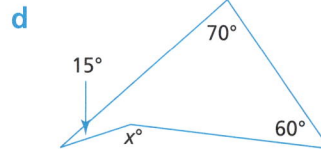

e

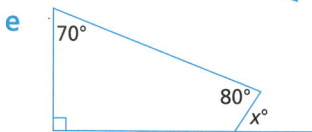

f

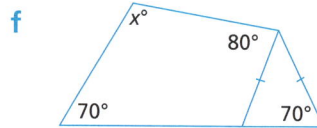

3 Find the value of the pronumerals, giving reasons:

a

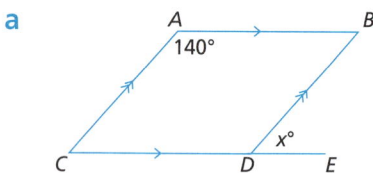

b

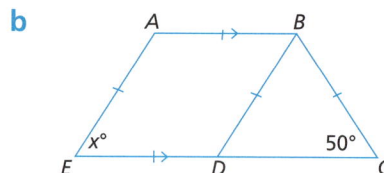

4 If *ABCD* is a parallelogram, find the value of *x*, giving reasons:

a

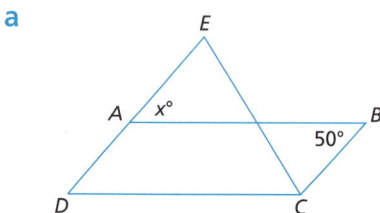

b

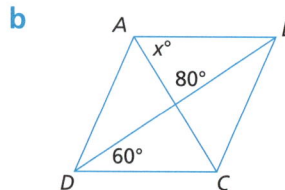

PAGE 137

20 MINUTES

INTERMEDIATE TEST

Part A Multiple Choice

1 The angle sum of a quadrilateral is:
  A 90°　　　　　**B** 180°　　　　　**C** 360°　　　　　**D** 400°　　　(1 mark)

2 The values of c and d are:
  A $c = 40°, d = 40°$　　**B** $c = 60°, d = 70°$
  C $c = 60°, d = 40°$　　**D** $c = 40°, d = 70°$　　　(1 mark)

3 Helen knows that two angles in a triangle are 40° and 57°. She concludes that the triangle is:
  A right-angled　　**B** obtuse-angled　　**C** isosceles　　**D** scalene　　(1 mark)

4 The value of x is: *Hint 1*
  A 50　　　　　**B** 115
  C 105　　　　**D** 110　　　(1 mark)

5 Louise drew a quadrilateral with diagonals that bisect at right angles. Her quadrilateral could **not** be a:
  A kite　　　　**B** square　　　　**C** rhombus　　　　**D** trapezium　　(1 mark)

6 A quadrilateral has two pairs of equal sides and one axis of symmetry. It must be a:
  A kite　　　**B** parallelogram　　　**C** rectangle　　　**D** trapezium　　(1 mark)

Part B Short Answer

7 Find the value of the pronumerals.　　　　　　　　　(2 marks each)
  a　　　　　　　　**b**　　　　　　　　**c**

8 Find the value of the pronumerals, giving reasons.　　　　(2 marks each)
  a　　　　　　　　**b**　　　　　　　　**c**

9 Find the value of the pronumerals, giving reasons for your answer.
  a　　　　　　　　**b**　　　　　　　　(3 marks each)

Your Feedback

$$\frac{\boxed{}}{24} \times 100\% = \boxed{} \%$$

PAGE 138

PAGE 161

Hint 1: First find the angles inside the isosceles triangle.

1 Find the value of the pronumerals:

a (1 mark)

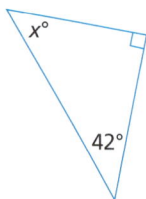

b (1 mark)

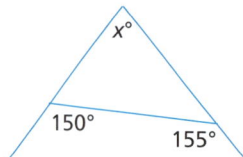

c (3 marks)

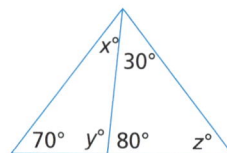

d (1 mark)

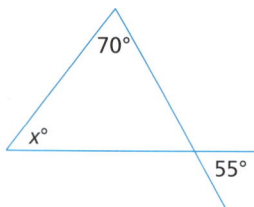

e (2 marks)

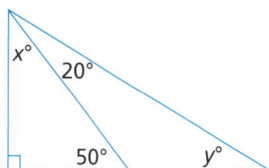

f (3 marks)

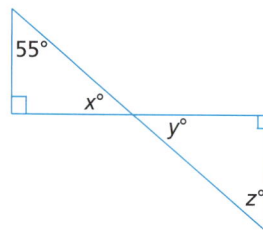

2 Write the value of the pronumerals:

a (2 marks)

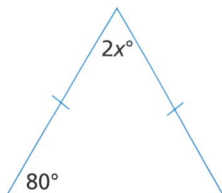

b (2 marks)

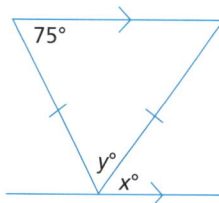

c (2 marks)

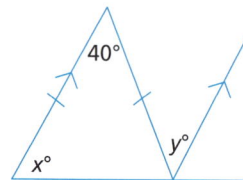

3 What is the value of each pronumeral?

a (2 marks)

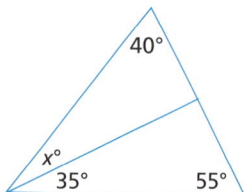

b (3 marks)

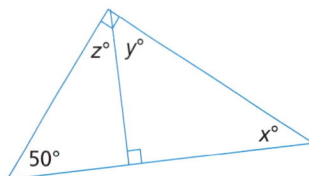

c (2 marks)

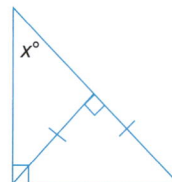

4 Find the value of the pronumerals:

a

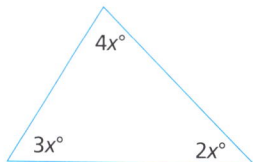

b (2 marks each)

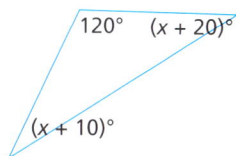

c

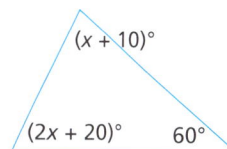

5 Find the pronumeral:

a

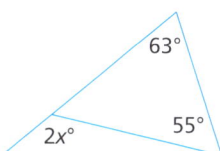

b

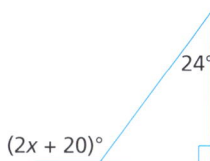

c

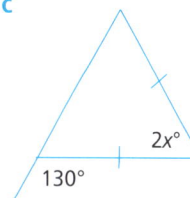

d

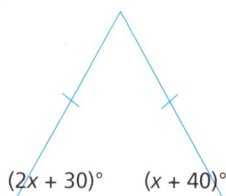

e

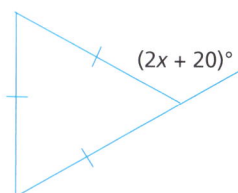

f (2 marks each)

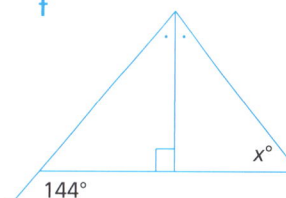

6 Write the value of the pronumeral:

a (1 mark)

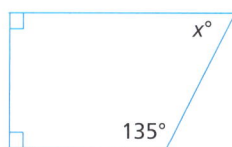

b (1 mark)

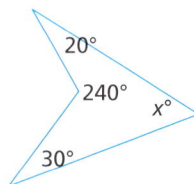

c (1 mark)

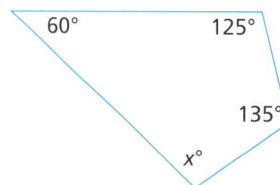

d (1 mark)

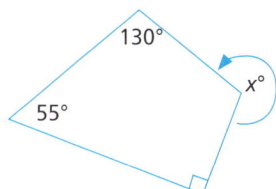

e (2 marks)

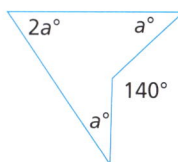

f (2 marks)

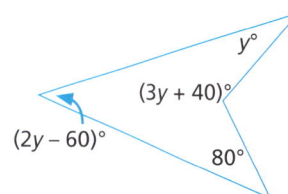

Your Feedback

$$\frac{}{50} \times 100\% = \boxed{} \%$$

PAGE 138

PAGE 161

PROBABILITY
Chance

1. Probability is the study of **chance**.

2. The probability of an **event** is expressed as a fraction, decimal or percentage.

3. An event will have a number of **outcomes**.
   For example, list the outcomes if a die is tossed. There are six outcomes: 1, 2, 3, 4, 5, 6.

4. A **simple event** is an event where each possible outcome is equally likely.

5. Probability ranges from **0** (impossible event) to **1** (certain event).

6. The **probablity of an event $Pr(E)$** is written as:

$$Pr(E) = \frac{\text{number of favourable outcomes}}{\text{number of possible outcomes}}$$

   For example, a bag contains three red balls and two blue balls. If a ball is chosen at random, what is the probability that the ball is red?

   $Pr(\text{red}) = \dfrac{3}{5}$

7. The **sum of all possible outcomes of an event is 1**.
   For example, a coin is tossed. Write down the possibility of throwing a:

   a head

   $\therefore Pr(\text{head}) = \dfrac{1}{2}$

   b tail

   $\therefore Pr(\text{tail}) = \dfrac{1}{2}$

   As these are the only two possible outcomes, the sum of the probabilities is $\dfrac{1}{2} + \dfrac{1}{2} = 1$.

8. When we identify **complementary events**, we can quickly determine probabilities.
   For example, a die is tossed. Find the probability of not tossing a 4.

   $Pr(\text{not tossing a 4}) = 1 - Pr(\text{tossing a 4})$
   $= 1 - \dfrac{1}{6}$
   $= \dfrac{5}{6}$

9. In some questions the outcomes are **not equally likely**.
   For example, the spinner illustrated is used to choose a number.
   What is the probability of spinning a 3?
   Two of the sectors are labelled with the number 3,

   so $Pr(\text{spinning a 3}) = \dfrac{2}{5}$

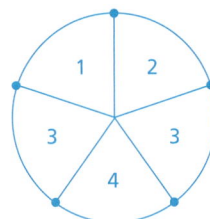

Checklist
Can you:

1. List all possible outcomes of a single event?
2. Recognise that the sum of probabilities is equal to 1?
3. Identify the complement of an event?
4. Find the probability of a complementary event?
5. Solve word problems involving probability?

1 A bag contains nine identical balls, numbered 1 to 9. A ball is selected at random from the bag. Find the probability that the number on the selected ball is:

a 3	**b** even	**c** odd
d not odd	**e** composite	**f** prime
g divisible by 3	**h** a factor of 15	**i** less than 7
j more than 4	**k** 3 or 5	**l** even or odd?

2 A die is rolled. Find the probability that the number is:

a a six	**b** less than 4	**c** not three
d not an odd number	**e** a square number	**f** a seven.

3 A bag contains 4 red marbles, 3 white marbles, 2 green marbles and a blue marble. A marble is chosen at random. What is the probability that the marble is:

a red?	**b** white?	**c** white or green?
d not blue?	**e** black?	**f** red, white or blue?

4 A jar contains jelly beans. The ratio of red jelly beans to white jelly beans is 4:3. If a jelly bean is selected at random, what is the probability of choosing a red jelly bean?

5 The circle illustrated represents a spinner where identical sectors are coloured using blue (*B*), red (*R*) or green (*G*) paint. What is the probability of spinning:

a red?

b green?

c not blue?

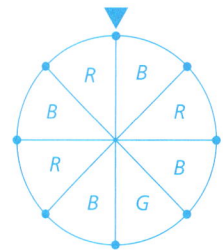

6 A jar contains 6 red, 4 black and 2 green jelly babies. A jelly baby is selected at random and eaten. What is the probability that the jar now contains 5 red jelly babies?

7 At a certain hospital the probabilty of a female birth last year was 0.53.

a What was the probability of a male birth?

b If there were 1200 births last year, how many were likely to be female?

8 Kalie uses the spinner illustrated to determine what she does tonight. What is the probability that she will:

a watch TV?

b not tidy her room?

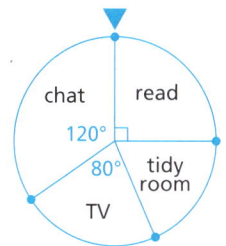

PAGE 140

PROBABILITY
Chance

Part A Multiple Choice

1 A bag contains 6 red cards and 4 blue cards. A card is chosen at random. What is the probability that the card is blue?

   A $\frac{4}{5}$ B $\frac{2}{5}$ C $\frac{2}{3}$ D $\frac{3}{5}$ (1 mark)

2 A die is thrown. What is the probability of not throwing a three? *Hint 1*

   A $\frac{1}{3}$ B $\frac{1}{6}$ C $\frac{1}{2}$ D $\frac{5}{6}$ (1 mark)

3 Each letter of the word PROBABILITY is written on identical cards and the eleven cards placed in a bag. If a card is drawn at random, what is the probability that the card is the letter B?

   A $\frac{1}{2}$ B $\frac{1}{11}$ C $\frac{2}{11}$ D $\frac{6}{11}$ (1 mark)

4 A card is selected from a normal deck of playing cards (52 cards). What is the probability that the card is a red seven?

   A $\frac{1}{26}$ B $\frac{1}{7}$ C $\frac{2}{7}$ D $\frac{2}{13}$ (1 mark)

5 In the game of 'lotto' there are 45 balls numbered 1 to 45. Peter predicts that the first number drawn will be higher than 40. The probability that Peter is correct is:

   A $\frac{1}{9}$ B $\frac{4}{45}$ C $\frac{1}{5}$ D $\frac{1}{41}$ (1 mark)

Part B Short Answer

6 A bag contains 4 red balls, 2 green balls and 2 white balls. A ball is chosen at random. What is the probability that the ball is:

   a red?   b white?   c not green?   (1 mark each)

7 100 000 tickets are sold in a lottery. Sharon buys 10 tickets.

   a Find the probability that Sharon wins first prize.   (1 mark)

   b Sharon does not win first prize. What is the probability she will win second prize? *Hint 2*   (2 marks)

8 The six faces of a die are renumbered as 1, 1, 2, 2, 2, 3. If the die is rolled, what is the probability that the number rolled is a 2 or a 3?   (2 marks)

9 A soccer club sold 100 raffle tickets. Mitchell bought ticket number 14.

   a Find the probability that Mitchell wins first prize.   (1 mark)

   b What is the probability that the winning ticket will be one off Mitchell's ticket number?   (1 mark)

10 A TV game show features a computer screen that rapidly flashes each of the nine squares illustrated, one at a time in random order. The contestant calls 'stop' and wins the amount displayed on the illustrated square. What is the probability the contestant wins:

$50	$0	$20
$80	$10	$0
$40	$0	$75

   a $50?   (1 mark)   b no money?   (1 mark)

   c at least $50   (1 mark)

Your Feedback

$\dfrac{\boxed{}}{18} \times 100\% = \boxed{}\ \%$

PAGE 141

PAGE 161

Hint 1: Use complementary events.
Hint 2: There are still 99 999 tickets left in the draw.

1   From the word CHANCE a letter is chosen at random. What is the chance that the letter is:

a   an A? b   a C?
c   a vowel? d   a consonant?
e   not a consonant? (1 mark each)

2   Two dice are rolled and their **sum** is calculated. The results are to be listed in a table.

a   Complete the table: (2 marks)

	1	2	3	4	5	6
1	2	3	4	5		
2	3	4				
3	4					
4						
5						
6						

b   Which is the most likely sum? (1 mark)
c   What is the probability that the sum will be:

i   odd? ii   less than 7?
iii   a square number? iv   prime?
v   divisible by 3? vi   a multiple of 4?
vii   a factor of 12? (1 mark each)

3   A bag contains numbered balls. The probability of selecting a 2 was $\frac{1}{2}$, a 3 was $\frac{1}{3}$. The remainder of the balls were numbered 1.

a   What is the smallest possible number of balls in the bag? (2 marks)
b   What is the probability of selecting:

i   a 1? (1 mark)
ii   less than 3? (1 mark)
iii   an odd number? (1 mark)

4   A die has been renumbered with the number 3 replaced with the number 2. If the die is rolled, what is the probability that it is:

a   a 2? (1 mark)
b   even? (1 mark)
c   less than 3? (1 mark)

5   A coloured ball is randomly chosen from a bag. The table shows the probabilities of the four colours.

	blue	green	red	yellow
probability	0.25	0.3		0.1

a   What was the probability of selecting a red ball? (1 mark)

b   If there were 40 balls in the bag, how many balls of each colour are there? (1 mark)
c   Explain why there cannot be 10 balls in the bag. (1 mark)
d   What is the smallest possible number of balls in the bag? (1 mark)

6   Two dice are rolled and their product is calculated. The results are to be listed in a table.

a   Complete the table: (2 marks)

	1	2	3	4	5	6
1						
2						
3						
4						
5						
6						

b   Which are the most likely products? (1 mark)
c   What is the probability that the product will be:

i   even? (1 mark)
ii   composite? (1 mark)
iii   a multiple of 4? (1 mark)
iv   a factor of 36? (1 mark)
v   prime and odd? (1 mark)
vi   prime or odd? (1 mark)

7   A bag contains balls which are of four different colours. It is twice as likely to choose an orange ball than it is to choose a pink ball. It is three times as likely to choose a pink ball than a green ball, and twice as likely to choose a red ball than a green ball.

a   Find the probability of choosing each colour. (2 marks)
b   What is the smallest possible number of balls in the bag? (1 mark)
c   If there are 72 balls in the bag, how many are red? (1 mark)
d   If the red balls were removed from the bag, what is the probability of choosing a green or an orange ball? (1 mark)

Your Feedback

$\frac{\quad}{41} \times 100\% = \boxed{}\%$

PAGE 141

PAGE 161

DATA REPRESENTATION
Data Representation and Interpretation

STUDY NOTES

1 Data can be represented in tabular form (e.g. **frequency distribution table**) or graphical form (e.g. **frequency histogram**, **frequency polygon**, **sector graph** or **column graph** etc.).

For example, given the completed frequency distribution table, draw a frequency histogram and polygon for the following **discrete** data.

Score	Tally	Frequency
41	IIII	5
42	IIII II	7
43	IIII IIII	10
44	IIII I	6
45	III	3

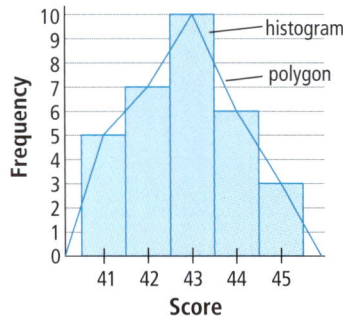

2 When data are **continuous**, they can be grouped in **class intervals** to make them easier to tabulate and graph.

For example, complete a frequency table for the following data.

21 39 28 36 33 32 27 24 32 34 29
25 33 40 28 31 27 26 26 34 34 38
21 23 35 39 32 22 35 24

Class interval	Class centre	Tally	Frequency
21–25	23	IIII II	7
26–30	28	IIII II	7
31–35	33	IIII IIII I	11
36–40	38	IIII	5

3 A **dot plot** can also be used to represent data in graphical form.

For example, use the dot plot to complete a frequency distribution table.

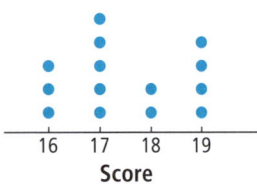

Score	Frequency
16	3
17	5
18	2
19	4

4 Another form of data representation is the **stem-and-leaf plot**.

For example, draw a back-to-back stem-and-leaf plot for the heights of boys and girls in class 7M1.

Boys (cm): 147, 138, 142, 143, 153, 158, 162, 157, 161, 155, 145, 153

Girls (cm): 138, 143, 145, 148, 151, 146, 163, 134, 143, 146, 148, 145

- Many girls' heights are **clustered** in the 140s.
- 163 cm is an **outlier** for the girls as it is a score which is much higher than the nearest score.

Boys		Girls
8	13	4 8
7 5 3 2	14	3 3 5 5 6 6 8 8
8 7 5 3 3	15	1
2 1	16	3

Checklist
Can you:

1 *Understand the terms discrete, continuous, clustered and outlier?* ☐

2 *Draw a frequency histogram and frequency polygon?* ☐

3 *Draw a dot plot and stem-and-leaf plot?* ☐

✔

1 Use the frequency table to draw a frequency histogram and polygon.

Score	Frequency
21	4
22	8
23	10
24	7
25	3

2 The masses (in kg) of students in class 7B are listed below. Complete the table.

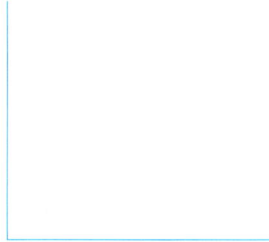

62 65 58 59 64
51 48 46 53 65
69 71 63 62 54
52 54 61 64 67
48 53 64 68 61
54 59 53 49 58

Class interval (kg)	Class centre (kg)	Tally	Frequency
46–50			
51–55			
56–60			
61–65			
66–70			
71–75			

3 Use the frequency histogram to complete the frequency distribution table.

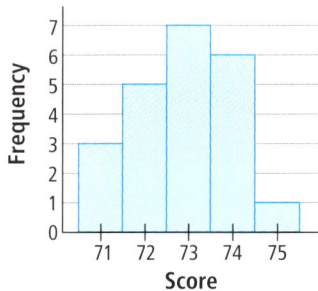

Score	Frequency

4 Draw a stem-and-leaf plot for the following data:

77 68 79 84 51 57 53 69 73 81 78 61 58 69 78 79

91 84 80 71 76 82 71 60 63 67 85 90 70 73 78 89

5 A stem-and-leaf plot records the scores in the year 7 English test. Transfer the data to the table.

Stem	Leaf
2	2 7 8 8 9
3	3 4 7 7 8 8 9
4	0 0 3 4 4 5 6
5	1 2 3 8 9
6	3 4 4 7 8 8

Class interval	Class centre	Frequency
20–29		
30–39		
40–49		
50–59		
60–69		

PAGE 143

Answers See worked solutions

1 A die is tossed 35 times and the results recorded below.

```
5  2  4  1  4  4  3  6  5
2  1  2  4  2  3  6  4  5
4  3  1  2  3  4  2  4  1
3  4  5  4  3  2  3  4
```

  a Complete a frequency table. (3 marks)

  b Draw a frequency histogram and frequency polygon. (3 marks)

  c How many times did a number less than 3 occur? (1 mark)

2 A survey is conducted to determine the hair colour of 72 students in year 7. The results are shown in the sector graph below.

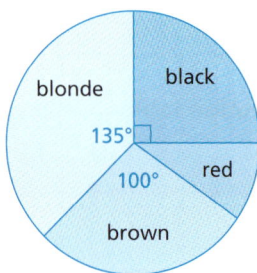

  a Complete the table below.
    Hint 1 (2 marks)

Colour	Angle	Frequency
blonde		
brown		
black		
red		

  b Draw a column graph. (3 marks)

3 The dot plot below shows the shoe sizes of 19 students.

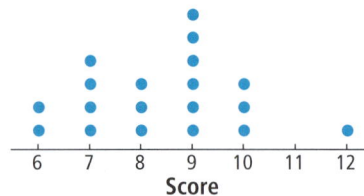

  a Identify the outlier. *Hint 2* (1 mark)

  b Draw a frequency table. (2 marks)

  c What is the most popular size? (1 mark)

  c What is the range of shoe sizes? (1 mark)

4 The stem-and-leaf plot below shows the results of a 'beep fitness' test for a class of students in Year 7. The data has been presented in tenths of a second. This means, for example, that 7.8 seconds is shown as 78 tenths of a second.

```
        Boys    Girls
            4 | 3  6  7
    9  7  5  2 | 5 | 0  1  6  7  7
          5  3 | 6 | 2  3  6  8
       8  6  6  2 | 7 | 8
 7  6  4  3  3  1 | 8 |
          5  2 | 9 |
```

  a Find the number of boys involved. (1 mark)

  b If the lowest score is 4.3, find the highest score for the class. (1 mark)

  c Draw a frequency table for the class. (3 marks)

  d Draw a frequency histogram and frequency polygon. (4 marks)

Hint 1: A revolution measures 360°.

Hint 2: An outlier is an individual score that is separate from other scores.

Your Feedback

$$\frac{\boxed{}}{26} \times 100\% = \boxed{}\%$$

PAGE 143

PAGE 161

1 The divided bar graph shows the way Marg spends her wage each week.

Rent	Food	Sav-ings	Other

a If she earns $1200 each week, how much does she spend on

  i food? (1 mark)

  ii rent? (1 mark)

b If she spends $360 on rent, how much does she

  i save? (1 mark)

  ii spend on food, savings and other activities? (1 mark)

2 A survey of ten students found their favourite colours. The results are shown in the dot plot. Draw a divided bar graph to represent the data. (2 marks)

Favourite Colours

3 The stem-and-leaf plot shows the results of a maths test. Complete the frequency table for the data. (1 mark)

Stem	Leaf
6	0 7 8
7	2 2 4 8 9
8	3 5 7 8
9	0 0 2 5

Marks	Students
60–69	
70–79	
80–89	
90–99	

4 A group of students was surveyed to find the number of pets at home. The results were recorded on a divided bar graph without labelling. There were twice as many dogs as cats. There were some rabbits and two birds.

a Label the graph. (1 mark)

b How many pet rabbits? (1 mark)

c If the data were recorded on a sector graph, what angle is used to represent dogs? (1 mark)

5 The graph shows the amount of time Liam spends on different activities at the gym.

Bike	Treadmill	Weights

a What percentage of the time does he spend on:

  i treadmill?   **ii** weights? (1 mark each)

b If he spends an hour at the gym, how long does he spend on the:

  i bike?   **ii** treadmill? (1 mark each)

c If he rides the bike for a quarter of an hour, how long does he spend on the:

  i treadmill?   **ii** weights? (1 mark each)

6 A survey of people found the state where they were born.

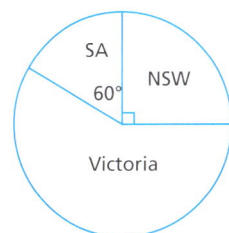

a Draw a divided bar graph for the data. (2 marks)

b If there were 36 people surveyed, how many were born in:

  i NSW?   **ii** Victoria? (1 mark each)

c If 18 people were born in NSW, how many were:

  i involved in the survey? (1 mark)

  ii born in SA? (1 mark)

  iii born in Victoria? (1 mark)

7 The table shows the masses of a group of students.

Girls	42, 53, 49, 45, 46, 40, 39, 51, 53
Boys	42, 46, 59, 46, 61, 47, 42, 49, 58

Complete the ordered back-to-back stem-and-leaf plot. (2 marks)

Girls		Boys
	3	
	4	
	5	
	6	

Your Feedback

$\dfrac{}{25} \times 100\% = \%$

PAGE 144

PAGE 161

DATA ANALYSIS
Data Representation and Interpretation

1. Data are collected using a census or a sample. A **census** involves collecting data about every individual in the **whole population**. For example, the Australian Bureau of Statistics (ABS) conducts a census of the Australian population every five years. A **sample** involves collecting data from **part of the population**. If a large enough sample is taken, we can get some idea about the whole population. For example, to ascertain the popularity of the Prime Minister, a phone call of 1000 adults might be conducted.

2. A calculator can be used in a **random sample**. For example, one thousand students are each allocated a number from 0 to 999. The random number generator on the calculator can be used to choose 20 students at random.

3. A sample is **biased** if it does not fairly represent the whole population. For example, a sample of 1000 adults to ascertain the popularity of the Prime Minister would be biased if all the adults sampled lived in the same suburb. In order to be fair, the sample would have to include adults from different parts of Australia and from different age groups.

4. **Measures of location** are mean, median and mode.

5. The **mean** ($\bar{x}$) is the average of a set of scores, where $\bar{x}$ = sum of scores ÷ number of scores.

   For example, find the mean of 3, 7, 6, 4, 2. $\quad \bar{x} = \dfrac{3 + 7 + 6 + 4 + 2}{5} = 4.4$

6. The mean can also be found by placing your **calculator in statistics (STAT) mode**. (Check the instructions that came with your calculator.)

7. The **median** is the middle of the scores when the scores are arrranged in order.
   For example, find the median of the following scores:

   a   4, 8, 8, 6, 2, 9, 1
   i.e. 1, 2, 4, 6, 8, 8, 9
   ∴ median is 6

   b   34, 4, 62, 48   i.e. 4, 34, 48, 62
   As there are an even number of scores, the
   median is the average of 34 and 48   ∴ median is 41

8. The **mode** is the most common score—the score with the highest frequency.
   For example, find the mode of the following scores:

   a   14, 4, 7, 4, 8, 11
   The number 4 occurs most often (twice)
   ∴ mode is 4

   b   9, 8, 6, 2, 3, 9, 7, 8
   The numbers 8 and 9 occur most often (twice each)
   ∴ mode is 8 and 9

9. A **measure of spread** is the range. The **range** of a set of scores is the highest score minus the lowest score. For example, find the range of the following scores:

   a   12, 8, 43, –4, 32
   Range is 43 –(–4) = 43 + 4   ∴ range is 47

   b   23.4, 1.3, 7.43, 4.02
   Range is 23.4 – 1.3   ∴ range is 22.1

10. Scores may be **clustered** together or an **outlier** might exist. An outlier is a score much lower or higher than other scores. For example, in the scores 3, 8, 5, 7, 6, 6, 31, 6, the scores are clustered about 6 and there is an outlier of 31.

Checklist
Can you:

1 Recognise the difference between a census and a sample?
2 Find measures of location (mean, median, mode)?
3 Use the calculator to find the mean?
4 Find a measure of spread (range)?

1 Would we use a sample or a census to answer the following statements?
   a What is the population of NSW?
   b Who is likely to be the next Prime Minister?
   c Who is 7M3's favourite teacher?
   d How many students in year 7 have braces?

2 A survey of 100 students is conducted to find out whether the students want a change in the school uniform.
   a What percentage of students do not want a change in the uniform?
   b Of those students who want a change, what percentage are female?

Uniform survey results

	Change	No change
Male	20	34
Female	20	26

3 Find the mean of the following:
   a $4, 7, 8, 4, 2$
   b $3, 11, 14, 7, 6, 7$
   c $0.4, 2.56, 3.84, 4$
   d $-4, 7, 6, 8, -2$

4 The mean of eight scores is 6. Find the value of the pronumeral, if the scores are:
   a $2, 5, 6, 10, 15, 3, x, 5$
   b $3, y, 6, 9, 2, -1, 4, 8$

5 Calculate the mean correct to 2 decimal places:
   a $3, 6, 8, 9, 2, 3, 3, 3, 5, 4, 4, 7, 8, 3, 9$
   b $12, 16, 13, 15, 12, 15, 18, 16, 15, 11, 18$

6 The mean of five scores is 10. If another score is added, the mean increases to 12. Find the new score.

7 Find the median of the following:
   a $35, 14, 6, 25, 11$
   b $98, 43, 56, 2, 76, 44, 41, 44, 58, 56$

8 What is the mode of:
   a $3, 17, 4, 3, 8, 14, 15$?
   b $12, -4, 9, 11, 9, 6, 81, 4, 12$?

9 Find the range of:
   a $12, 7, 4, 2, 5$
   b $3, 6, -1, -15, 2, 7, 4, 6, 8, 2, -1, 0, 11$

10 Two groups of students were given the following marks for their French assignments:
   Group 1: $5, 5, 6, 7, 6, 7, 5, 7, 6, 6$ Group 2: $9, 8, 7, 2, 4, 7, 5, 8, 7, 3$
   Compare the groups in regard to:
   a mean   b median   c mode   d range

11 The following scores are arranged in ascending order. The median is the same as the range. Find the value of x:
   a $2, 3, 5, x, 8, 8, 9$
   b $x, 2, 2, 4, 5, 5$

PAGE 145

DATA ANALYSIS
Data Representation and Interpretation

INTERMEDIATE TEST

Part A Multiple Choice

1 The mean of the scores 4, 7, 2, 8, 6, 4, 3, 0, 1, 5 is:
   A 3   B 4   C 5   D 35.2   (1 mark)

2 The median of the scores 4, x, 2, 10 is 6. The value of x is:
   A 4   B 6   C 8   D 9   (1 mark)

3 Find the mode of the scores 4, 2, 8, 6, 4, 5, 7, 12, 8, 4.
   A 2   B 3   C 4   D 5   (1 mark)

4 The range of the scores 4, 2, 5, –1, y, 3 is 10. The value of y could be:
   A 11   B 8   C 9   D 10   (1 mark)

5 Five students scored marks in their English and science
   tests as noted in the table. Which one of the following
   is correct?
   A The range of English marks is 11.
   B The mode of the science marks is 75.
   C The median of the English marks is more than the median of the science marks.
   D The mode of the English marks is less than the mode of the science marks.   (1 mark)

   Test marks

Students	A	B	C	D	E
English	68	71	68	80	74
Science	75	68	73	79	79

Part B Short Answer

6 For the scores 9, 6, 5, 5, 2, 3, 5, find the:
   a mean   b median   c mode   d range   (1 mark each)

7 For the scores 4, 0, 3, 5, 11, –3, 6, 3, 5, 9, find the:
   a mean   b median   c mode   d range   (1 mark each)

8 After four maths tests Jo's mean is 76. As an incentive, her parents have offered to buy
   her a mobile phone if she can increase the mean to 80 following her next test. What mark
   will Jo need to score to receive the phone? *Hint 1*   (2 marks)

9 In February the Harvey family
   decided to record the age and
   height of each member of the
   family. The results appear in
   the table. Find the mean age
   and mean height of the
   Harvey family as at February.

   Age and height: Harveys

	Cliff	Anne	Fiona	Craig	Jason
Age (years)	42	42	14	11	6
Height (cm)	176	172	165	158	145

   (2 marks)

10 The heights, in cm, of the players on two junior boys basketball teams are as follows:
    Tigers: 163, 168, 171, 163, 165, 166, 172, 160   Eagles: 171, 163, 170, 173, 159, 172, 164, 164
    Compare the two teams, commenting on measures of location and spread. *Hint 2*   (4 marks)

Your Feedback

$$\frac{\boxed{}}{21} \times 100\% = \boxed{} \%$$

PAGE 146

PAGE 161

Hint 1: First find the sum of the four scores.
Hint 2: Find the mean, median, mode and range
   of both teams.

1 The mean mass of Ben, Ken and Len is 52 kg. If Ben's mass is 48 kg and Ken's mass is 50 kg, what is Len's mass? (2 marks)

2 A company's mean profit for the first four months of the year was $120 000. The profit in May was $150 000 and in June $180 000. What was the mean monthly profit in the six months? (2 marks)

3 A set of four different numbers has a range of 6 and a mean of 6. None of the numbers are 6. What is a possible set of numbers? (1 mark)

4 The median of four scores is 6.5. If the range is 3 and the mode is 7, find the four scores. (1 mark)

5 A score was added to the set of scores:

4   6   6   8   8   12

What was the new score if the new

a mode is 6?   **b** mean is 7?
c median is 7?   **d** range is 12? (1 mark each)

6 The mean of five scores is 9. When one of the scores changes, the mean increases by 2. What is the change in the score? (2 marks)

7 The number of goals scored by Mark's football team in five games is listed below:

4   2   4   2   2

In the sixth game, no goals were scored. Comment on the change to the:

a mode   **b** median
c range   **d** mean   (1 mark each)

8 A maths quiz taken by five students is marked out of 10 and the results are whole numbers. Give a possible set of students' results, if the:

a median is 6, the range is 6, mode is 6 and the mean is 7. (1 mark)

b median is 6, the range is 9, mode is 6 and the mean is 5. (1 mark)

9 In four games a hockey team scored an average of three goals. In the fifth game the team won by five goals, and their overall game average increased by one goal. What was the final score in the fifth game? (2 marks)

10 Find the mean, mode, median and range of the following:

a 0.4, 0.04, 0.4, 0.04, 4, 0.4 (4 marks)
b $\frac{1}{4}, \frac{1}{2}, \frac{3}{4}, \frac{1}{3}, \frac{1}{4}$ (4 marks)
c 4, −3, 2, −1, −1, 1, −2 (4 marks)

11 The mean of four scores is 8. When another two scores are included, the mean increases by 4. If one of the new scores is 12, what is the other new score? (2 marks)

12 A set of seven scores has a median of 6. Two new scores are added to the set. What will be the new median, if the new scores are 5 and 10? (1 mark)

13 The mean of a set of ten marks is 4. When another two marks are included, the mean doubles. What is the mean of the two additional scores? (2 marks)

14 The heights of students in a class were recorded and the average was 140 cm. Joshua and Mia were absent. When their heights were included in the class data, the mean height did not change. If Joshua's height was 143 cm, what was Mia's height? (2 marks)

15 Sheridan has completed four tests and her mean mark is 70%. What mark (as a percentage) will she need to get in her next test to increase the mean to 75% (2 marks)

16 This set of data is arranged in ascending order.

1,   3,   4, x,   8,   8.

What will be the value of x, if the:

a mean is 5? (2 marks)
b median is 6? (1 mark)

17 The mean temperature over five mornings in a ski village was −3 °C. When the temperature had been measured on the sixth morning the mean had increased by one degree. What was the temperature on the sixth morning? (2 marks)

18 Here are three scores: $x, 4, y$. The median and the range are both 3. What are the missing scores? (2 marks)

19 The Bardy family has four boys and two girls. The mean age of the boys is 12 and the mean age of the girls is 6. What is the mean age of the six children? (2 marks)

Your Feedback

$\dfrac{\boxed{}}{50} \times 100\% = \boxed{}\%$

📋 PAGE 146

📝 PAGE 161

1 A **frequency table** can be used to find **measures of location**:
- **mean**—by inserting an additional column, frequency × score (*fx*);
- **median**—by using the frequency column to find the middle score;
- **mode**—the score with the highest frequency;
- **range**—highest score minus lowest score.

For example, complete the table (right) and then find the mean, median and mode.

Mean = $\dfrac{\Sigma fx}{\Sigma f}$ [Σ means 'sum of']

$\quad\quad = \dfrac{102}{19} = 5.37$ (correct to 2 decimal places)

Median: the scores have been arranged in ascending order. There are 19 scores, so the middle score will be the 10th score. Working down the frequency column from the top row, we can see that the 10th score is a 5 (there are four scores of 4 and six scores of 5)
∴ median = 5.

Score (*x*)	Frequency (*f*)	*fx*
4	4	16
5	6	30
6	7	42
7	2	14
Totals	$\Sigma f = 19$	$\Sigma fx = 102$

Mode: the score with the highest frequency of 7 was 6   ∴ mode = 6.

2 A **dot plot**, **frequency histogram** or **frequency polygon** can also be used to find measures of location:
- **mean**—by using the formula, sum of scores ÷ number of scores;
- **median**—by crossing off the high and low scores in pairs to find the middle score;
- **mode**—the score with the tallest column. For example, find the mean, median and mode of the data represented by the dot plot at right.

Mean = $\dfrac{(16 \times 3) + (17 \times 4) + (18 \times 6) + (19 \times 4) + (20 \times 2)}{4 + 7 + 5 + 3 + 1}$

$\quad\quad = \dfrac{340}{19} = 17.89$ (correct to 2 decimal places)

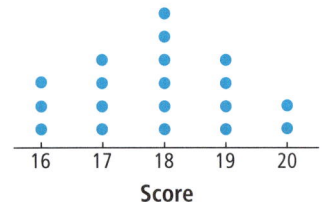

Median: cross off high and low scores in pairs. We end in the middle column   ∴ median = 18
Mode = 18

3 A **stem-and-leaf plot** can also be used to find measures of location:
- **mean**—by using a formula or the calculator;
- **median**—by crossing off the high and low scores in pairs to find the middle score;
- **mode**—look for the most common score.

For example, find the mean, median and mode of the data represented by the stem-and-leaf plot at right.
Mean: place calculator in STAT mode   ∴ mean = 82
Median: first ensure that the stem-and-leaf plot is ordered, cross off high and low scores in pairs. We are left with scores 80 and 82.   ∴ median = 81 [half-way between 80 and 82]   Mode: = 87

6	0 3 4 9
7	0 0 1 2 6 8 9
8	0 2 7 7 7 9
9	3 5 6 7 9
10	2 2

Checklist
Can you:

1 Calculate the mean, median, mode and range from a frequency table?   ☐
2 Calculate the mean, median, mode and range from a dot plot, histogram or polygon?   ☐
3 Calculate the mean, median, mode and range from a stem-and-leaf plot?   ☐

1 The results of a maths quiz are recorded:

16 18 17 14 17 18 15 17 16 13 19 17 15 17 19 17
16 18 19 19 18 17 19 18 16 16 18

  a Complete a frequency distribution table. Include *fx* (each score times its frequency) and totals of frequency and *fx*.

  b Find: **i** the mean of the results   **ii** the median   **iii** the mode   **iv** the range

  c What fraction of results is less than 17?

  d If a result is chosen at random, what is the probability that it is greater than 17?

2 **a** Complete the frequency distribution table at right.

  b Find: **i** the mean of the scores   **ii** the median
            iii the mode   **iv** the range

  c How many scores are less than the mode?

  d If a score is chosen at random, what is the probability that it is greater than the mean?

Score (x)	Frequency (f)	fx
3	7	
5		35
	12	
10		
Totals	$\Sigma f = 30$	$\Sigma fx = 180$

3 Data are collected on the number of cars owned by families living in a suburban street. The results are depicted in the histogram at right.

  a Find: **i** the mean of the scores   **ii** the median
            iii the mode   **iv** the range

  b If a household is chosen at random, what is the probability that the family owns three cars?

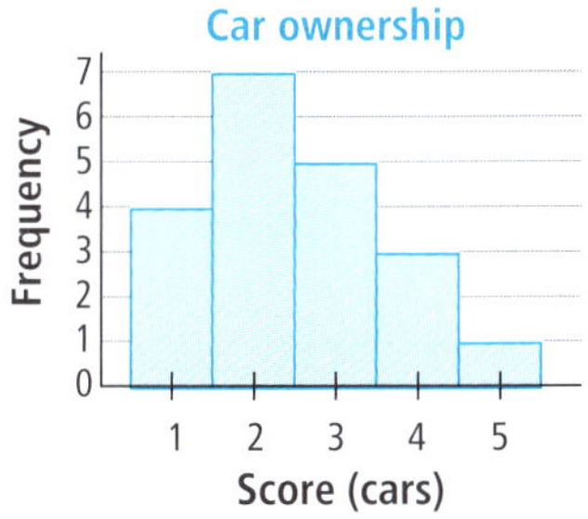

Car ownership

4 The contents of twenty packets of toothpicks were counted and the results summarised in the dot plot at right.

  a Find: **i** the mean of the scores   **ii** the median
            iii the mode   **iv** the range

  b What percentage of packets contained less than 150 toothpicks?

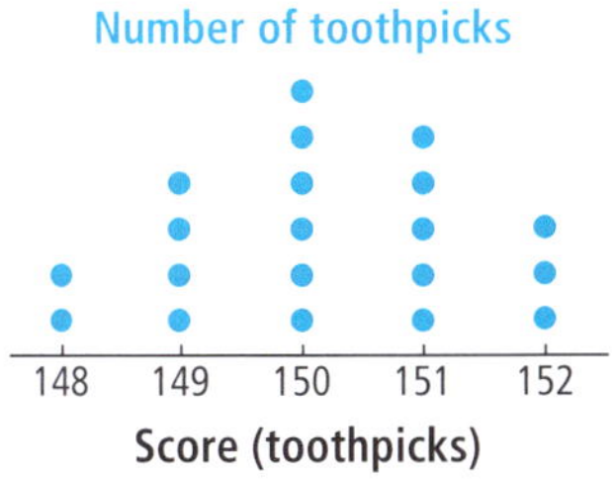

Number of toothpicks

5 The results of a test were recorded in the stem-and-leaf plot at right.

  a Find: **i** the mean of the scores   **ii** the median
            iii the mode   **iv** the range

  b What percentage of scores are less than the mean? Give your answer to one decimal place.

Test results

5	0 2 9
6	0 4 7 8
7	2 4 8 8 9
8	1 5 9

PAGE148

INTERPRETING DATA FROM GRAPHS

Data Representation and Interpretation

20 MINUTES

INTERMEDIATE TEST

Part A Multiple Choice

1 The □ in the table at right represents a digit in the stem-and-leaf plot. The scores are arranged in ascending order. If the median has the same value as the range, then □ is: *Hint 1*

1	2 8
2	0 4 5 6 9
3	0 3 3 5 7 8
4	1 3 5 □

A 5 **B** 6 **C** 7 **D** 8 (1 mark)

2 The value of *y* in this frequency table is: *Hint 2*

A 30 **B** 35
C 40 **D** 45

Score (*x*)	Frequency (*f*)	*fx*
2	5	
4		32
5		*y*
	3	
Totals	Σ*f* = 25	Σ*fx* = 108

(1 mark)

3 The median of the data represented by this frequency table is 6 and the mode is two more than the range. If *x* < *y* then the value of *x* is:

A 1 **B** 2 **C** 3 **D** 4

Score	Frequency
x	5
y	8

(1 mark)

Part B Short Answer

4 Use the dot plot to find the:

a mean of the scores (2 marks)
b mode (1 mark)
c median (1 mark)
d range (1 mark)

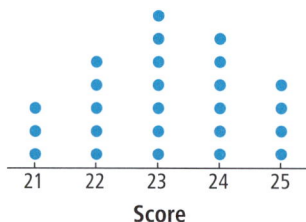

5 A survey of fifteen students was conducted to find the number of tablets in the family household. The results appear in the frequency histogram.

a Find the following: *Hint 3*

  i the mean score to 1 decimal place (2 marks)
  ii the median (1 mark)
  iii the mode (1 mark)
  iv the range (1 mark)

b A student is chosen at random. What is the probability that there is one tablet in the family household? (1 mark)

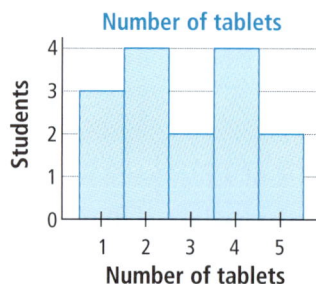

Hint 1: First find the median.
Hint 2: Complete the frequency table.
Hint 3: The data could be summarised in a frequency table.

Your Feedback

$$\frac{}{14} \times 100\% = \boxed{}\%$$

PAGE 149

PAGE 161

INTERPRETING DATA FROM GRAPHS
Data Representation and Interpretation

30 MINUTES

ADVANCED TEST

1 The stem-and-leaf plot shows the results of a science test.

Stem	Leaf
5	0 9
6	2 3 7 9
7	0 0 4 5 6
8	2 3 7
9	1

What are the mode, range and median?
(3 marks)

2 A set of scores is recorded in a table.

Score	Frequency
6	3
7	5
8	4
9	8
10	11

What are the mode, range and median? (3 marks)

3 Consider the dot plot.

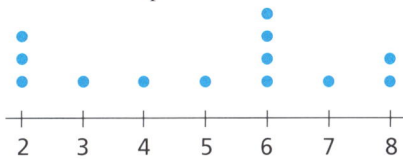

What are the mode, range, median and mean?
(4 marks)

4 A back-to-back stem-and-leaf plot records the heights, in cm, of a group of young people.

Boys		Girls
	13	3 7
9 7 7 6 3	14	2 5 8 9
8 4 4 4 0 0	15	0 0 4 5
5 5 3	16	1

a What is the mode, range and median of the boys? (3 marks)
b What is the mode, range and median of the girls? (3 marks)
c What is the mode, range and median of the whole group? (3 marks)
d A person is chosen at random. What is the probability that the person has a height of 150 cm? (1 mark)

5 A set of scores has been recorded in a table:

Score	Frequency
4	5
5	x
6	2

What are the possible values of x, if the:
a median is 4? **b** mode is 5?
c mean is 4.7? (1 mark each)

6 A stem-and-leaf plot is shown below.

Stem	Leaf
3	a 3 4
4	0 0 5 7 b
5	2 3 4 4 4
6	5 8 9

What is the value of:
a a, if the range is 37? (1 mark)
b b, if the median is 50.5? (1 mark)

7 The boys and girls in a year seven class are surveyed to find the number of mobile phones in their homes.

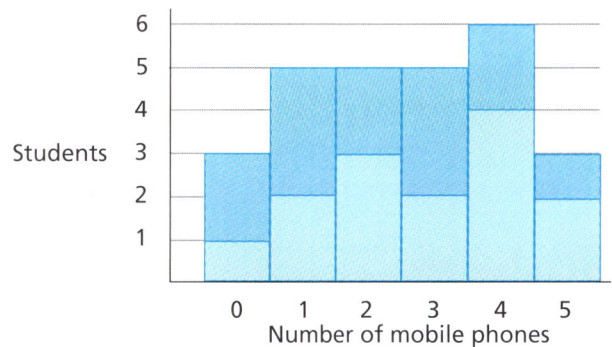

Key ▢ : Boys ▢ : Girls

a How many students were surveyed? (1 mark)
b How many girls were surveyed? (1 mark)
c How many boys had 5 mobiles in their homes? (1 mark)
d What was the total number of mobile phones? (2 marks)
e What was the modal number of phones for the:
  i group? **ii** girls? (1 mark each)
f What was the median for the:
  i group? **ii** girls? (1 mark each)
g Find the mean number of phones for the:
  i group **ii** girls (1 mark each)

Your Feedback

$\dfrac{\boxed{}}{36} \times 100 = \boxed{}$ %

PAGE 150

PAGE 161

Know what to expect

- **Find out** from your teacher exactly what topics will be assessed in the exam.
- Yearly exams normally test **all work covered** throughout the year.
- **Determine what format** is being used for the exam. Are there multiple-choice questions? Will calculators be allowed in any part of the exam?

Show all working

- **Read the instructions** on the exam paper—marks may be allocated for working.
- Even when **marks are not allocated**, working is important and it is rewarded, even though your answer may be incorrect.
- **Never use correction fluid**—just put a line through any incorrect working. Let your teacher see all your work.

Allocate your time

- Ensure you are **working through the paper efficiently** and not spending too much time on each question, only to find you run out of time at the end of the exam.

Understand mark allocations

- **Questions worth more marks** are often more complex and difficult. Working is crucial in these types of questions.

Reread and check

- Once you have **completed a question**, rather than moving to the next, reread that question to make sure you have in fact answered the correct question. This will only take a second or two.
- If you **finish the exam** with time still remaining, check your answers—often mistakes are found and can be corrected.

Use quality diagrams

- Diagrams should be of **good quality, large and drawn with a lead pencil**. Use an eraser, not correction fluid, to delete mistakes.

Be ready

- Finally, you need to be **prepared for the exam**.
- Always **study Mathematics actively**. Active study means using pen and paper to make notes, writing down difficult questions and their solutions, and recording rules to learn.

SAMPLE EXAM PAPERS
Level of difficulty—Average

90 MINUTES

PAPER 1

Part A Multiple Choice   **(10 marks)**

1 The lowest common multiple of 6 and 8 is:

    A 12   B 18   C 24   D 48   (1 mark)

2 Find the value of $12 - 4 \times 3$

    A 0   B 24   C 18   D 12   (1 mark)

3 $\dfrac{3}{4}$ is the same as:

    A $\dfrac{9}{16}$ B $\dfrac{24}{30}$ C $\dfrac{5 \times 3}{5 \times 4}$ D $\dfrac{5 + 3}{5 + 4}$ (1 mark)

4 If $\dfrac{?}{4} = \dfrac{12}{16}$, the missing value is

    A 1   B 2   C 3   D 4   (1 mark)

5 Simplify $\dfrac{3}{5} - \dfrac{1}{10}$

    A $\dfrac{1}{10}$ B $\dfrac{2}{5}$ C $\dfrac{1}{2}$ D $\dfrac{23}{50}$ (1 mark)

6 Find the product of $\dfrac{3}{4}$ and $\dfrac{2}{3}$

    A $\dfrac{1}{2}$ B $\dfrac{5}{12}$ C $\dfrac{1}{12}$ D $1\dfrac{5}{12}$ (1 mark)

7 Simplify $1.76 - 0.4$

    A 1.72   B 1.36   C 1.32   D 1.08   (1 mark)

8 The diagram shows a kite. How many lines of symmetry are there?

    A 1   B 2   C 3   D 4   (1 mark)

9 Keeley saves $6 out of her allowance of $20. The percentage of her allowance she saves is:

    A 6%   B 12%   C 20%   D 30%   (1 mark)

10 The median of 2, 5, 12, 8, 6, 3, 1 is:

    A 5   B 6   C 11   D 1   (1 mark)

Your Score

☐ ÷ 10

PAGE 151

Part B   **Short Answer**   **(30 marks)**

11   What is the mode of $5, 3, 6, 2, 3, 6, 9, 3, 5, 8$?   (1 mark)

12   Write the complement of $72°$.   (1 mark)

13   Write in numerals: three hundred and sixty thousand, eight hundred and twenty.   (1 mark)

14   Evaluate $12 \div 4 \times 2$ (1 mark)

15   Find the reciprocal of $2\frac{1}{2}$ (1 mark)

16   What fraction of the shape is shaded?   (1 mark)

17   Evaluate $2 - 1\frac{3}{5}$ (1 mark)

18   Find the sum of $\frac{1}{2}, \frac{1}{4}$ and $\frac{1}{8}$ (1 mark)

19   Rewrite the following in decimal form: $4 + 0.7 + 0.002 + 0.000\,05$ (1 mark)

20   On the number line locate with an X the position of 2.47.   (1 mark)

21   Evaluate $3.2 - 1.047$ (1 mark)

22   Find the quotient of 4.8 and 0.006 (1 mark)

23   Find the value of $(-4) - 2 + 6$ (1 mark)

24   Arrange in descending order: $-12, 6, 3, -1, 0$ (1 mark)

25   Rewrite $7a^2b^3$ in expanded form.   (1 mark)

26   Complete the rule for the table.

x	0	1	2	3	4
y	−1	0	1	2	3

(1 mark)

27   Simplify $4x - 3x + 2x$ (1 mark)

28   Simplify $4 : 14$ (1 mark)

29   Evaluate $-2 - (-3)$ (1 mark)

30   Find the value of x, if $2x - 1 = 7$ (1 mark)

31   Find the perimeter of the hexagon.   12.2 cm   (1 mark)

32   What is the range of the scores $4, 8, 2, 7, 11$?   (1 mark)

33 On a number line, what number is 4 units to the left of –1? (1 mark)

34 Find the area of a parallelogram with a base of 1.2 cm and a height of 0.7 cm. (1 mark)

35 Find the area of the rectangle in cm². (1 mark)

45 cm

1 m

36 Find the area of a triangle with base 16 cm and perpendicular height of 8 cm. (1 mark)

37 Each water bottle contains 600 mL. If a carton contains 24 bottles, what is the total amount of water, in litres, in each carton. (1 mark)

38 Find the value of x. (1 mark)

121° $x°$

39 Three angles in a quadrilateral are 120°, 40° and 70°. What is the size of the other angle? (1 mark)

40 During a season, six out of eight netballers have played in the centre position. What percentage of the team have not played centre? (1 mark)

Your Score

30

PAGE 151

Part C **Show All Working** **(60 marks)**

41 Complete a factor tree for 84 and express it as a product of its prime factors. (2 marks)

42 Twins Peter and Paul both have hiccups. Peter hiccups every four seconds and Paul every six seconds. If they hiccup at the same instant, how long before they hiccup together again? (2 marks)

43 Evaluate $15 \div 5 + 3 \times 7$ (2 marks)

44 Todd cuts a wooden plank of length 10 metres into two pieces in the ratio 2:3. What is the length of the shorter piece? (2 marks)

45 Sean discovers that $\frac{12}{15}$ and $\frac{x}{10}$ can be simplified to give the same equivalent fraction.

What is the value of x? (2 marks)

46 What fraction is $3.60 of $10? (2 marks)

47 Evaluate $2\frac{1}{2} + 3\frac{1}{3}$ (2 marks)

48 Find the value of $\frac{4}{5} + \frac{2}{3} \times \frac{3}{5}$ (2 marks)

49 Evaluate $\left(2\frac{1}{2}\right)^2$ (2 marks)

50 Find the cost of $3\frac{1}{2}$ metres of pipe at \$14 per metre. (2 marks)

51 Express $\frac{7}{9}$ as a recurring decimal. (2 marks)

52 Evaluate $0.4 + 1.6 \div 4$ (2 marks)

53 At the swimming carnival, Rhonda scored the following from the diving judges:
7.5, 8.0, 6.5, 7.5 and 8.0. What was Rhonda's average score? (2 marks)

54 At the Khemlani Rug Sale, Sean purchased a rug measuring 4.5 m by 2.5 m.
Find the area of the rug. (2 marks)

55 A bag contains 15 balls. Four of the balls are red, three are green and the remainder is blue.
  a How many blue balls are in the bag? (1 mark)
  b If a ball is chosen at random from the bag, what is the probability that it is blue? (1 mark)

56 Find 16% of \$40. (2 marks)

57 Find the values of the pronumerals: (2 marks)

58 **a** On the number plane plot the points:
     $A(1, -3)$, $B(1, 4)$, $C(-3, 4)$, $D(-3, -3)$ (1 mark)
  b Join the points to form $ABCD$.
     What type of polygon is $ABCD$? (1 mark)

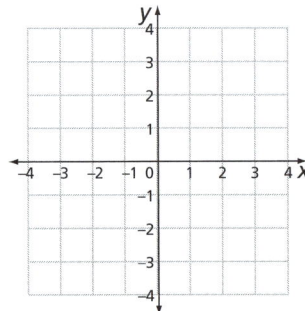

59 Simplify $4a \times 3 - 18a \div 6$ (2 marks)

60 Evaluate $(14 \div 7) \times 3 + 4 \times 2$ (2 marks)

61 **a** By letting the number be x, express the following in symbols:
     'The product of four and a number is equal to twenty-four' (1 mark)
  b Use your equation to find the value of x. (1 mark)

62 One hundred lunchboxes were checked to find the type of fruit students bring to school.

No fruit	Apples	Mandarins	Other

Using the graph: **a** What is the most popular fruit that these students brought to school? (1 mark)
                b How many students brought apples to school? (1 mark)

63 On the right are the admission charges to Funworld.

  a Find the cost of admission of Mrs Peters with her two sons, Jarrod (4 years) and Frodo (9 years). (1 mark)

  b How much will be saved when a Family Pass is purchased compared to separate tickets for two adults and two children? (1 mark)

Adult	$55
Students 12 and over	$48
Children (5–11)	$36
Senior card holders	$40
Family Pass *	$165
*2 adults and 2 children	

64 Find the cost of fencing a paddock in the shape of a rectangle measuring 15.5 metres by 10.5 metres, when fencing costs $9 per metre. (2 marks)

65 The stem-and-leaf plot shows the waiting times for people in a doctor's surgery on one afternoon. Find:

  a the range (1 mark)

  b the median (1 mark)

```
0 | 8 9
1 | 4 5 5 7 8
2 | 3 6
```

66 Complete the table. (2 marks)

Score (x)	Frequency (f)	fx
14	2	
15	3	
16	5	
Totals	$\Sigma f =$	$\Sigma fx =$

67 Calculate the mean for the data in the table in question 26. (2 marks)

68 A phone originally priced at $189 is discounted by $69.50. Find the new price. (2 marks)

69 Find the value of the pronumerals. (2 marks)

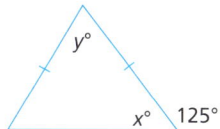

$y°$

$x°$ $125°$

70 Peanuts are sold in four differently sized packets: 100 g for $2.20, 200 g for $4.10, 400 g for $8.00 and 500 g for $10.20. Which packet gives the best value? (2 marks)

Your Score

[ ]

60

PAGE 152

Your Feedback—Paper 1

[ ] + [ ] + [ ] = [ ]/100 = [ ] %

Part A   Part B   Part C

PAGE 161

Part A **Multiple Choice** **(10 marks)**

1 Which of the following is not equal to 6?

A $4^2 - 5 \times 2$ **B** $\sqrt{4 \times 9}$ **C** $10 + 2 \div 2$ **D** $\dfrac{3 \times 8}{2 \times 2}$ (1 mark)

2 Which of the following number lines correctly shows X where $X = \dfrac{2}{3}$?

A **B**

C **D** (1 mark)

3 The fraction $\dfrac{3}{5}$ as a decimal is:

A 0.3 **B** 0.5 **C** 0.35 **D** 0.6 (1 mark)

4 A decimal has been rounded to the nearest hundredth as 1.67
The original number could have been:

A 1.66 **B** 1.675 **C** 1.662 **D** 1.674 (1 mark)

5 The product of 1.6 and 0.04 is:

A 0.064 **B** 0.64 **C** 6.4 **D** 64 (1 mark)

6 The rule used for this table is:

A $y = x - 1$ **B** $y = 3x - 1$
C $y = x + 2$ **D** $y = 2x + 1$

x	0	1	2	3
y	−1	2	5	8

(1 mark)

7 Simplify $30a \div 3 + 2 \times 2a$

A $18a$ **B** $14a$ **C** $12a$ **D** $12a^2$ (1 mark)

8 The perimeter of a square is 16 mm. The area of the square is:

A 4 mm^2 **B** 8 mm^2 **C** 16 mm^2 **D** 64 mm^2 (1 mark)

9 Which of the following is true?

A $a = 75, b = 75$ **B** $a = 105, b = 75$
C $a = 75, b = 105$ **D** $a = 105, b = 105$

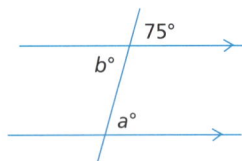

(1 mark)

10 The supplement of 64° is:

A 26° **B** 32° **C** 116° **D** 128° (1 mark)

Your Score

[ ]

10

PAGE 153

Part B **Short Answer** **(30 marks)**

11 True or false? 47 644 is divisible by 6 (1 mark)

12 Write in symbols:
The sum of twelve and five is less than or equal to the product of two and eleven. (1 mark)

13 Evaluate $23 \times 47 + 77 \times 47$ (1 mark)

14 Express 40 cents as a fraction of $2.40 (1 mark)

15 Find the value of x, if $\dfrac{4}{x} = \dfrac{56}{70}$ (1 mark)

16 Find $\dfrac{3}{5}$ of $30 (1 mark)

17 Express $\dfrac{1}{8}$ as a decimal. (1 mark)

18 Find the value of y, if $0.02 \times y = 8$ (1 mark)

19 Find the value of 47.62×10^2 (1 mark)

20 Evaluate $\sqrt{9} \times \sqrt{36} \times \sqrt{4}$ (1 mark)

21 At 6 am the temperature was $-3°$ and by noon it had risen to $9°$. What was the increase in temperature? (1 mark)

22 If $y = 4$, find the value of $3y^2$ (1 mark)

23 If $p = 0.6$ and $q = 1.2$, find $\dfrac{4p}{q}$ (1 mark)

24 Simplify $4a - 2b - 3a + 6b$ (1 mark)

25 Simplify $3a \times 2b - 4ab \times 5$ (1 mark)

26 Find the value of x. (1 mark)

27 Simplify $2 : 2.40 (1 mark)

28 Find the range of the scores $2, 5, -3, 6, -1$. (1 mark)

29 What is 15% of 6 metres? (1 mark)

30 Find the area of the rectangle in square centimetres. (1 mark)

31 Find the mean of $3, 7, 4, 2, 8$ and 12. (1 mark)

32 Find the volume of a cube with side 4 cm. (1 mark)

33 Find the area. 40 cm / 120 cm (1 mark)

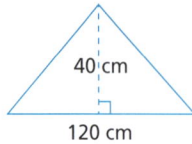

34 If $a = -2$ and $b = -7$, find the value of $b - a$. (1 mark)

35 A 2-litre bottle of lemonade costs \$2.40. Find the cost per millilitre. (1 mark)

36 Find the value of the pronumeral. 120° 72° 110° $x°$ (1 mark)

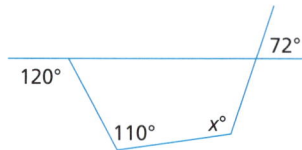

37 What percentage is 30 seconds of 5 minutes? (1 mark)

38 The circle is split into 12 equal parts. The sectors are numbered using the digits 1, 2 and 3. Find the probability of spinning an odd number? (1 mark)

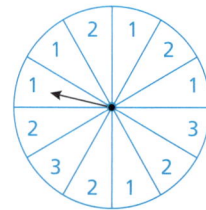

39 Roberta wrote the following on five separate cards.:

0.21   18% $\dfrac{1}{20}$ $\dfrac{1}{5}$ 3%

She then arranged them in ascending order along a table. What card is in the middle? (1 mark)

40 How many lines of symmetry does an equilateral triangle have? (1 mark)

Your Score

☐
___
30

PAGE 154

Part C **Show All Working** **(60 marks)**

41 Complete a factor tree for 360 and express it as a product of its prime factors, written in index form. (2 marks)

42 **a** List the primes between 20 and 30. (1 mark)
   b List the composites between 45 and 55. (1 mark)

43 Evaluate $\dfrac{30 \times 4}{4 + 6}$ (2 marks)

44 Solve the equation $2x + 1 = 7$ (2 marks)

45 A diamond ring is purchased for $600 and later sold for $800. Write the profit expressed as a fraction of the cost price. (2 marks)

46 Simplify $\dfrac{10 \times 8 \times 6 \times 4}{20 \times 16 \times 3 \times 2}$ (2 marks)

47 Scott conducted a survey of those who regularly attend his church.

Males 30 years and over: $\dfrac{1}{5}$, males under 30 years old: $\dfrac{3}{8}$, females 30 years and over: $\dfrac{1}{4}$.

What fraction of the congregation is female, aged under 30 years old? (2 marks)

48 Simplify $3\dfrac{2}{3} - 1\dfrac{1}{4}$ (2 marks)

49 Evaluate $1\dfrac{3}{4} \div \dfrac{9}{10}$ (2 marks)

50 What is the product of $2\dfrac{1}{4}$ and its reciprocal? (2 marks)

51 Half of the thirty students in 7P are boys, and three-fifths of the girls have blonde hair. How many blonde haired girls are in 7P? (2 marks)

52 Express $\dfrac{4}{11}$ as a recurring decimal. (2 marks)

53 Arrange the following in ascending order: $\dfrac{3}{5}$, $0.\dot{6}$, $\dfrac{29}{50}$, $\dfrac{14}{25}$ (2 marks)

54 Find the value of $(1.2)^2 - (0.5)^2$ (2 marks)

55 Each shirt requires 1.4 metres of material. How many shirts can be made from 8 metres of material? (2 marks)

56 Petrol costs 162.2 cents per litre. How much will Lisa pay for 30 litres? (2 marks)

57 The travel graph shows a journey of Jerome driving home from a holiday. Jerome was travelling home but got a phone call from the resort telling him he had left his laptop behind.

a How many kilometres did Jerome drive? (1 mark)

b Between what times was Jerome driving the fastest? (1 mark)

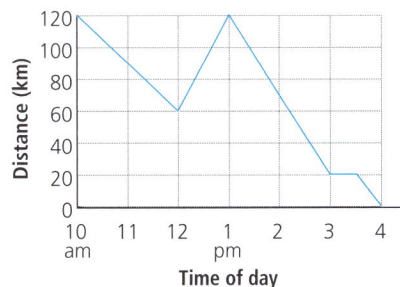

58 If $x = 3$ is a solution of the equation $2x - k = 5$, what is the value of k? (2 marks)

59 a Write the rule for the table linking a and b. (1 mark)

b Find the value of p. (1 mark)

a	0	2	4	6	10
b	3	7	11	15	p

60 Simplify $15ab \div 5a + 3 \times 4b$ (2 marks)

61 Find the area of the trapezium.   (2 marks)

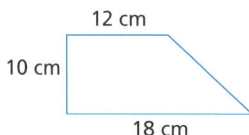

12 cm
10 cm
18 cm

62 *ABCD* is a parallelogram. Find the coordinates of *D*.   (2 marks)

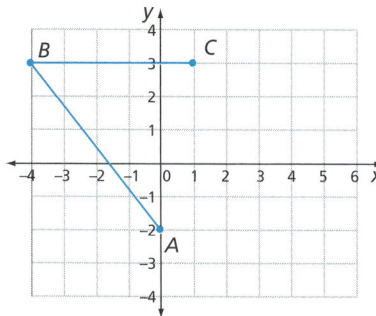

63 The shoe sizes of a group of year 7 students were recorded in the histogram.
  a How many students participated in the survey?   (1 mark)
  b Find the range of shoe sizes.   (1 mark)

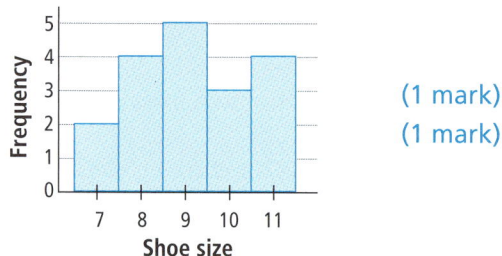

64 A die is rolled. What is the probability of rolling a number which is:
  a less than 6?   (1 mark)
  b prime?   (1 mark)

65 Eleni surveyed the houses in her street to find the number of cars driven by residents. She recorded the results in the dot plot shown. Find the:
  a mode   (1 mark)
  b median   (1 mark)

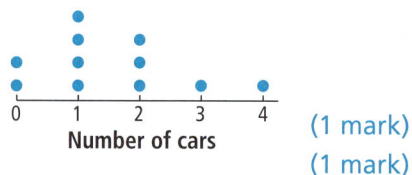

66 Find the area of the shaded region.   (2 marks)

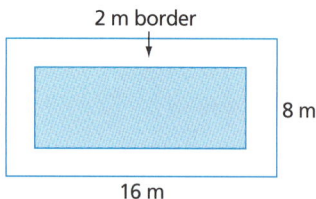

2 m border
8 m
16 m

67 Terri wrote these number patterns but left a number out. What are the missing numbers?
  a 8, 5, 2, _____, −4   (1 mark)
  b 1.4, 1.25, 1.1, _____, 0.8   (1 mark)

68 Find the value of *x*, giving reasons.   (2 marks)

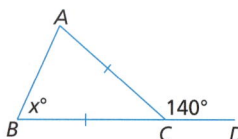

69 From a two-litre carton of orange juice, Darcie pours 300 mL. What percentage of the juice remains in the carton?   (2 marks)

70 Mrs Bryden gave her students a quiz and recorded the results.

    a How many students did the quiz?   (1 mark)

    b Find the median mark.   (1 mark)

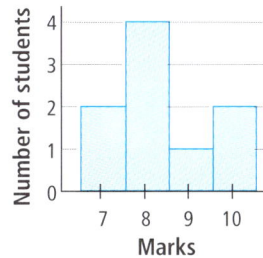

Your Score

[ ]
60

PAGE 155

Your Feedback—Paper 2

$$\frac{\boxed{}}{\text{Part A}} + \frac{\boxed{}}{\text{Part B}} + \frac{\boxed{}}{\text{Part C}} = \frac{\boxed{}}{100} = \boxed{}\%$$

PAGE 161

Part A **Multiple Choice** **(10 marks)**

1 Which of the following numbers has a factor of 6?
  A 187 B 244 C 342 D 999 (1 mark)

2 Find the value of $\frac{3}{5} \div \frac{3}{4}$

  A $1\frac{1}{4}$ B $\frac{4}{5}$ C $3\frac{3}{4}$ D $\frac{1}{2}$ (1 mark)

3 Which of the following is arranged in ascending order?
  A $\frac{1}{2}, \frac{2}{3}, \frac{3}{4}$ B $\frac{1}{2}, \frac{3}{4}, \frac{2}{3}$ C $\frac{3}{4}, \frac{2}{3}, \frac{1}{2}$ D $\frac{2}{3}, \frac{1}{2}, \frac{3}{4}$ (1 mark)

4 The value of X could be:

  A $\frac{2}{3}$ B $\frac{5}{8}$ C $\frac{4}{5}$ D $\frac{5}{9}$ (1 mark)

5 Which of the following is equal to 0.2?

  A $\sqrt{0.4}$ B $3.6 \div 1.8$ C $\frac{4.8}{2.4}$ D $0.6 \div 3$ (1 mark)

6 The missing number in the sequence $5, 2, \_\_\_, -4, -7$ is:
  A 1 B 0 C −1 D −2 (1 mark)

7 $-3 - (-1)$ equals:
  A −2 B 2 C −4 D 4 (1 mark)

8 If $a = 3$, $b = 4$, which of the following is true?
  A $2a + b = 5$ B $3b - a = 8$ C $2a - b = 3$ D $ab - 2 = 10$ (1 mark)

9 The table is completed for $y = 3 - x$
Which of the following is true?

x	−3	−2	−1	0
y	a	b	c	d

  A $a = 0$ B $b = 5$ C $c = 2$ D $d = -3$ (1 mark)

10 The value of x is:

  A 130 B 50 C 80 D 65 (1 mark)

Your Score

[ ]
___
10

PAGE 156

Part B   Short Answer   **(30 marks)**

11   What number am I? I am a multiple of 4, 5 and 6. I lie between 100 and 150.   (1 mark)

12   Find the volume of a rectangular prism with dimensions 1.2 cm, 0.8 cm and 0.4 cm.   (1 mark)

13   Write in symbols: the cube root of the sum of seven and nine is not equal to the square of the difference between nine and four.   (1 mark)

14   Insert grouping symbols to make a true statement: $14 - 2 + 7 \div 3 + 4 = 7$ (1 mark)

15   What fraction is half-way between $\frac{1}{3}$ and $\frac{1}{2}$?   (1 mark)

16   Simplify $\frac{4}{5} + \frac{3}{4}$ (1 mark)

17   Rewrite in ascending order: $\frac{4}{5}$, 0.73, 0.728, $\frac{2}{3}$ (1 mark)

18   Evaluate $\dfrac{4.5 + 1.5}{0.3}$ (1 mark)

19   Find the value of $(1 - 0.4)^2$ (1 mark)

20   The average minimum temperature over three consecutive days was $0\,°C$. If the temperature on Monday was $-4\,°C$ and Tuesday $1\,°C$, what was the minimum temperature on Wednesday?   (1 mark)

21   If $a = 4$ and $b = 3$, find the value of $a^2 + b^2$ (1 mark)

22   Terry buys p pizzas at $\$d$ each. How much change will he receive from $\$m$?   (1 mark)

23   Find the area of the triangle.   4a cm   7a cm   (1 mark)

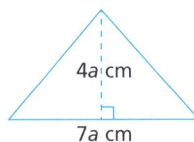

24   Simplify $4a^2 - (4a)^2$ (1 mark)

25 $ABDE$ is a parallelogram and $BD = BC$. $\angle BAE = 130°$. Find the size of $\angle BCD$.   (1 mark)

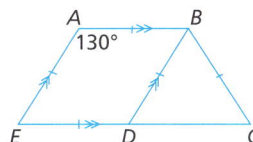

26   The product of five and the sum of a number and two is equal to fifteen. Find the number.   (1 mark)

27 Find the perimeter of *ABCD*. (1 mark)

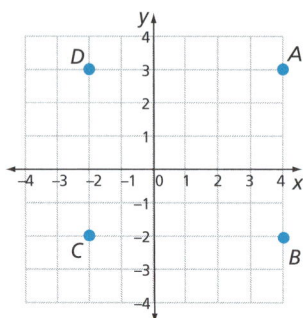

28 Convert *y* kilometres to millimetres. (1 mark)

29 Last weekend Fiona visited her aunt. Her car uses petrol at the rate of 9 litres for every 100 km it travels. On Saturday she travelled 240 km and on Sunday 160 km. If petrol costs $1.50 per litre, what did the weekend trip cost Fiona? (1 mark)

30 Liu averages 1 min 12 s for each lap of a training circuit. How long will it take her to complete 10 laps? (1 mark)

31 Find the area of the triangle. (1 mark)

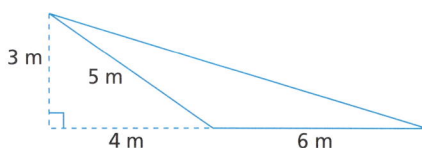

32 The volume of a cube is 125 cm³. Find the area of one of its square faces. (1 mark)

33 Find the value of *x*. (1 mark)

34 A tap drips 0.25 mL in every drop. If it drips every 4 seconds, how much water is lost every hour? (1 mark)

35 If $a = -1$ and $b = -4$, evaluate $12 - (a - b)$. (1 mark)

36 If the median of the scores in the stem-and-leaf plot is 55, what is the missing number? (1 mark)

```
3 | 2 3
4 | 5 6 8
5 | 2 □ 8 9
6 | 4 7 8
```

37 If *AB* is to be parallel to *CD*, what is the size of ∠*DHF*? (1 mark)

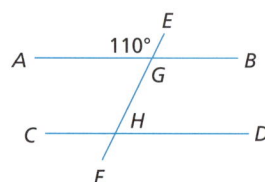

38 Solve $\dfrac{4}{x} = 2$ (1 mark)

39 Ed uses fertiliser which costs 40 cents per 10 m². Find the cost of fertlising a rectangular paddock measuring 20 metres by 18 metres. (1 mark)

40 In the diagram $\angle ABC = \angle ADE = 90°$ and $AD = DB = DE = 2$ cm. What percentage of $\triangle ABC$ is shaded? (1 mark)

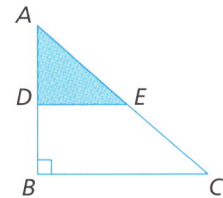

Your Score

30

PAGE 156

Part C **Show All Working** **(60 marks)**

41 Using a factor tree, find the square root of 784. (2 marks)

42 The mean of four scores is 16. Another score is included and the mean increases by two. What is the score that has been added? (2 marks)

43 Evaluate $3^2 + 4 \times 5 - 3$ (2 marks)

44 Find the profit as a fraction of the cost price. (2 marks)

Cost price	Selling price	Profit
	$6.50	$1.50

45 Evaluate $947 \div 24$, writing your answer in the form: $947 = \_\_\_\_ \times 24 + \_\_\_\_$ (2 marks)

46 On a tram the ratio of men to women is 3:5. If there are 8 more women than men, how many women are on the tram? (2 marks)

47 Evaluate $9300 \div 200$ (2 marks)

48 One sixth of the rectangle is shaded. If two thirds of the remaining squares are now shaded, what fraction of the rectangle remains unshaded? (2 marks)

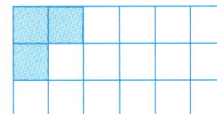

49 Find the value of $2\frac{1}{4} - 1\frac{3}{5}$ (2 marks)

50 Two and a half kilograms of cheese costs $15. Find the cost per kilogram. (2 marks)

51 Evaluate $3\frac{1}{2} \div 2\frac{1}{3}$ (2 marks)

52 Simplify $\dfrac{\frac{4}{5}+\frac{1}{2}}{\frac{4}{5}-\frac{1}{2}}$ (2 marks)

53 A tree is currently at three quarters of its final height. If presently it is 12 metres high, find its final height. (2 marks)

54 Express $\dfrac{26}{99}$ as a recurring decimal. (2 marks)

55 Jason used 14.4 litres to paint 4 identical rooms. How much paint will be required to paint seven rooms? (2 marks)

56 Evaluate $(0.21 \div 0.7)^2$ (2 marks)

57 Find the value of $(4.85 \times 10^3) \div (0.5 \times 10^2)$ (2 marks)

58 Listed are four scores arranged in ascending order: $4, 6, x, y$. If the range and the median are both 8, find the mean. (2 marks)

59 In a church youth group the ratio of boys to girls is $2:3$. On a 'bring your friends' night all the boys bring 2 male friends each, while the girls bring a female friend each. What is the new ratio of boys to girls? (2 marks)

60 Evaluate $\dfrac{5^2 - 2^2 - 1^2}{\sqrt{3^2 + 4^2}}$ (2 marks)

61 Larry the lumberjack takes six minutes to saw a log into three pieces. How long will it take him to saw a similar log into six pieces? (2 marks)

62 A cruise ship has 2400 passengers. There are women, men and children on the ship. Three in every eight passengers are men and one in three passengers is a woman. How many children are on the cruise? (2 marks)

63 At a party Jill noticed the handshakes between people as they were introducing each other. She recorded the number of handshakes for different groupings of people. Jill summarised the information in the table below.

2 people   3 people   4 people

a Complete the table. (1 mark)

People (p)	2	3	4	5
Handshakes (h)	1	3		

b Jill realises that the values in the handshakes row form a special group of numbers. What sort of numbers are they? (1 mark)

64 'The sum of three consecutive odd numbers is 27.'

    a By letting the smallest number be x, rewrite the statement as an equation.   (1 mark)

    b Solve the equation to find the numbers.   (1 mark)

65 Antoinette's half-yearly results were recorded.

    a In which subject(s) did Antoinette score more than 75?   (1 mark)

    b What is the average of the four results?   (1 mark)

Half-yearly exam results

Mark — English, maths, science, geography — *Subject*

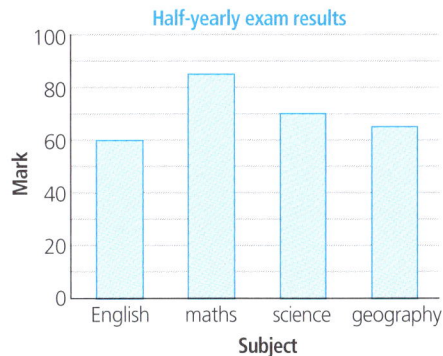

66 The length of a rectangle is 8 cm and its perimeter is 26 cm. If the dimensions are doubled, what is the area of the new rectangle?   (2 marks)

67 Three-eights of the students in a group cannot swim. There are eight more swimmers than non-swimmers. How many students are in the group?   (2 marks)

68 A folder costs twice as much as a ruler which costs twice as much as a pencil. Sam bought twice as many rulers as pencils and half as many folders as rulers. If a folder costs $1.20 and Sam bought two rulers, how much change does he get from $10?   (2 marks)

69 After a discount of 40% is applied, the cost of insuring Bob's house is $720. What is the cost of insuring the house if he had no discount?   (2 marks)

70 Payne's Electrical Repairs charge a call-out fee of $40 plus $3 per minute for domestic work. This information is summarised in the table below:

Minutes (t)	0	10	20	30	40
Cost in $ (C)	40	70	100	130	160

    a Write a formula linking cost (C) and time (t).   (1 mark)

    b How long will the repairman be working if he charges $115?   (1 mark)

Your Score

[ ] / 60

PAGE 158

Your Feedback—Paper 3

$$\frac{\boxed{}}{\text{Part A}} + \frac{\boxed{}}{\text{Part B}} + \frac{\boxed{}}{\text{Part C}} = \frac{\boxed{}}{100} = \boxed{}\%$$

PAGE 161

MULTIPLES, FACTORS AND PRIMES
SKILLS CHECK   PAGE 2

1 a 7, 14, 21, 28, 35
  b 11, 22, 33, 44, 55
  c 13, 26, 39, 52, 65

2 a 3: 3, 6, 9, 12, **15**, …
    5: 5, 10, **15**, …
    LCM is 15
  b 10: 10, 20, 30, 40, 50, **60**, …
    12: 12, 24, 36, 48, **60**, …
    LCM is 60
  c 3: 3, 6, 9, **12**, 15, 18, 21, 24, …
    4: 4, 8, **12**, 16, 20, 24, …
    6: 6, **12**, 18, 24, …
    LCM is 12

3 a True
  b True

4 a 20: 1, 2, 4, 5, 10, 20
  b 36: 1, 2, 3, 4, 6, 9, 12, 18, 36
  c 40: 1, 2, 4, 5, 8, 10, 20, 40

5 a 12: 1, 2, 3, **4**, 6, 12
    16: 1, 2, **4**, 8, 16
    HCF is 4
  b 18: 1, 2, 3, **6**, 9, 18
    24: 1, 2, 3, 4, **6**, 8, 12, 24
    HCF is 6
  c 10: 1, 2, **5**, 10
    20: 1, 2, 4, **5**, 10, 20
    25: 1, **5**, 25
    HCF is 5

6 a 2, 3, 5, 7
  b 29, 31, 37
  c 23
  d 101, 103, 107, 109

7 a 4, 6, 8, 9, 10
  b 21, 22, 24, 25, 26, 27, 28
  c 9, 15
  d 42, 44, 45, 46, 48, 49

8 a True [as factors are 1, 2, 4]
  b False [as factors are 1, 3, 7, 21]
  c False [as 29 is also prime]
  d True [as 12, 14, 15, 16, 18 are composite]

9 a

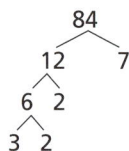

∴ 60 = 3 × 2 × 5 × 2
    = 2^2 × 3 × 5

  b

∴ 84 = 3 × 2 × 2 × 7
    = 2^2 × 3 × 7

  c

∴ 150 = 3 × 5 × 5 × 2
    = 2 × 3 × 5^2

10 a True. Last digit is a 5
  b True. Sum of digits is 12, which is divisible by 3
  c False. 35 is not divisible by 4
  d True. Last digit is 0
  e False. Last digit is not even or 0
  f True. Sum of digits is 9, which is divisible by 9
  g False. Last three digits are 124, which is not divisible by 8
  h True. Divisible by 2 (last digit is even) and sum of digits is 12, which is divisible by 3.

MULTIPLES, FACTORS AND PRIMES
INTERMEDIATE TEST   PAGE 3

1 Multiples of 4: 4, 8, **12**, …
  Multiples of 6: 6, **12**, 18, …
  ∴ LCM is 12   **B** ✓   (1 mark)

2 As 7 + 8 = 15, and 15 is divisible by 3
  ∴ 3 is a factor of 78   **A** ✓
    (1 mark)

3 861 has factor of 3 as
  8 + 6 + 1 = 15   **C** ✓   (1 mark)

4 Multiples of 4 are …, 72, 76, …   **B** ✓   (1 mark)

5 Primes are 83, 89 only i.e. 2 primes   **A** ✓   (1 mark)

6 97 is prime   **D** ✓   (1 mark)

7 a 48, 52, 56, 60, 64, 68   ✓✓
  b 78, 84, 90, 96, 102   ✓✓
    (4 marks)

8 a Either 23 875 or 23 870
    ∴ 5 (or 0) ✓
  b Either 476 124, or 476 424, or 476 724, as the sum of the digits is divisible by 3 and each number is divisible by 2.
    ∴ 1 (or 4 or 7) ✓ (2 marks)

9 Division method:

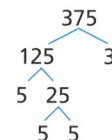

As no remainder, then 3 is a factor of 375 ✓
Factor tree method:

∴ 375 = 3 × 5 × 5 × 5
∴ 3 is a factor ✓   (2 marks)

10 a

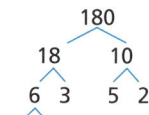

∴ 180 = 2 × 2 × 3 × 3 × 5 ✓
  b

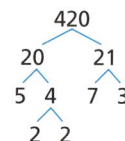

∴ 420 = 2 × 2 × 3 × 5 × 7 ✓
    (6 marks)

11 a Try 45 and 90 as they are divisible by 3 and 5; but 90 is between 89 (prime) and 91 (composite)
    ∴ number is 90 ✓✓
  b Try 60 and 72 as they are divisible by 4 and 6; but 72 is divisible by 9.
    ∴ number is 72 ✓✓
    (4 marks)

12 Multiples of 8: 8, 16, **24**, …
Multiples of 6: 6, 12, 18, **24**, …
∴ 24 is LCM
∴ meet after 24 minutes ✓✓
(2 marks)

13 Multiples of 7: 7, 14, …, **84**, …
Multiples of 12: 12, 24, …, **84**, …
∴ 84 is LCM
∴ drip together after 84 s
(i.e. 1 min 24 s)
∴ drip at 10:01:24 am ✓✓
(2 marks)

14 Multiples of 4: 4, …, **60**, …
Multiples of 5: 5, …, **60**, …
Multiples of 6: 6, …, **60**, …
∴ 60 is LCM
∴ smallest number is 60 ✓✓
(2 marks)

MULTIPLES, FACTORS AND PRIMES
ADVANCED TEST   PAGE 4

1 **a** Primes: 2, 3, 5, 7, 11, 13, 17, 19, 23, 29, 31, 37, 41, 43, 47
∴ 15 numbers ✓
Percentage prime
$= \dfrac{15}{50} \times 100\%$
$= 30\%$ ✓

b Composite:
As $50 - 15 - 1 = 34$,
∴ 34 numbers are composite ✓
Percentage composite
$= \dfrac{34}{50} \times 100\%$
$= 68\%$ ✓   (4 marks)

2 **a** 32: 1, 2, **4**, 8, 16, 32
52: 1, 2, **4**, 13, 26, 52
highest common factor of 4 ✓

b 120: 1, 2, 3, 4, 5, 6, 8, 10, 12, 15, 20, 24, **30**, 40, 60, 120
150: 1, 2, 3, 5, 6, 10, 15, 25, **30**, 50, 75, 150
∴ highest common factor of 30 ✓

c 75: 1, 3, 5, 15, 25, **75**
225: 1, 3, 5, 9, 15, 25, 45, **75**, 225
∴ highest common factor of 75 ✓   (3 marks)

3 **a** 16: 16, 32, **48**, 60, …
24: 24, **48**, 72, …
∴ lowest common multiple of 48 ✓

b 15: 15, 30, 45, 60, **75**, 90, 105, …
25: 25, 50, **75**, …
∴ lowest common multiple of 75 ✓

c 25: 25, 50, 75, 100, 125, 150, 175, **200**, 225, …
40: 40, 80, 120, 160, **200**, 240, …
∴ lowest common multiple of 200 ✓   (3 marks)

4 Consider the lowest common multiple:
3: 3, 6, 9, …, 57, **60**, 63, …
4: 4, 8, 12, …, 56, **60**, 64, …
5: 5, 10, 15, …, 55, **60**, 65, … ✓
∴ lowest common multiple of 60
∴ every 60th bag has all three items ✓   (2 marks)

5 **a**
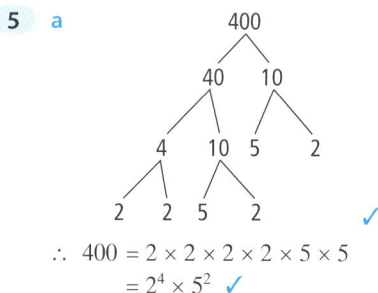
∴ $400 = 2 \times 2 \times 2 \times 2 \times 5 \times 5$
$= 2^4 \times 5^2$ ✓

b
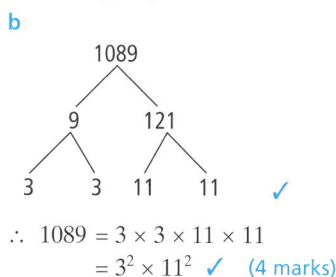
∴ $1089 = 3 \times 3 \times 11 \times 11$
$= 3^2 \times 11^2$ ✓   (4 marks)

6 Consider the lowest common multiple:
6: 6, 12, 18, **24**, 30, …
8: 8, 16, **24**, 32, …
∴ lowest common multiple of 24 ✓
As $60 \times 5 = 300$, then
No. of times $= 300 \div 24$
$= 100 \div 8$
$= 12.5$
∴ the lights blink together 12 times ✓   (2 marks)

7 As 1, 2 and 3 are factors of 6, then need to only consider multiples of 4, 5 and 6. ✓
4: 4, 8, 12, …, 56, **60**, 64, …
5: 5, 10, 15, …, 55, **60**, 65, …
6: 6, 12, 18, …, 54, **60**, 66, …
∴ the smallest number is 60 ✓   (2 marks)

8 From the pattern, 4 to the power of odd has last digit = 4, and 4 to the power of even has last digit = 6. As 2014 is even, then last digit is 6. ✓   (1 mark)

9 Consider the highest common factor:
24: 1, 2, 3, 4, **6**, 8, 12, 24
30: 1, 2, 3, 5, **6**, 10, 15, 30
∴ highest common factor of 6 ✓
∴ there are 6 possible groups ✓
(each with 4 year seven students)   (2 marks)

10 • divisible by 9: digits add to 9
• multiple of 6: even
• middle digit prime
∴ 630 ✓   (1 mark)

11 72: 1×72, 2×36, 3×24, 4×18, 6×12, 8×9, 9×8, 12×6, 18×4, 24×3, 36×2, 72×1
Can only use
6×12, 8×9, 9×8, 12×6 ✓
∴ only four arrangements possible ✓   (2 marks)

12 **a** $3^2 \times 7^2 = (3 \times 7)^2$
$= 21 \times 21$
$= 21 \times 20 + 21$
$= 441$ ✓✓

b $3^2 \times 2^4 \times 5^2 = 3^2 \times 4^2 \times 5^2$
$= (3 \times 4 \times 5)^2$
$= 60^2$
$= 3600$ ✓✓   (4 marks)

13 Consider the highest common factor: ✓
48: 1, 2, 3, 4, 6, 8, **12**, 16, 24, 48
60: 1, 2, 3, 5, 6, 10, **12**, 15, 20, 30, 60
∴ highest common factor of 12
∴ Jay will need 12 containers ✓
(each with 4 choc-chip and 5 anzac biscuits)   (2 marks)

14 a Multiples of 6 are even and digits add to a multiple of 3: 84, 372, 480

∴ 3 numbers ✓

b Multiples of 8: 224, 480

∴ 2 numbers ✓ *(2 marks)*

15 Possible dimensions:

$48 \times 1, 24 \times 2, 16 \times 3, 12 \times 4, 8 \times 6$ ✓

∴ 5 different perimeters ✓ *(2 marks)*

16 Consider the lowest common multiple: ✓

5: 5, 10, 15, …, 115, **120**, 125, …

8: 8, 16, 24, …, 112, **120**, 128, …

12: 12, 24, 36, …, 108, **120**, 132, …

∴ lowest common multiple of 120

∴ Laura picked 120 oranges ✓ *(2 marks)*

17 Consider the highest common factor:

160: 1, 2, 4, **5**, …

120: 1, 2, 3, 4, **5**, …

75: 1, 2, 3, **5**, …

∴ highest common factor of 5

∴ there are 5 matching bracelets ✓

As $120 \div 5 = 24$, then she uses 24 red beads on each bracelet. ✓ *(2 marks)*

18 As 3 m = 300 cm and 2.4 m = 240 cm, then we need to find the highest common factor of 300 and 240:

300: 1, 2, 3, 4, 5, 6, 10, 15, 20, 30, 50, **60**, 75, 100, 150, 300

240: 1, 2, 3, 4, 5, 6, 8, 10, 12, 15, 16, 20, 30, 40, 48, **60**, 80, 120, 240

∴ highest common factor is 60

∴ largest tile is 60 cm by 60 cm ✓

As $300 \div 60 = 5$ and $240 \div 60 = 4$, and $5 \times 4 = 20$, then 20 tiles are required. ✓ *(2 marks)*

NUMBERS AND DIRECTED NUMBERS
SKILLS CHECK   PAGE 6

1 a $70 \div 10 = 7$

b $5 + 3 + 8 < 18$

c $365\,000 > 10^3$

d $3^2 + 2^3 = 17$

e $5(4 + 2) = 30$

f $(8 + 7)^2 \geq 100$

2 a $15 - 3 \times 4 = 15 - 12 = 3$

b $12 - (3 - 2) = 12 - 1 = 11$

c $40 \div 5 \times 2 = 16$

d $3 \times 2 + 4 \times 6 = 6 + 24 = 30$

e $11(2 + 5 \times 3) = 11 \times (2 + 15)$
$$= 11 \times 17 = 187$$

f $21 \div (4 + 3) = 21 \div 7 = 3$

3 a $(4 + 6) \div (2 + 3) = 10 \div 5 = 2$

b $(8 \times 7 - 9 \times 6)^2 = (56 - 54)^2$
$$= 2^2$$
$$= 4$$

c $\sqrt{3 \times 4 \times 3 \times 4} = \sqrt{3 \times 3} \times \sqrt{4 \times 4}$
$$= 3 \times 4$$
$$= 12$$

d $\dfrac{12 \times 4}{6 \times 2} = \dfrac{48}{12}$
$$= 4$$

e $\dfrac{42 \div 7 + 3 \times 3}{21 - 3 \times 2} = \dfrac{6 + 9}{21 - 6}$
$$= \dfrac{15}{15}$$
$$= 1$$

f $\sqrt{\dfrac{5 \times 7 + 1}{6 \times 3 \div 2}} = \sqrt{\dfrac{35 + 1}{9}}$
$$= \sqrt{\dfrac{36}{9}}$$
$$= \dfrac{6}{3}$$
$$= 2$$

4 ∴ $225 = 5 \times 3 \times 3 \times 5$
$$= 15 \times 15$$
∴ $\sqrt{225} = 15$

```
        225
       /   \
      5     45
           /  \
          9    5
         / \
        3   3
```

5 a Descending order is from highest to lowest.

∴ $8, 5, -3, -6, -10$

b Descending order: $4, 0, -2, -8, -32$

6 a Ascending order is from lowest to highest.

∴ $-6, -1, 3, 4, 5$

b $-4, -3, -1, 2, 8$

7

$-8\ -7\ -6\ -5\ -4\ -3\ -2\ -1\ 0\ 1\ 2\ 3\ 4\ 5\ 6\ 7\ 8$

a $5 - 3 = 2$ **b** $1 - 3 = -2$

c $-2 - 3 = -5$

8

$-8\ -7\ -6\ -5\ -4\ -3\ -2\ -1\ 0\ 1\ 2\ 3\ 4\ 5\ 6\ 7\ 8$

a $2 + 6 = 8$ **b** $-1 + 6 = 5$

c $-8 + 6 = -2$

9 a $-6 < -2$ **b** $5 > -6$

c $-3 < 2$

10
a $-3 + 5 = 2$
b $-5 + 2 = -3$
c $4 - 7 = -3$
d $-3 - 2 = -5$
e $-3 + 7 = 4$
f $-2 + 8 = 6$
g $2 + (-3) = 2 - 3 = -1$
h $-2 - (-4) = -2 + 4 = 2$
i $3 - (+2) = 3 - 2 = 1$
j $-2 - (-1) = -2 + 1 = -1$
k $9 + (-2) = 9 - 2 = 7$
l $3 + (-5) = 3 - 5 = -2$

11
a $4 \times -3 = -12$
b $-2 \times -5 = 10$
c $-4 \times 6 = -24$
d $-7 \times -3 = 21$
e $8 \times -5 = -40$
f $(-2)^2 = -2 \times -2 = 4$
g $12 \div -3 = -4$
h $-8 \div -4 = 2$
i $18 \div -2 = -9$
j $-21 \div 7 = -3$
k $22 \div -2 = -11$
l $-30 \div -5 = 6$

NUMBERS AND DIRECTED NUMBERS
INTERMEDIATE TEST   PAGE 7

1 $16 - 4 \times 3 = 16 - 12$
$= 4$ **D** ✓   (1 mark)

2 Try each of the alternatives …
$20 - 4 \times 2 = 20 - 8$
$= 12$ **D** ✓   (1 mark)

3 $\dfrac{12 \times 4}{4 \times 3 \times 2} = \dfrac{48}{24}$
$= 2$ **D** ✓   (1 mark)

4 $24 - \{(10 \div [2 + 3] \times 3) + 6\}$
$= 24 - \{10 \div 5 \times 3 + 6\}$
$= 24 - \{6 + 6\}$
$= 12$ **B** ✓   (1 mark)

5 $18, 11, 4, …$ is subtracting 7.
The next number is $4 - 7 = -3$
   C ✓   (1 mark)

6 Temperature rises means adding
$-2 + 5 = 3$ $\therefore 3°$ **B** ✓
   (1 mark)

7
a $16 - 3 \times (2 + 3) = 16 - 3 \times 5$
$= 16 - 15$

$= 1$ ✓✓
b $\sqrt{9 + 3 - 4 \times 2} = \sqrt{9 + 3 - 8}$
$= \sqrt{4}$
$= 2$ ✓✓
   (4 marks)

8
576 ✓✓
$8 \quad 72$
$4 \quad 2 \quad 36 \quad 2$
$2 \quad 2 \quad 6 \quad 6$

$576 = 2 \times 2 \times 2 \times 2 \times 6 \times 6$
$\sqrt{576} = \sqrt{2 \times 2 \times 2 \times 2 \times 6 \times 6}$
$= 2 \times 2 \times 6$
$= 24$ ✓ (3 marks)

9
a $18 + 7 < 4 \times 9$ ✓
b $63 \div 9 \geq 43 - 39$ ✓ (2 marks)

10
a $11 - [3 + 12 \div 6] - 2 = 4$ ✓
b $8 + 2 \times [16 - 3 \times 4] - 5$
$= 11$ ✓   (2 marks)

11 A word problem such as:
'The temperature this morning
was $-6\,°C$ and then rose
by $10\,°C$. What is the new
temperature?' ✓✓   (2 marks)

12 If -3 represents 3 floors below
ground level and 'going up 12
floors' means $+12$, then 'down 2
floors' means -2.
$\therefore \ -3 + 12 - 2 = 7$
the seventh floor ✓✓   (2 marks)

13
a $-4 + 2 \times 3 = -4 + 6$
$= 2$ ✓
b $5 - 4 \times 3 = 5 - 12$
$= -7$ ✓
c $12 \div 4 - 2 \times 5 = 3 - 10$
$= -7$ ✓
d $(18 - 7) - (3 + 6) = 11 - 9$
$= 2$ ✓
e $5 - 3 \times 7 = 5 - 21$
$= -16$ ✓
f $(3 - 5)(4 - 7) = -2 \times -3$
$= 6$ ✓
g $(3 - 6)^2 = (-3)^2$
$= 9$ ✓
h $(5 - 10) \div (3 - 8) = (-5) \div (-5)$
$= 1$ ✓
   (8 marks)

NUMBERS AND DIRECTED NUMBERS
ADVANCED TEST   PAGE 8

1
a $12 + 16 \leq 6 \times 11$ ✓
b $8 \div (4 + 2) \neq 10$ ✓
c $10(4 + 5) < 100 - 2$ ✓
d $(4 + 3)^2 > 3^3$ ✓
e $\sqrt{20 - 4} = 2^2$ ✓   (5 marks)

2
a $4 + 7 \times 2 - 3 \times 4 = 6$ ✓
b $9 \times 5 - 10 \times 2 \times 2 = 5$ ✓
c $24 \div 4 + 3 \times 8 \div 4 = 12$ ✓
   (3 marks)

3
a $4 \times (5 - 2 + 6) = 36$ ✓
b $[16 - (2 + 3)] \times 2 - 4 = 18$ ✓
c $24 \div (2 + 6) \times 6 \div (6 \div 2) = 6$
   ✓   (3 marks)

4 Evaluate
a $25 - 4 \times 3 + 10 \div 2$
$= 25 - 12 + 5$ ✓
$= 18$ ✓
b $3(11 - 2 \times 4) = 3 \times (11 - 8)$ ✓
$= 3 \times 3$
$= 9$ ✓
c $(12 + 3 \times 2)(11 - 3^2)$ ✓
$= (12 + 6)(11 - 9)$
$= 18 \times 2$
$= 36$ ✓
d $\dfrac{14 + 4}{2 \times 3} = \dfrac{18}{6}$ ✓
$= 3$ ✓
e $\sqrt{15 - 3 \times 2} = \sqrt{15 - 6}$ ✓
$= \sqrt{9}$
$= 3$ ✓
f $(18 - 4 \times 2)^3 = (18 - 8)^3$ ✓
$= 10^3$
$= 1000$ ✓
g $4[2 + 3(15 - 3 \times 4)]$ ✓
$= 4[2 + 3(15 - 12)]$
$= 4[2 + 3 \times 3]$
$= 4[2 + 9]$
$= 44$ ✓
h $\sqrt{\dfrac{18 + 6 \times 3}{18 - 3 \times 3}} = \sqrt{\dfrac{18 + 18}{18 - 9}}$ ✓
$= \sqrt{\dfrac{36}{9}}$
$= \sqrt{4}$
$= 2$ ✓
i $\dfrac{1}{2}(12 - 2 \times 3) = \dfrac{1}{2}(12 - 6)$ ✓

$= 3$ ✓

j $(2^2 + 2 \times 3)^3 - (2^2 + 2 \times 3)^2$
$= (4 + 6)^3 - (4 + 6)^2$ ✓
$= 1000 - 100$
$= 900$ ✓

(20 marks)

5 **a**

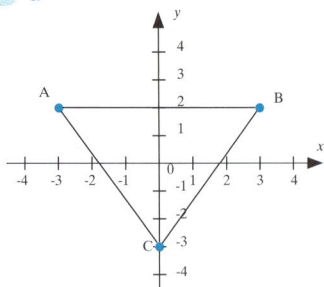

$\text{Area} = \dfrac{1}{2} \times 6 \times 5$

$= 15$

∴ area is 15 units^2 ✓ (2 marks)

6

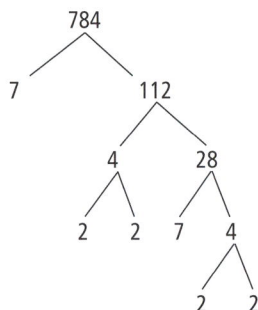

∴ $784 = 2^4 \times 7^2$
$= (2^2 \times 7) \times (2^2 \times 7)$
∴ $\sqrt{784} = 2^2 \times 7$
$= 28$ ✓ (2 marks)

7 **a** 17, 11, 5, **–1, –7** ✓

b –83, –67, –51, **–35, –19** ✓

(2 marks)

8 **a** $62 \times 2 + 48$ ✓
∴ $62 \times 2 + 48 = 124 + 48$
$= 172$
∴ cost is $172 ✓

b $42 + 48 \times 2$ ✓
$42 + 48 \times 2 = 42 + 96$
$= 138$
∴ cost is $138 ✓

c $48 \times 11 + 62 + 42$ ✓
∴ $48 \times 11 + 62 + 42$
$= 538 + 62 + 42$
$= 632$
∴ cost is $632 ✓ (6 marks)

---

9 $3 + 2 \times 2$ ✓
∴ $3 + 2 \times 2 = 3 + 4$
$= 7$
∴ cost is $7 ✓ (2 marks)

10 $690 + 80 \times 6 + 100 \times 10$ ✓
∴ $690 + 80 \times 6 + 100 \times 10$
$= 690 + 480 + 1000$
$= 2170$
∴ total savings of $2170 ✓ (4 marks)

11 **a** $7 - 5 \times 6 = 7 - 30$
$= -23$ ✓

b $4 \times 9 - 10 \times 6 = 36 - 60$
$= -24$ ✓

c $-6 + 4 \times 3 - 16 \div 4$
$= -6 + 12 - 4$
$= 2$ ✓

d $-5 - 5 - 5 - 5 = -20$ ✓

(4 marks)

12

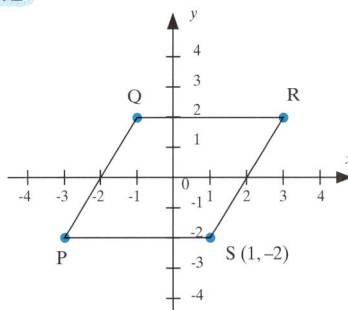

∴ S(1, –2) ✓ (2 marks)

13 **a** □ + ✿ $= -5 + -3$
$= -5 - 3$
$= -8$ ✓

b (✿ – □)^3 $= (-3 - -5)^3$
$= (-3 + 5)^3$
$= 2^3$
$= 8$ ✓ (2 marks)

14 $\text{Average} = \dfrac{5 + (-1) + (-2) + 4}{4}$ ✓

$= \dfrac{5 - 1 - 2 + 4}{4}$

$= \dfrac{6}{4}$

$= 1\dfrac{1}{2}$

∴ average temperature is $1\dfrac{1}{2}°$ ✓

(2 marks)

---

1 **a** $\dfrac{8}{16} = \dfrac{8 \times 1}{8 \times 2} = \dfrac{1}{2}$

b $\dfrac{10}{30} = \dfrac{10 \times 1}{10 \times 3} = \dfrac{1}{3}$

c $\dfrac{15}{45} = \dfrac{15 \times 1}{15 \times 3} = \dfrac{1}{3}$

d $\dfrac{80}{120} = \dfrac{40 \times 2}{40 \times 3} = \dfrac{2}{3}$

e $\dfrac{48}{60} = \dfrac{12 \times 4}{12 \times 5} = \dfrac{4}{5}$

f $\dfrac{55}{75} = \dfrac{5 \times 11}{5 \times 15} = \dfrac{11}{15}$

2 **a** $\dfrac{2}{3} = \dfrac{\mathbf{6}}{9}$
∴ missing number is 6

b $\dfrac{5}{\mathbf{9}} = \dfrac{20}{36}$
∴ missing number is 9

c $\dfrac{2}{5} = \dfrac{\mathbf{10}}{25}$
∴ missing number is 10

d $\dfrac{4}{7} = \dfrac{28}{\mathbf{49}}$
∴ missing number is 49

e $\dfrac{\mathbf{5}}{8} = \dfrac{35}{56}$
∴ missing number is 5

f $\dfrac{4}{\mathbf{25}} = \dfrac{16}{100}$
∴ missing number is 25

3 **a** $\dfrac{7}{3} = 2\dfrac{1}{3}$

b $\dfrac{14}{5} = 2\dfrac{4}{5}$

c $\dfrac{9}{2} = 4\dfrac{1}{2}$

4 **a** $2\dfrac{1}{2} = \dfrac{5}{2}$

b $1\dfrac{3}{4} = \dfrac{7}{4}$

c $5\dfrac{1}{3} = \dfrac{16}{3}$

5 **a** $\dfrac{4}{12} = \dfrac{1}{3}$

b $\dfrac{3}{15} = \dfrac{1}{5}$

c $\dfrac{50}{400} = \dfrac{1}{8}$ [as $4 = 400c]

WORKED SOLUTIONS

d $\dfrac{20}{200} = \dfrac{1}{10}$ [as 2 m = 200 cm]

e $\dfrac{45}{120} = \dfrac{3}{8}$ [as 2 min = 120 s]

f $\dfrac{7}{1000}$ [as 1 m = 1000 mm]

6 a As $2 = \dfrac{2}{1}$, then reciprocal is $\dfrac{1}{2}$

b For $\dfrac{1}{3}$ the reciprocal is $\dfrac{3}{1} = 3$

c For $\dfrac{2}{7}$ the reciprocal is $\dfrac{7}{2} = 3\dfrac{1}{2}$

d For $\dfrac{5}{8}$ the reciprocal is $\dfrac{8}{5} = 1\dfrac{3}{5}$

e As $1\dfrac{1}{4} = \dfrac{5}{4}$, then reciprocal is $\dfrac{4}{5}$

f As $3\dfrac{2}{3} = \dfrac{11}{3}$, then reciprocal is $\dfrac{3}{11}$

7 a As $\dfrac{2}{3} = \dfrac{4}{6}$ and $\dfrac{1}{2} = \dfrac{3}{6}$

$\therefore \dfrac{2}{3} > \dfrac{1}{2}$

b As $\dfrac{3}{5} = \dfrac{9}{15}$ and $\dfrac{2}{3} = \dfrac{10}{15}$

$\therefore \dfrac{3}{5} < \dfrac{2}{3}$

c As $\dfrac{7}{10} = \dfrac{21}{30}$ and $\dfrac{2}{3} = \dfrac{20}{30}$

$\therefore \dfrac{7}{10} > \dfrac{2}{3}$

8 a $\dfrac{4}{5} = \dfrac{24}{30}$, $\dfrac{2}{3} = \dfrac{20}{30}$, $\dfrac{1}{2} = \dfrac{15}{30}$

$\therefore$ order is $\dfrac{1}{2}, \dfrac{2}{3}, \dfrac{4}{5}$

b $\dfrac{3}{4} = \dfrac{18}{24}$, $\dfrac{2}{3} = \dfrac{16}{24}$, $\dfrac{7}{8} = \dfrac{21}{24}$

$\therefore$ order is $\dfrac{2}{3}, \dfrac{3}{4}, \dfrac{7}{8}$

BASIC FRACTION CONCEPTS
INTERMEDIATE TEST   PAGE 11

1 Try each of the alternatives ...

As $\dfrac{24}{36} = \dfrac{12 \times 2}{12 \times 3}$

$= \dfrac{2}{3}$ **D** ✓   (1 mark)

---

2 Number line is marked in twelfths.

i.e. $X = \dfrac{9}{12} = \dfrac{3}{4}$ **C** ✓   (1 mark)

3 $\dfrac{45}{90} = \dfrac{?}{10}$

i.e. $\dfrac{45}{90} = \dfrac{9 \times 5}{9 \times 10}$

$= \dfrac{5}{10}$ $\therefore$ 5   **B** ✓
(1 mark)

4 8 out of 12 $= \dfrac{8}{12} = \dfrac{2}{3}$ **C** ✓
(1 mark)

5 As $\dfrac{1}{4} = \dfrac{2}{8}$ and $\dfrac{1}{2} = \dfrac{4}{8}$

$\therefore$ in between $\dfrac{2}{8}$ and $\dfrac{4}{8}$

is $\dfrac{3}{8}$ **D** ✓   (1 mark)

6 Rewrite with same denominators:

$\dfrac{41}{50} = \dfrac{82}{100}$, $\dfrac{3}{4} = \dfrac{75}{100}$, $\dfrac{4}{5} = \dfrac{80}{100}$,

$\dfrac{17}{20} = \dfrac{85}{100}$

Descending means from largest to smallest,

$\therefore \dfrac{17}{20}, \dfrac{41}{50}, \dfrac{4}{5}, \dfrac{3}{4}$ ✓✓
(2 marks)

7 a $\dfrac{?}{10} = \dfrac{27}{30}$

$\therefore \dfrac{?}{10} = \dfrac{3 \times 9}{3 \times 10}$

$\therefore ? = 9$

i.e. missing number is 9   ✓

b $\dfrac{33}{54} = \dfrac{?}{18}$

$\therefore \dfrac{3 \times 11}{3 \times 18} = \dfrac{?}{18}$

$\therefore ? = 11$

i.e. missing number is 11   ✓
(2 marks)

8 Profit = selling price – cost price

$= \$35 - \$25$

$= \$10$ ✓

Profit as a fraction of cost $= \dfrac{10}{25}$ ✓

$= \dfrac{2}{5}$

$\therefore$ profit is $\dfrac{2}{5}$ of cost price   ✓
(3 marks)

---

9 Walkers = 1150 – (250 + 500)

$= 1150 - 750$

$= 400$ ✓

Fraction of walkers $= \dfrac{400}{1150} = \dfrac{8}{23}$

$\therefore \dfrac{8}{23}$ of students walk to school
✓   (2 marks)

10 Twins total runs = 67 + 83

$= 150$

Fraction $= \dfrac{150}{350}$ ✓

$= \dfrac{3}{7}$

$\therefore \dfrac{3}{7}$ of runs scored by the twins ✓
(2 marks)

BASIC FRACTION CONCEPTS
ADVANCED TEST   PAGE 12

1 a As $3 \times 27 = 81$, then $2 \times 27 = 54$

$\therefore$ missing number is 54   ✓

b As $108 \div 12 = 9$, then $72 \div 12 = 6$

$\therefore$ missing number is 6   ✓

c As $56 \div 8 = 7$, then $96 \div 8 = 12$

$\therefore$ missing number is 12   ✓

d As $55 \div 11 = 5$, then $132 \div 11 = 12$

$\therefore$ missing number is 12   ✓
(4 marks)

2 a $\dfrac{53}{7} = 7\dfrac{4}{7}$ ✓

b $\dfrac{94}{5} = 18\dfrac{4}{5}$ ✓

c $\dfrac{403}{4} = 100\dfrac{3}{4}$ ✓   (3 marks)

3 a $3\dfrac{7}{9} = \dfrac{34}{9}$ ✓

b $5\dfrac{11}{12} = \dfrac{71}{12}$ ✓

c $9\dfrac{8}{11} = \dfrac{107}{11}$ ✓   (3 marks)

4 a $\dfrac{7}{24}$, $\dfrac{1}{2} = \dfrac{12}{24}$, $\dfrac{3}{8} = \dfrac{9}{24}$, $\dfrac{5}{12} = \dfrac{10}{24}$ ✓

$\therefore \dfrac{7}{24}, \dfrac{3}{8}, \dfrac{5}{12}, \dfrac{1}{2}$ ✓

WORKED SOLUTIONS

b $\dfrac{3}{5} = \dfrac{24}{40}, \dfrac{13}{20} = \dfrac{26}{40}, \dfrac{3}{4} = \dfrac{30}{40}, \dfrac{27}{40}$ ✓

$\therefore \dfrac{3}{5}, \dfrac{13}{20}, \dfrac{27}{40}, \dfrac{3}{4}$ ✓ (4 marks)

5 $\dfrac{23}{32}, \dfrac{5}{8} = \dfrac{20}{32}, \dfrac{11}{16} = \dfrac{22}{32},$

$\dfrac{3}{4} = \dfrac{24}{32}, \dfrac{21}{32}$

$\therefore \dfrac{3}{4}, \dfrac{23}{32}, \dfrac{11}{16}, \dfrac{21}{32}, \dfrac{5}{8}$ ✓

$\therefore$ the middle fraction is $\dfrac{11}{16}$ ✓

(2 marks)

6 a As $1\dfrac{3}{4} = \dfrac{7}{4}$, then the

reciprocal is $\dfrac{4}{7}$ ✓

b As $3\dfrac{5}{6} = \dfrac{23}{6}$, then the

reciprocal is $\dfrac{6}{23}$ ✓

c For $\dfrac{3}{a}$, the reciprocal is $\dfrac{a}{3}$ ✓

d As $x = \dfrac{x}{1}$, then the reciprocal

is $\dfrac{1}{x}$ ✓ (4 marks)

7 Firstly, $200 - 120 = 80$

Fraction not read $= \dfrac{80}{200}$

$= \dfrac{2}{5}$ ✓

(1 mark)

8 The reciprocal of the reciprocal
means that the original fraction
has not changed.

$\therefore \dfrac{5}{8}$ ✓ (1 mark)

9 As $30 - (5 + 3) = 22$,

then fraction $= \dfrac{22}{30}$

$= \dfrac{11}{15}$ ✓ (1 mark)

10 a $4\dfrac{3}{5} = \dfrac{23}{5}$

$= \dfrac{46}{10}$

$\therefore$ 46 tenths ✓

---

b $45\dfrac{1}{2} = \dfrac{91}{2}$

$= \dfrac{182}{4}$

$\therefore$ 182 quarters ✓

c $2\dfrac{2}{3} = \dfrac{8}{3}$

$= \dfrac{32}{12}$

$\therefore$ 32 twelfths ✓ (3 marks)

11 a $\dfrac{26}{40} = \dfrac{13}{20}$ ✓

b $\dfrac{8}{20} = \dfrac{2}{5}$ ✓

c $\dfrac{14}{26} = \dfrac{7}{13}$ ✓ (3 marks)

12 a $\dfrac{5}{10} = \dfrac{1}{2}$ ✓

b $\dfrac{2}{10} = \dfrac{1}{5}$ ✓

c $\dfrac{4}{10} = \dfrac{2}{5}$ ✓ (3 marks)

13 a $\dfrac{20}{300} = \dfrac{1}{15}$ ✓

b $\dfrac{50}{1\,000\,000} = \dfrac{1}{20\,000}$ ✓

c $\dfrac{2}{2\,000\,000} = \dfrac{1}{1\,000\,000}$ ✓

d $\dfrac{40}{14\,400} = \dfrac{1}{360}$ ✓ (4 marks)

14 Total distance $= 210$ km

Fraction $= \dfrac{150}{210}$

$= \dfrac{5}{7}$ ✓ (1 mark)

USING FRACTIONS
SKILLS CHECK   PAGE 14

1 a $\dfrac{3}{5} + \dfrac{1}{5} = \dfrac{4}{5}$

b $\dfrac{3}{10} + \dfrac{7}{10} = \dfrac{10}{10} = 1$

c $\dfrac{3}{8} + \dfrac{7}{8} = \dfrac{10}{8} = 1\dfrac{2}{8} = 1\dfrac{1}{4}$

2 a $\dfrac{3}{10} + \dfrac{1}{3} = \dfrac{9 + 10}{30} = \dfrac{19}{30}$

b $\dfrac{4}{5} + \dfrac{3}{4} = \dfrac{16 + 15}{20} = 1\dfrac{11}{20}$

---

c $\dfrac{3}{4} + \dfrac{5}{8} = \dfrac{6 + 5}{8} = 1\dfrac{3}{8}$

3 a $1 - \dfrac{2}{3} = \dfrac{3}{3} - \dfrac{2}{3} = \dfrac{1}{3}$

b $2 - \dfrac{3}{4} = 1\dfrac{1}{4}$

c $5 - \dfrac{1}{6} = 4\dfrac{5}{6}$

4 a $\dfrac{7}{10} - \dfrac{2}{10} = \dfrac{5}{10} = \dfrac{1}{2}$

b $\dfrac{9}{10} - \dfrac{2}{3} = \dfrac{27 - 20}{30} = \dfrac{7}{30}$

c $\dfrac{3}{4} - \dfrac{3}{8} = \dfrac{6 - 3}{8} = \dfrac{3}{8}$

5 a $\dfrac{4}{5} \times \dfrac{3}{4} = \dfrac{3}{5}$

b $\dfrac{1}{2}$ of $\dfrac{4}{5} = \dfrac{1}{2} \times \dfrac{4}{5} = \dfrac{2}{5}$

c $\dfrac{2}{5} \times \dfrac{5}{6} \times \dfrac{1}{3} = \dfrac{1}{9}$

d $\dfrac{3}{4}$ of $12 = \dfrac{3}{4} \times \dfrac{12}{1} = 9$

e $\left(\dfrac{3}{4}\right)^2 = \dfrac{3}{4} \times \dfrac{3}{4} = \dfrac{9}{16}$

f $\dfrac{7}{10}$ of $35 = \dfrac{7}{10} \times \dfrac{35}{1} = 24\dfrac{1}{2}$

6 a $\dfrac{3}{4} \div \dfrac{1}{2} = \dfrac{3}{4} \times \dfrac{2}{1} = \dfrac{3}{2} = 1\dfrac{1}{2}$

b $\dfrac{4}{5} \div 2 = \dfrac{4}{5} \times \dfrac{1}{2} = \dfrac{2}{5}$

c $12 \div \dfrac{1}{2} = \dfrac{12}{1} \times \dfrac{2}{1} = 24$

7 a $\dfrac{4}{5} \times \dfrac{3}{4} = \dfrac{3}{5}$

b $\dfrac{7}{10} \div \dfrac{4}{5} = \dfrac{7}{10} \times \dfrac{5}{4} = \dfrac{7}{8}$

8 a $\dfrac{3}{5} \times \dfrac{5}{6} + \dfrac{1}{2} \times \dfrac{4}{5} = \dfrac{1}{2} + \dfrac{2}{5}$

$= \dfrac{5 + 4}{10}$

$= \dfrac{9}{10}$

b $\left(\dfrac{1}{2} + \dfrac{1}{3}\right) \div \left(\dfrac{1}{2} - \dfrac{1}{3}\right) = \dfrac{5}{6} \div \dfrac{1}{6} = 5$

9 a $2 + 3 + \dfrac{1}{2} + \dfrac{1}{3} = 5 + \dfrac{3 + 2}{6}$

$= 5\dfrac{5}{6}$

b $4 - 2 + \dfrac{1}{2} - \dfrac{1}{4} = 2 + \dfrac{2 - 1}{4} = 2\dfrac{1}{4}$

WORKED SOLUTIONS

c $\dfrac{5}{4} \times \dfrac{10}{3} = \dfrac{25}{6} = 4\dfrac{1}{6}$

d $4\dfrac{1}{3} \div 3\dfrac{1}{2} = \dfrac{13}{3} \div \dfrac{7}{2}$

$= \dfrac{13}{3} \times \dfrac{2}{7}$

$= \dfrac{26}{21} = 1\dfrac{5}{21}$

e $\dfrac{5}{2} \times \dfrac{5}{2} = \dfrac{25}{4} = 6\dfrac{1}{4}$

f $\dfrac{2}{1} \div \dfrac{7}{2} = \dfrac{2}{1} \times \dfrac{2}{7} = \dfrac{4}{7}$

USING FRACTIONS
INTERMEDIATE TEST   PAGE 15

1 $\dfrac{2}{5} + \dfrac{1}{3} \times \dfrac{3}{5} = \dfrac{2}{5} + \dfrac{1}{5}$

$= \dfrac{3}{5}$ **C** ✓

(1 mark)

2 12 people means 3 × original recipe

∴ $3 \times \dfrac{3}{4} = \dfrac{3}{1} \times \dfrac{3}{4}$

$= \dfrac{9}{4}$

$= 2\dfrac{1}{4}$

i.e. $2\dfrac{1}{4}$ cups   **A**   ✓ (1 mark)

3 Try each alternative.

$36 \div \dfrac{1}{6} = 36 \times 6$

$= 216 \neq 6$ **C** ✓

(1 mark)

4 Still 25 km of the total 60 km.

∴ fraction to travel

$= \dfrac{25}{60}$

$= \dfrac{5}{12}$ **C** ✓   (1 mark)

5 a $\dfrac{1}{4} + \dfrac{1}{2}$ i.e. $\dfrac{3}{4}$

∴ $\dfrac{3}{4}$ of the rectangle shaded ✓

b $\dfrac{1}{2} \times \dfrac{3}{4}$ i.e. $\dfrac{1}{2}$ of $\dfrac{3}{4} = \dfrac{3}{8}$

∴ $\dfrac{3}{8}$ of the rectangle shaded
✓

(2 marks)

6 Number of lots $= 49 \div 3\dfrac{1}{2}$

$= \dfrac{49}{1} \div \dfrac{7}{2}$

$= \dfrac{49}{1} \times \dfrac{2}{7}$

$= 14$

∴ 14 lots in subdivision ✓✓

(2 marks)

7 a $5\dfrac{3}{5} - 3\dfrac{2}{3} = 5 - 3 + \dfrac{3}{5} - \dfrac{2}{3}$

$= 2 + \dfrac{9 - 10}{15}$ ✓

$= 2 + \dfrac{-1}{15}$ ✓

$= 1\dfrac{14}{15}$ ✓

b $2\dfrac{1}{4} \times 2\dfrac{2}{3} = \dfrac{9}{4} \times \dfrac{8}{3}$ ✓✓

$= 6$ ✓   (6 marks)

8 Fraction to run $= 1 - \left(\dfrac{3}{5} + \dfrac{1}{3}\right)$

$= 1 - \dfrac{9 + 5}{15}$

$= 1 - \dfrac{14}{15}$

$= \dfrac{1}{15}$ ✓

Distance yet $= \dfrac{1}{15} \times 45$

$= 3$

∴ 3 km to travel ✓   (2 marks)

9 Spent $= \dfrac{5}{8} \times \dfrac{12}{1}$

$= 7.5$

∴ she spends $7.50/week ✓

(1 mark)

10 a Quantity $= \dfrac{3}{4} \times \dfrac{5000}{1}$

$= 3750$

∴ 3750 L presently in tank ✓

b New quantity $= \dfrac{9}{10} \times \dfrac{5000}{1}$

$= 4500$ ✓

∴ after rain 4500 L in tank

∴ 750 L of water added ✓

(3 marks)

USING FRACTIONS
ADVANCED TEST   PAGE 16

1 a $\dfrac{2}{5} + \dfrac{1}{2} + \dfrac{3}{10} = \dfrac{4 + 5 + 3}{10}$ ✓

$= \dfrac{12}{10}$

$= 1\dfrac{2}{10}$

$= 1\dfrac{1}{5}$ ✓

b $\dfrac{7}{8} + \dfrac{3}{4} + \dfrac{1}{2} = \dfrac{7 + 6 + 4}{8}$ ✓

$= \dfrac{17}{8}$

$= 2\dfrac{1}{8}$ ✓

c $1\dfrac{2}{3} + \dfrac{3}{4} = 1 + \dfrac{8 + 9}{12}$ ✓

$= 1 + \dfrac{17}{12}$

$= 2\dfrac{5}{12}$ ✓

d $2\dfrac{4}{5} + 1\dfrac{1}{2} = 3 + \dfrac{8 + 5}{10}$ ✓

$= 3 + \dfrac{13}{10}$

$= 4\dfrac{3}{10}$ ✓

e $5\dfrac{3}{4} + 3\dfrac{7}{10} = 8 + \dfrac{15 + 14}{20}$ ✓

$= 8 + \dfrac{29}{20}$

$= 9\dfrac{9}{20}$ ✓

(10 marks)

2 a $\dfrac{9}{10} - \dfrac{2}{5} - \dfrac{1}{2} = \dfrac{9 - 4 - 5}{10}$ ✓

$= 0$ ✓

b $6 - 3\dfrac{2}{5} = 3 - \dfrac{2}{5}$ ✓

$= 2\dfrac{3}{5}$ ✓

WORKED SOLUTIONS

c $3\frac{4}{5} - 1\frac{2}{3} = 2 + \frac{4}{5} - \frac{2}{3}$ ✓

$= 2 + \frac{12 - 10}{15}$

$= 2\frac{2}{15}$ ✓

d $3\frac{2}{5} - 2\frac{7}{10} = 1 + \frac{4 - 7}{10}$ ✓

$= 1 + \frac{-3}{10}$

$= 1 - \frac{3}{10}$

$= \frac{7}{10}$ ✓

e $4\frac{1}{3} - 1\frac{5}{6} = 3 + \frac{1}{3} - \frac{5}{6}$

$= 3 + \frac{2 - 5}{6}$ ✓

$= 3 + \frac{-3}{6}$

$= 3 - \frac{1}{2}$

$= 2\frac{1}{2}$ ✓ (10 marks)

3 a $2\frac{2}{5} \times 5 = \frac{13}{5} \times \frac{5^1}{1}$ ✓

$= 13$ ✓

b $1\frac{2}{3} \times 2\frac{1}{5} = \frac{5^1}{3} \times \frac{11}{5_1}$ ✓

$= \frac{11}{3}$

$= 3\frac{2}{3}$ ✓

c $3\frac{1}{4} \times 3\frac{1}{3} = \frac{13}{4_2} \times \frac{10^5}{3}$ ✓

$= \frac{65}{6}$

$= 10\frac{5}{6}$ ✓

d $(2\frac{2}{3})^2 = \frac{8}{3} \times \frac{8}{3}$

$= \frac{64}{9}$

$= 7\frac{1}{9}$ ✓

e $(5\frac{1}{2})^2 = \frac{11}{2} \times \frac{11}{2}$

$= \frac{121}{4}$

$= 30\frac{1}{4}$ ✓ (8 marks)

4 a $1\frac{2}{3} \div 5 = \frac{5}{3} \times \frac{1}{5_1}$ ✓

$= \frac{1}{3}$ ✓

b $8 \div 1\frac{3}{5} = \frac{8}{1} \div \frac{8}{5}$

$= \frac{8^1}{1} \times \frac{5}{8_1}$ ✓

$= 5$ ✓

c $\frac{5}{8} \div 4\frac{1}{6} = \frac{5}{8} \div \frac{25}{6}$

$= \frac{5^1}{8_4} \times \frac{6^3}{25_5}$ ✓

$= \frac{3}{20}$ ✓

d $3\frac{1}{2} \div 1\frac{3}{4} = \frac{7}{2} \div \frac{7}{4}$

$= \frac{7^1}{2_1} \times \frac{4^2}{7_1}$ ✓

$= 2$ ✓

e $\dfrac{1\frac{2}{3}}{2\frac{1}{2}} = 1\frac{2}{3} \div 2\frac{1}{2}$

$= \frac{5}{3} \div \frac{5}{2}$ ✓

$= \frac{5^1}{3} \times \frac{2}{5_1}$

$= \frac{2}{3}$ ✓ (10 marks)

5 a $\dfrac{\frac{2}{3}+\frac{1}{2}}{\frac{2}{3}-\frac{1}{2}} = \left(\frac{2}{3}+\frac{1}{2}\right) \div \left(\frac{2}{3}-\frac{1}{2}\right)$

$= \frac{4+3}{6} \div \frac{4-3}{6}$ ✓

$= \frac{7}{6} \div \frac{1}{6}$

$= \frac{7}{6_1} \times \frac{6^1}{1}$

$= 7$ ✓

b $\frac{4}{5} \times 1\frac{2}{3} - \frac{5}{6} \div \frac{2}{3}$

$= \frac{4}{5_1} \times \frac{5^1}{3} - \frac{5}{6_2} \times \frac{3^1}{2}$ ✓

$= \frac{4}{3} - \frac{5}{4}$

$= \frac{16 - 15}{12}$

$= \frac{1}{12}$ ✓ (4 marks)

6 Difference $= \frac{2}{3} - \frac{5}{8}$

$= \frac{16 - 15}{24}$

$= \frac{1}{24}$

∴ one-twenty-fourth of tank = 300

Whole tank = 300 × 24

= 7200

∴ the tank holds 7200 litres ✓

As the tank is now two-thirds full, it needs another one-third:

∴ $\frac{1}{3} \times 7200 = 2400$

∴ another 2400 litres fills the tank ✓ (2 marks)

7 Total area $= 25\frac{1}{4} + 14\frac{2}{3}$

$= 39 + \frac{1}{4} + \frac{2}{3}$ ✓

$= 39 + \frac{3 + 8}{12}$

$= 39\frac{11}{12}$

∴ area is $39\frac{11}{12}$ hectares ✓ (2 marks)

8 Total time $= 1\frac{3}{4} \times 7$

$= \frac{7}{4} \times \frac{7}{1}$ ✓

$= \frac{49}{4}$

$= 12\frac{1}{4}$

∴ total time of $12\frac{1}{4}$ hours ✓ (2 marks)

9 We can work backwards:

If two-thirds given to sister, then one-third = 48

$$\text{amount before sister} = 48 \times 3$$
$$= 144$$

If one-quarter given to brother, then

$$\text{three-quarters} = 144$$
$$\text{amount before brother} = 144 \div 3 \times 4$$
$$= 192$$

∴ Jacob originally had 192 stamps ✓

$$\text{Brother's stamps} = \frac{1}{4} \times 192$$
$$= 48$$
$$\text{Remaining stamps} = 192 - 48$$
$$= 144$$
$$\text{Sister's stamps} = \frac{2}{3} \times 144$$
$$= 96$$
$$\text{Difference} = 96 - 48$$
$$= 48$$

∴ Jacob gave 48 more stamps to his sister than to his brother ✓ (2 marks)

10 As $1 - \frac{3}{5} = \frac{2}{5}$, then

two-fifths of Ethan's savings = 120 ✓

$$\text{Ethan's savings} = 120 \div 2 \times 5$$
$$= 300$$

∴ Ethan saved $300, Sophie saved $180

∴ total savings is $480 ✓ (2 marks)

11 Firstly, $\frac{1}{3} + \frac{1}{6} = \frac{2+1}{6}$

$$= \frac{3}{6}$$
$$= \frac{1}{2} ✓$$

∴ half of pole always in water or sea-bed.

As 2 + 1 = 3, then 3 m above water.

∴ the mooring pole is 6 metres long. ✓ (2 marks)

12 We can work backwards:

If saved one-quarter, then three-quarters left = 360

$$\text{Amount before savings} = 360 \div 3 \times 4$$
$$= 480 ✓$$

If food was one-fifth, then

$$\text{four-fifths remainder} = 480$$
$$\text{Amount before food} = 480 \div 4 \times 5$$
$$= 600$$

If rent was one-third, then

$$\text{two-thirds wage} = 600$$
$$\text{Wage} = 600 \div 2 \times 3$$
$$= 900$$

∴ Ned is paid $900 per week ✓ (2 marks)

BASIC DECIMAL CONCEPTS

SKILLS CHECK   PAGE 18

1 **a** 5 hundredths (2nd decimal place)

b 5 tenths (1st decimal place)

c 5 hundred thousandths (5th decimal place)

2 **a** 0.64 (as 3 < 5)

b 0.49 (as 6 ≥ 5)

c 0.19 (as 5 ≥ 5)

3 **a** 4 decimal places

b 4 decimal places

c 1 decimal place

4 **a** 6.982 (as 5 ≥ 5)

b 21.890 (as 1 < 5)

c 0.001 (as 9 ≥ 5)

5 **a** $\frac{78}{100} = 0.78$

b 0.1 + 0.05 = 0.15

c 0.02 + 0.003 = 0.023

6 **a** $2 + 0.5 + 0.03 \quad \left(= 2 + \frac{5}{10} + \frac{3}{100} \right)$

b $0.03 + 0.005 \quad \left(= \frac{3}{100} + \frac{5}{1000} \right)$

c $0.003 + 0.00009 \quad \left(= \frac{3}{1000} + \frac{9}{100\,000} \right)$

7 **a** 2.400, 2.041, 2.410, 2.104

∴ 2.041, 2.104, 2.4, 2.41

b 6.402, 6.024, 6.240, 6.040

∴ 6.024, 6.04, 6.24, 6.402

8 **a** Halfway between 2.5 and 3 i.e. 2.75

b Each unit represents 0.02 i.e. 4.24

9 **a** $\frac{3}{4} = \frac{75}{100} \quad ∴ 0.75$

Or $4\overline{)3.00}^{\,0.75}$ i.e. $\frac{3}{4} = 0.75$

b $\frac{12}{25} = \frac{48}{100} \quad ∴ 0.48$

Or $25\overline{)12.00}^{\,0.48}$ i.e. $\frac{12}{25} = 0.48$

c $\frac{19}{50} = \frac{38}{100} \quad ∴ 0.38$

Or $50\overline{)19.00}^{\,0.38}$ i.e. $\frac{19}{50} = 0.38$

d $8\overline{)7.000}$ i.e. $\dfrac{7}{8} = 0.875$
   $\dfrac{0.875}{}$

e $9\overline{)4.000\,00}$ i.e. $\dfrac{4}{9} = 0.\dot{4}$
   $\dfrac{0.444\,...}{}$

f $11\overline{)3.000\,000}$ i.e. $\dfrac{3}{11} = 0.\dot{2}\dot{7}$
   $\dfrac{0.272\,7\,...}{}$

10 a $0.8 = \dfrac{8}{10} = \dfrac{4}{5}$

b $0.08 = \dfrac{8}{100} = \dfrac{2}{25}$

c $0.071 = \dfrac{71}{1000}$

d $0.105 = \dfrac{105}{1000} = \dfrac{21}{200}$

e $0.880 = \dfrac{880}{1000} = \dfrac{22}{25}$

f $0.1001 = \dfrac{1001}{10\,000}$

11 a   As $0.125 = \dfrac{1}{8}$,

   the reciprocal is 8

b   As $1.25 = 1\dfrac{1}{4} = \dfrac{5}{4}$,

   the reciprocal is $\dfrac{4}{5}$

c   As $3.2 = 3\dfrac{1}{5} = \dfrac{16}{5}$,

   the reciprocal is $\dfrac{5}{16}$

BASIC DECIMAL CONCEPTS
INTERMEDIATE TEST   PAGE 19

1   As $\dfrac{1}{2} = 0.5$ and $\dfrac{3}{4} = 0.75$, then
   the decimal between 0.5 and
   0.75 is 0.6. **C** ✓   (1 mark)

2   Answer must be 8.657 as this
   rounded to 1 decimal place is 8.7
   i.e. missing number is 6 **C** ✓
                                    (1 mark)

3   Try each alternative …
   i.e. 7.200, 7.260, 7.248, 7.253
   ∴ closest to 7.250 is
   7.248 **C** ✓   (1 mark)

---

4 $\dfrac{3}{10} + \dfrac{61}{100}$ $= 0.3 + 0.61$
   $= 0.30 + 0.61$
   $= 0.91$ **A** ✓
                    (1 mark)

5   For $\dfrac{2}{3}$, $3\overline{)2.000\,00}$
                          $\dfrac{0.666\,...}{}$
   i.e. $\dfrac{2}{3} = 0.67$ correct to 2 dec. pl.

                    B ✓   (1 mark)

6 $0.065 = \dfrac{6}{100} + \dfrac{5}{1000}$ **C** ✓
                                    (1 mark)

7   Nearest thousandth is to 3
   decimal places
   ∴ 0.028 **A** ✓   (1 mark)

8   Rewriting $\dfrac{5}{8}$ as a decimal:

   $8\overline{)5.000}$ ∴ $\dfrac{5}{8} = 0.625$ ✓
   $\dfrac{0.625}{}$

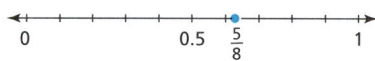

                          ✓   (2 marks)

9 a   Rewriting each as decimals:
   0.68, $\dfrac{3}{5} = 0.6$,

   $0.\dot{6} = 0.666\,...,\dfrac{62}{100} = 0.62$ ✓

   ∴ $\dfrac{3}{5}$, $\dfrac{62}{100}$, $0.\dot{6}$, 0.68   ✓

b
   Rewriting each as decimals: ✓
   1.34, $1\dfrac{19}{50} = 1.38$, $1\dfrac{1}{3} = 1.333\,...$, 1.3

   ∴ 1.3, $1\dfrac{1}{3}$, 1.34, $1\dfrac{19}{50}$ ✓
                          (4 marks)

10   As $\dfrac{1}{11} = 0.\dot{0}\dot{9}$, $\dfrac{2}{11} = 0.\dot{1}\dot{8}$
   we see a pattern developing,
   i.e. $\dfrac{3}{11} = 0.\dot{2}\dot{7}$ and so on

   ∴ $\dfrac{6}{11} = 0.\dot{5}\dot{4}$ ✓   (1 mark)

---

11 a   They both involve the same
   six numbers, assembled in
   triples. ✓

b   Taking the pattern from part
   a and that $13 - 5 = 8$

   then $\dfrac{8}{13} = 0.\dot{6}1538\dot{4}$ ✓

   [check by calculator]

c   They are all repeating
   decimals involving six digits.
   Patterns exist in pairs of
   fractions with denominators
   of 13, i.e. in $\dfrac{4}{13}$ the first

   3 digits in the repeated
   decimal gives the last 3 digits

   for $\dfrac{9}{13}$, and vice versa. ✓✓
                          (4 marks)

BASIC DECIMAL CONCEPTS
ADVANCED TEST   PAGE 20

1 a $\dfrac{5}{10} + \dfrac{3}{100} + \dfrac{9}{10\,000} = 0.5309$ ✓

b $\dfrac{7}{100} + \dfrac{9}{1000} + \dfrac{1}{10\,000} = 0.0791$
                                          ✓
                          (2 marks)

2 a   24.9818 = 24.98 ✓
b   0.025\,08 = 0.03 ✓
c   1.9898 = 1.99 ✓
d   2.0999 = 2.10 ✓
e   149.4049 = 149.40 ✓
                          (5 marks)

3 a   209.7932 = 209.793 ✓
b   0.006\,78 = 0.007 ✓
c   0.666\,66 = 0.667 ✓
d   8671.9006 = 8671.901 ✓
e   11.372\,499 = 11.372 ✓
                          (5 marks)

4 a   54.5: 50 and 0.5
   As $0.5 \times 100 = 50$, then it is
   100 times bigger ✓
b   259.75: 50 and 0.05
   As $0.05 \times 1000 = 50$, then it is
   1000 times bigger ✓
c   514.0356: 500 and 0.005
   As $0.005 \times 100\,000 = 500$,
   then it is
   100\,000 times bigger ✓
                          (3 marks)

WORKED SOLUTIONS

5 **a** $0.7 = \frac{7}{10}$. The reciprocal is $\frac{10}{7}$, or $1\frac{3}{7}$ ✓

b $0.4 = \frac{4}{10}$. The reciprocal is $\frac{10}{4}$, or $2\frac{1}{2}$ ✓

c $0.81 = \frac{81}{100}$. The reciprocal is $\frac{100}{81}$, or $1\frac{19}{81}$ ✓

d $2.6 = \frac{26}{10}$. The reciprocal is $\frac{10}{26}$, or $\frac{5}{13}$ ✓

e $1.001 = 1\frac{1}{1000} = \frac{1001}{1000}$. The reciprocal is $\frac{1000}{1001}$ ✓

(5 marks)

6 **a** $\frac{5}{12}$ $12\overline{)5.000000}$ ... $0.4166...$

∴ $\frac{5}{12} = 0.41\dot{6}$ ✓✓

b $\frac{17}{40}$ $40\overline{)17.000}$ ... 0.425

∴ $\frac{17}{40} = 0.425$ ✓✓

c $\frac{7}{11}$ $11\overline{)7.000000}$ ... $0.6363...$

∴ $\frac{7}{11} = 0.\dot{6}\dot{3}$ ✓✓

d $\frac{6}{7}$ $7\overline{)6.00000000000}$ ... 0.857142871

∴ $\frac{6}{7} = 0.\dot{8}5714\dot{2}$ ✓✓

(8 marks)

7 **a** $\frac{7}{8} = 0.875$, 0.85, 0.9, $\frac{4}{5} = 0.8$ ✓

∴ $\frac{4}{5}, 0.85, \frac{7}{8}, 0.9$ ✓

b $\frac{34}{50} = 0.68$, 0.66, $\frac{2}{3} = 0.\dot{6}$, 0.67 ✓

∴ $0.66, \frac{2}{3}, 0.67, \frac{34}{50}$ ✓

(4 marks)

8 1 nanosecond = 0.000 000 001 second ✓   (1 mark)

9 **a** $\frac{5}{8} = 0.625$

∴ $\frac{5}{8} < 0.635$ ✓

b $\frac{7}{9} = 0.\dot{7}$,

∴ $0.78 > \frac{7}{9}$ ✓   (2 marks)

10 **a** 2.420, 2.403, 2.400, 2.030, 2.430

∴ 2.03, 2.4, **2.403**, 2.42, 2.43

∴ third decimal is 2.403 ✓

b 4.500, 4.054, 4.405, 4.045, 4.040

∴ 4.04, 4.045, **4.054**, 4.405, 4.5

∴ third decimal is 4.054 ✓   (2 marks)

11 **a**

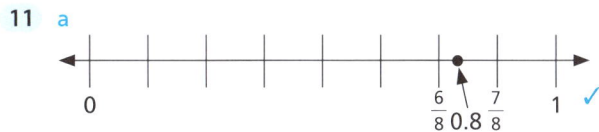

0.8 is between $\frac{6}{8} = 0.75$, and $\frac{7}{8} = 0.875$

b

0.3 is between $\frac{1}{4} = 0.25$, and $\frac{1}{2} = 0.5$

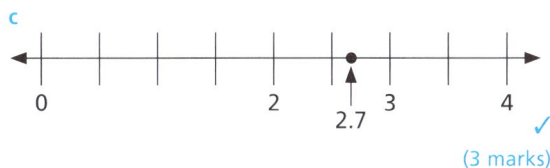

c

(3 marks)

12 **a** Suzy with 22.05 s ✓

b Jasmine with 22.3 s ✓

c Rose with 22.91 s ✓   (3 marks)

13 **a** $\frac{3000}{10000}, \frac{3400}{10000}, \frac{3040}{10000}, \frac{3024}{10000}$

∴ largest is $\frac{34}{100} = 0.34$ ✓

b $\frac{65}{1000}, \frac{64}{100}, \frac{600}{1000}, \frac{604}{1000}$

∴ largest is $\frac{64}{100} = 0.64$ ✓   (2 marks)

USING DECIMALS
SKILLS CHECK   PAGE 22

1 **a** 5.20 + 0.34 = 5.54

b 0.030 + 0.012 = 0.042

c 12.00 + 2.10 + 5.03 = 19.13

d −4.1 + 5.0 = 0.9

e 14.00 + 7.06 = 21.06

f $10.00 + $3.13 = $13.13

2 **a** 1.00 − 0.23 = 0.77

b 14.0 − 1.3 = 12.7

c 0.6 − 0.4 − 0.1 = 0.1

d 0.3 − 0.5 = −0.2

e −3.2 − 1.4 = −4.6

f $1.00 − $0.95 = $0.05

3 **a** As 3 × 5 = 15, then 0.3 × 5 = 1.5

b As 16 × 4 = 64, then 1.6 × 4 = 6.4

c As 13 × 4 = 52, then 1.3 × 0.4 = 0.52

d As 45 × 3 = 135, then 4.5 × 0.3 = 1.35

WORKED SOLUTIONS

e As $7 \times 7 = 49$, then 0.7×0.7
$= 0.49$

f As $4 \times 4 = 16$, then $0.04 \times 0.04 = 0.0016$

4 a $5 \overline{)1.5} \quad \therefore 0.3$
0.3

b $4 \overline{)3.80} \quad \therefore 0.95$
0.95

c $0.55 \div 0.5 = 5.5 \div 5 = 1.1$

d $10 \div 0.1 = 100 \div 1 = 100$

e $24 \div 0.04 = 2400 \div 4 = 600$

f $1.08 \div 0.9 = 10.8 \div 9 = 1.2$

5 a $\ldots \times 100$: move dec. 2 pl. to right $\therefore 150$

b $\ldots \times 1000$: move dec. 3 pl. to right $\therefore 7345$

c As $10^4 = 10000$
i.e. $\ldots \times 10000$: move dec. 4 pl. right $\therefore 160380$

d $\ldots \div 10$: move dec. 1 pl. to left $\therefore 1.678$

e $\ldots \div 100$: move dec. 2 pl. to left $\therefore 0.24$

f As $10^3 = 1000$
i.e. $\ldots \div 1000$: move dec. 3 pl. to left $\therefore 0.0000563$

6 a $0.4 \times 3 + 1.6 = 1.2 + 1.6$
$= 2.8$

b $(3.2 \div 4)^2 = (0.8)^2$
$= 0.64$

c $\dfrac{2.3 + 1.7}{0.4} = \dfrac{4}{0.4}$
$= 40 \div 4$
$= 10$

7 a $0.650 + 1.344 = 1.994$

b $1.85 - 0.60 = 1.25$

c As $176 \times 4 = 704$
then $1.76 \times 0.04 = 0.0704$

d $5.5 \div 0.05 = 550 \div 5$
$= 110$

e Average
$= \dfrac{0.3 + 0.6 + 0.2 + 0.1}{4}$
$= \dfrac{1.2}{4}$
$= 0.3$

f $\sqrt{0.36} = 0.6$
[as $0.6 \times 0.6 = 0.36$]

8 a $7.876 - 4.500 = 3.376$

b $3.000 - 1.056 = 1.944$

c $2.97 \div 1.1 = 29.7 \div 11$
$= 2.7$

d $4.5 \div 900 = 0.005$
i.e. $900 \overline{)4.50}$
0.005

9 $32 \div 1.2 = 320 \div 12$
$= 26\dfrac{8}{12} \quad \therefore 27$ boxes

10 $45 \times \$0.80 = \$36$
$\therefore$ cost is $\$36$

USING DECIMALS
INTERMEDIATE TEST   PAGE 23

1 $4.5 \div 0.5 = 45 \div 5$
$= 9$ **B** ✓   (1 mark)

2 As $24 \times 3 = 72$
$\therefore 0.24 \times 3 = 0.72$ **A** ✓(1 mark)

3 Try each of the alternatives.
$(0.2)^2 = 0.2 \times 0.2$
$= 0.04$
$\neq 0.4$ **B** ✓   (1 mark)

4 Half of $4.75 = \dfrac{4.75}{2}$
$= 2.375$ **B** ✓
(1 mark)

5 $48, 12, 3, 0.75, \ldots$
We are dividing by 4,
$\therefore$ next term $= 0.75 \div 4$
i.e. $4 \overline{)0.7500}$
0.1875
$\therefore$ next term is 0.1875 **D** ✓
(1 mark)

6 $1.4 \times 0.5 + (0.6)^2 = 0.7 + 0.36$
$= 1.06$ **C** ✓
(1 mark)

7 $2000 \times 0.942 = 2 \times 1000 \times 0.942$
$= 2 \times 942$
$= 1884$
$\therefore$ US$\$1884$ **A** ✓   (1 mark)

8 An answer such as 'Jenny bought 0.25 metres of material which costs $\$0.50$ per metre. Find the cost of the purchase.' ✓✓
(2 marks)

9 Average weight of
4 watermelons $= 3.6$ kg
Total weight of
4 watermelons $= 3.4 \times 4$
$= 14.4$
$\therefore$ 4 watermelons weigh 14.4 kg ✓
After 1 watermelon is sold, average weight of
3 watermelons $= 4$ kg
Total weight of
3 watermelons $= 4 \times 3$
$= 12$
$\therefore$ 3 watermelons weigh 12 kg ✓
Weight of sold
watermelon $= 14.4 - 12$
$= 2.4$ kg
$\therefore$ sold watermelon weighed
2.4 kg ✓   (3 marks)

10 a Cost $= 1.589 \times 40$
$= 63.56$
$\therefore$ petrol cost $\$63.56$ ✓✓

b Distance $= 12.3 \times 40$
$= 492$
$\therefore$ car is able to travel
492 km ✓✓   (4 marks)

11 a Number of cans
needed $= 250 \div 60$
$= 4.1\dot{6}$
$\therefore$ Bruce will buy 5 cans ✓✓

b Cost $= \$62.50 \times 5$
$= \$312.50$
$\therefore$ paint will cost $\$312.50$ ✓✓
(4 marks)

USING DECIMALS
ADVANCED TEST   PAGE 24

1 a $12.3 + 3.45$
$= 15.75$ ✓

$12.30 +$
3.45
$\overline{15.75}$

b $2.08 + 17 + 0.092$
$= 19.172$ ✓

$2.080 +$
17.000
0.092
$\overline{19.172}$

c $12 - 3.5$
$= 8.5$ ✓

$12.0 -$
3.5
$\overline{8.5}$

d $5.09 - 3.8$
$= 1.29$ ✓

$5.09 -$
3.80
$\overline{1.29}$

e $5 - 2.9817$
$= 2.0183$ ✓

$\begin{array}{r} 5.0000 - \\ 2.9817 \\ \hline 2.0183 \end{array}$

(5 marks)

2 a $3.4 \times 4 = 13.6$ ✓
b $1.08 \times 5 = 5.4$ ✓
c $19.002 \times 400 = 7600.8$ ✓
d $5.2 \times 0.08 = 0.416$ ✓
e $(0.09)^2 = 0.0081$ ✓ (5 marks)

3 a $4.6 \div 5$
$= 0.92$ ✓

$\begin{array}{r} 0.92 \\ 5\overline{)4.60} \end{array}$

b $16.18 \div 4$
$= 4.045$ ✓

$\begin{array}{r} 4.065 \\ 4\overline{)16.180} \end{array}$

c $45.81 \div 0.03$
$= 4581 \div 3$
$= 1527$ ✓

$\begin{array}{r} 1527 \\ 4\overline{)4581} \end{array}$

d $\dfrac{123}{0.6} = \dfrac{1230}{6}$
$= 205$ ✓

$\begin{array}{r} 205 \\ 6\overline{)1230} \end{array}$

e $\dfrac{0.8545}{0.05} = \dfrac{85.45}{5}$
$= 17.09$ ✓ (5 marks)

$\begin{array}{r} 17.09 \\ 5\overline{)85.45} \end{array}$

4 a 87.3×2.3
$= 200.79$ ✓✓

$\begin{array}{r} 873 \times \\ 23 \\ \hline 2619 \\ 17460 \\ \hline 20079 \end{array}$

b 37.6×0.078
$= 2.9328$ ✓✓

$\begin{array}{r} 376 \times \\ 78 \\ \hline 3008 \\ 26320 \\ \hline 29328 \end{array}$

(4 marks)

5 a $1.7 - 12.2$
$= -10.5$ ✓

$\begin{array}{r} 12.2 - \\ 1.7 \\ \hline 10.5 \end{array}$

b $-0.4 - (-4.2) = -0.4 + 4.2$
$= 4.2 - 0.4$
$= 3.8$ ✓

c $-3.2 + (-1.04)$
$= -3.2 - 1.04$
$= -4.24$ ✓

$\begin{array}{r} 3.20 + \\ 1.04 \\ \hline 4.24 \end{array}$

(3 marks)

6 a $4.2 - (2.3 + 1.002)$
$= 4.2 - 3.302$ ✓
$= 0.898$ ✓

$\begin{array}{r} 4.200 - \\ 3.302 \\ \hline 0.898 \end{array}$

b $5 - 2.3 \times 0.8 = 5 - 1.84$ ✓

$\begin{array}{r} 23 \times \\ 8 \\ \hline 184 \end{array}$

$\begin{array}{r} 5.00 - \\ 1.84 \\ \hline 3.16 \end{array}$

$= 3.16$ ✓

c $1.64 \div 0.2 - (0.5)^2$

$\begin{array}{r} 8.2 \\ 2\overline{)16.4} \end{array}$

$= 8.2 - 0.25$ ✓
$= 7.95$ ✓

$\begin{array}{r} 8.20 - \\ 0.25 \\ \hline 7.95 \end{array}$

d $\dfrac{1.6 + 1.1}{1.6 - 1.1} = \dfrac{2.7}{0.5}$ ✓

$= \dfrac{27}{5}$

$= 5.4$ ✓

e $(0.5 + 2.4 \div 4)^2 = (0.5 + 0.6)^2$ ✓
$= 1.1^2$
$= 1.21$ ✓

(10 marks)

7 0.789276×600

$\begin{array}{r} 789276 \times \\ 600 \\ \hline 473565600 \end{array}$

$= 473.5656$
∴ approximately $473.57 ✓

(1 mark)

8 $43.85 \times 6 = 263.10$
∴ Tessa rides 263.1 km ✓

(1 mark)

9 Savings $= 74.50 \times 12 - 682$
$= 894 - 798$
$= 96$
∴ $96 is saved ✓ (1 mark)

10 Petrol $= 11.3 \times 4.5$

$\begin{array}{r} 113 \times \\ 45 \\ \hline 565 \\ 4520 \\ \hline 5085 \end{array}$

∴ the car uses 50.85 L ✓✓

(2 marks)

11 Payment $= 217.2 \div 3$

$\begin{array}{r} 72.4 \\ 3\overline{)217.2} \end{array}$

$= 72.4$
∴ each paid $72.40 ✓ (1 mark)

12 Growth $= 1.7 - 0.83$

$\begin{array}{r} 1.70 - \\ 0.83 \\ \hline 0.87 \end{array}$

∴ Otis grew 0.87 m ✓ (1 mark)

13 Average
$= (11.3 + 10.2 + 9.5 + 10.4 + 11.1) \div 5$
✓
$= 52.5 \div 5$
$= 105 \div 10$
$= 10.5$
∴ the average is 10.5 m ✓
(2 marks)

14 Difference $= 23.5 - 19.7$
$= 3.8$
∴ the difference is 3.8° ✓
(1 mark)

15 Number $= 94.5 \div 1.5$ ✓
$= 189 \div 3$
$= 63$
∴ there are 63 DVDs in the
stack ✓ (2 marks)

16 a Petrol mass $= 32.4 \times 0.72$ ✓

$\begin{array}{r} 324 \times \\ 72 \\ \hline 648 \\ 22680 \\ \hline 23328 \end{array}$

$= 23.328$
∴ the mass is 23.328 kg ✓

b Diesel quantity $= 16.4 \div 0.82$ ✓
$= 1640 \div 82$

$\begin{array}{r} 20 \\ 82\overline{)1640} \end{array}$

$= 20$
∴ there is 20 L of diesel ✓

c Petrol quantity $= 30 \div 1.5$
$= 60 \div 3$
$= 20$ ✓
Petrol mass $= 20 \times 0.72$
$= 14.4$
∴ adds 14.4 kg of mass ✓

d Mass of sea water $= 1.02 \times 20$
$= 20.4$ ✓
As $20.4 - 20 = 0.4$, then sea
water is 0.4 kg heavier. ✓

(8 marks)

WORKED SOLUTIONS

BASIC PERCENTAGE CONCEPTS
SKILLS CHECK — PAGE 26

1

a $\dfrac{71}{100} \times \dfrac{100}{1}\% = 71\%$

b $\dfrac{3}{100} \times \dfrac{100}{1}\% = 3\%$

c $\dfrac{7}{25} \times \dfrac{100}{1}\% = 28\%$

d $\dfrac{3}{5} \times \dfrac{100}{1}\% = 60\%$

e $\dfrac{17}{20} \times \dfrac{100}{1}\% = 85\%$

f $\dfrac{3}{8} \times \dfrac{100}{1}\% = 37.5\% = 37\frac{1}{2}\%$

g $\dfrac{2}{3} \times \dfrac{100}{1}\% = 66.\dot{6}\% = 66\frac{2}{3}\%$

h $1\dfrac{1}{4} \times \dfrac{100}{1}\% = 125\%$

i $\dfrac{7}{1000} \times \dfrac{100}{1}\% = 0.7\%$ or $\dfrac{7}{10}\%$

2

a $\dfrac{16}{100} = \dfrac{4}{25}$

b $\dfrac{6}{100} = \dfrac{3}{50}$

c $\dfrac{95}{100} = \dfrac{19}{20}$

d $\dfrac{12\frac{1}{2}}{100} = \dfrac{25}{200} = \dfrac{1}{8}$

e $\dfrac{5\frac{1}{4}}{100} = \dfrac{21}{400}$

f $\dfrac{\frac{3}{5}}{100} = \dfrac{3}{500}$

3

a $\dfrac{111}{100} = 1\dfrac{11}{100}$

b $\dfrac{186}{100} = 1\dfrac{86}{100} = 1\dfrac{43}{50}$

c $\dfrac{550}{100} = 5\dfrac{50}{100} = 5\dfrac{1}{2}$

4

a $0.4 \times 100\% = 40\%$

b $0.07 \times 100\% = 7\%$

c $0.019 \times 100\% = 1.9\%$

d $1.6 \times 100\% = 160\%$

e $1.05 \times 100\% = 105\%$

f $0.125 \times 100\% = 12.5\%$

5

a $32 \div 100 = 0.32$

b $6 \div 100 = 0.06$

c $120 \div 100 = 1.2$

d $8.5 \div 100 = 0.085$

e $12.5 \div 100 = 0.125$

f $7.25 \div 100 = 0.0725$

6

a $0.16 \times 700 = 112 \quad \therefore\ \$112$

b $0.08 \times 72 = 5.76 \quad \therefore\ \$5.76$

c $1.01 \times 280 = 282.8 \quad \therefore\ \$282.80$

d $1.25 \times 4000 = 5000 \quad \therefore\ \$5000$

e $0.035 \times 2000 = 70 \quad \therefore\ \$70$

f $0.0575 \times 600 = 34.5 \quad \therefore\ \$34.50$

7

a $0.06 \times 300 = 18 \quad \therefore\ 18\ cm$

b $0.30 \times 120 = 36$
$\therefore\ 36\ seconds$

c $1.08 \times 12 = 12.96$
$\therefore\ 12.96\ mm$

d $0.21 \times 12 = 2.52 \quad \therefore\ 2.52\ kg$

e $1.35 \times 40 = 54 \quad \therefore\ 54\ km$

f $0.045 \times 2000 = 90 \quad \therefore\ 90\ mL$

8

a $\dfrac{14}{56} \times \dfrac{100}{1}\% = 25\%$

b $\dfrac{20}{120} \times \dfrac{100}{1}\% = 16.\dot{6}\%$
$= 16\dfrac{2}{3}\%$

9

a $\dfrac{420}{2100} \times \dfrac{100}{1}\% = 20\%$

b $\dfrac{15}{120} \times \dfrac{100}{1}\% = 12.5\%$

BASIC PERCENTAGE CONCEPTS
INTERMEDIATE TEST — PAGE 27

1 $1.06 \times 100\% = 106\%$ **A** ✓
(1 mark)

2 $0.18 \times 50 = 9.00$
$\therefore\ 18\%$ of $\$50 = \$9$ **A** ✓
(1 mark)

3 One revolution $= 360°$
$\therefore\ \dfrac{120}{360} \times 100\% = 33.\dot{3}\%$
$= 33\dfrac{1}{3}\%$ **C** ✓
(1 mark)

4 $42\% = \dfrac{42}{100} = 0.42$
Try each of the alternatives.
$\therefore\ $ closest to $\dfrac{43}{100}$ **B** ✓ (1 mark)

5 Measure the rectangles.
$\therefore\ \dfrac{4.8}{8} \times 100\% = 60\%$ **B** ✓
(1 mark)

6 Males $= 50 - 24$
$= 26$
$\therefore\ \%$ males $= \dfrac{26}{50} \times 100\%$
$= 52\%$ **D** ✓
(1 mark)

7

Students	Votes
Brown	64
Black	**18**
Green	48
White	70

a Black received 18 votes. ✓

b White (70 votes) ✓

c $\%$ green $= \dfrac{48}{200} \times 100\%$
$= 24\%$ ✓ (3 marks)

8

a Australian Rules $= 1$ cm out of 8 cm ✓
$= \dfrac{1}{8} \times 160$
$= 20$
$\therefore\ 20$ boys play Australian Rules ✓

b Soccer $= \dfrac{3}{8} \times 100\%$ ✓
$= 37.5\%$
$\therefore\ 37.5\ \%$ play soccer ✓
(4 marks)

9

a Geography angle
$= 360 - (40 + 80 + 60 + 120)$ ✓
$= 60$
$\therefore\ $ geography angle is $60°$ ✓

b i $\%$ maths $= \dfrac{120}{360} \times 100\%$ ✓
$= 33.\dot{3}\%$
$= 33\dfrac{1}{3}\%$
$\therefore\ $ percentage who selected maths is $33\dfrac{1}{3}\%$ ✓

ii $\%$ science $= \dfrac{80}{360} \times 100\%$ ✓
$= 22.\dot{2}\%$
$= 22\dfrac{2}{9}\%$
$\therefore\ $ percentage who selected science is $22\dfrac{2}{9}\%$ ✓ (6 marks)

WORKED SOLUTIONS

BASIC PERCENTAGE CONCEPTS
ADVANCED TEST   PAGE 28

1 a $\dfrac{37}{40} = \dfrac{37}{40} \times \dfrac{100}{1}$ %

$= \dfrac{370}{4}$ %

$= 92.5\%$ ✓

b As $\dfrac{21}{25} = \dfrac{84}{100} = 84\%$

$\therefore 284\%$ ✓

c $\dfrac{17}{1000} \times \dfrac{100}{1}$ % $= \dfrac{17}{10}$ %

$= 1.7\%$ ✓

d $\dfrac{3}{500} \times \dfrac{100}{1}$ % $= \dfrac{3}{5}$ %

$= 0.6\%$ ✓

e $1.003 \times 100\% = 100.3\%$ ✓

f $0.0009 \times 100\% = 0.09\%$ ✓

(6 marks)

2 a $\dfrac{3}{4}$ % $= \dfrac{\frac{3}{4}}{100}$

$= \dfrac{3}{400}$ ✓

b $7\dfrac{4}{5}$ % $= \dfrac{7\frac{4}{5}}{100}$

$= \dfrac{\frac{39}{5}}{100}$

$= \dfrac{39}{500}$ ✓

c $15.5\% = \dfrac{15.5}{100}$

$= \dfrac{31}{200}$ ✓   (3 marks)

3 a $270 \div 100 = 2.7$

$\therefore 2.7$ ✓

b $0.03 \div 100 = 0.0003$

$\therefore 0.0003$ ✓

c $5.05 \div 100 = 0.0505$

$\therefore 0.0505$ ✓

d $7\dfrac{4}{5} = 7.8$

$7.8 \div 100 = 0.078$

$\therefore 0.078$ ✓

e $20\dfrac{17}{20} = 20.85$

$20.85 \div 100 = 0.2085$

$\therefore 0.2085$ ✓   (5 marks)

4 a $\dfrac{^1\cancel{20}}{_2\cancel{160}} \times \dfrac{\cancel{100}^{25}}{1}$ % $= \dfrac{25}{2}$ %

$= 12.5\%$ ✓

b $\dfrac{3}{1000} \times \dfrac{100}{1}$ % $= \dfrac{3}{10}$ %

$= 0.3\%$ ✓

c $\dfrac{^3\cancel{15}}{_2\cancel{40}} \times \dfrac{\cancel{100}^{25}}{1}$ % $= \dfrac{75}{2}$ %

$= 37.5\%$ ✓

d $\dfrac{\frac{1}{2}}{2} = \dfrac{1}{4}$ [mult. num. & den. by 2]

$= \dfrac{1}{_1\cancel{4}} \times \dfrac{\cancel{100}^{25}}{1}$ %

$= 25\%$ ✓

e $\dfrac{2\frac{1}{4}}{10} = \dfrac{9}{40}$ [mult. num. & den. by 4]

$= \dfrac{9}{_2\cancel{40}} \times \dfrac{\cancel{100}^{5}}{1}$ %

$= \dfrac{45}{2}$ %

$= 22.5\%$ ✓

f $\dfrac{^5\cancel{15}}{_2\cancel{24}} \times \dfrac{\cancel{100}^{25}}{1}$ % $= \dfrac{125}{2}$ %

$= 62.5\%$ ✓

g $\dfrac{1}{1\,000\,000} \times \dfrac{100}{1}$ % $= \dfrac{1}{10\,000}$ %

$= 0.0001\%$ ✓

h $\dfrac{\frac{1}{2}}{10} = \dfrac{1}{20}$ [mult. num. & den. by 2]

$= \dfrac{1}{_1\cancel{20}} \times \dfrac{\cancel{100}^{5}}{1}$ %

$= 5\%$ ✓   (8 marks)

5 a 23% of $400 = 0.23 \times 400$

$= 92$

$\therefore \$92$ ✓

b $12\dfrac{1}{4}$ % of $\$800 = 0.1225 \times 800$

$= 98$

$\therefore \$98$ ✓

c 120% of $60 = 1.2 \times 60$

$= 72$ ✓

d 95% of $200 = 0.95 \times 200$

$= 190$ ✓

e 16% of 3 mg $= 0.16 \times 3$

$= 0.48$

$\therefore 0.48$ mg ✓   (5 marks)

6 $100 - (75 + 16) = 9$

$\therefore 9\%$ of alloy is zinc ✓

9% of $65 = 0.09 \times 65$

$= 5.85$

$\therefore 5.85$ kg ✓   (2 marks)

7 Increase $= 4\%$ of 960

$= 0.04 \times 960$

$= 38.4$

$\therefore \$38.40$ ✓

New Pay $= \$960 + \$38.40$

$= \$998.40$

$\therefore$ Charlotte's new pay is $\$998.40$ ✓

(2 marks)

8 % incorrect $= 100 - 80$

$= 20$ ✓

Number incorrect $= 20\%$ of 40

$= 0.2 \times 40$

$= 8$

$\therefore$ he got 8 questions incorrect ✓

(2 marks)

9 % males $= 100 - 60$

$= 40$

40% of membership $= 24$ ✓

10% of membership $= 24 \div 4$

$= 6$

100% of membership $= 6 \times 10$

$= 60$

$\therefore$ there are 60 members in the club ✓   (2 marks)

10 a No. drawn $= 20 - (11 + 5)$

$= 4$ ✓

% drawn $= \dfrac{^1\cancel{4}}{_1\cancel{20}} \times \dfrac{\cancel{100}^{20}}{1}$ %

$= 20\%$

$\therefore$ the team drew 20% of the games ✓

b 3 out of 4 games were nil-all.

$\therefore$ 1 out of 4 games the team scored. ✓

$\therefore 25\%$ of the games ✓

(4 marks)

Excel SMARTSTUDY YEAR 7 MATHEMATICS   **117**

WORKED SOLUTIONS

11 a Distance increase = 20% of 2.4
$$= 0.2 \times 2.4$$
$$= 0.48$$
$\therefore$ 0.48 km ✓
New distance = 2.4 + 0.48
$$= 2.88$$
$\therefore$ Isaac will run 2.88 km ✓

b 120% of last week = 4.8
10% of last week = 4.8 ÷ 12
$$= 0.4 ✓$$
100% of last week = 0.4 × 10
$$= 4$$
$\therefore$ Mim ran 4 km last week ✓

c 20% of this week = 1.6
100% of this week = 1.6 × 5
$$= 8$$
$\therefore$ Liam runs 8 km this week and 9.6 km next week ✓
Distance increase = 0.2 × 9.6
$$= 1.92$$
$\therefore$ 1.92 km
New distance = 9.6 + 1.92
$$= 11.52$$
$\therefore$ Liam runs 11.52 km the week after ✓ **(6 marks)**

12 15% of school pop = 120
5% of school pop = 120 ÷ 3
$$= 40 ✓$$
100% of school pop = 40 × 20
$$= 800$$
As 800 − 120 = 680, then 680 students not in year 12. ✓
(2 marks)

13 Total = 350 + 500 + 800 + 250 + 100 = 2000 ✓
King percentage $= \dfrac{35\cancel{0}}{20\cancel{00}} \times \dfrac{\cancel{100}}{1}\%$
$$= \dfrac{35}{2}\%$$
$$= 17.5\%$$
$\therefore$ King received 17.5% of the votes ✓ **(2 marks)**

14 Let Seth have 1 coin. Jo has 3 coins and Ryan has 6 coins.
Total coins = 1 + 3 + 6
$$= 10 ✓$$
Ryan percentage $= \dfrac{6}{10} \times \dfrac{100}{1}\%$
$$= 60\%$$
$\therefore$ Ryan has 60% of the coins ✓ **(2 marks)**

RATIOS
SKILLS CHECK PAGE 30

1 There are 12 boys and 18 girls.

a $12:18 = \dfrac{12}{6}:\dfrac{18}{6} = 2:3$

b $18:12 = 3:2$

c $30:12 = \dfrac{30}{6}:\dfrac{12}{6} = 5:2$

2 a $5:8$

b $8:5$

c $15:12 = \dfrac{15}{3}:\dfrac{12}{3} = 5:4$

d $8:12 = \dfrac{8}{4}:\dfrac{12}{4} = 2:3$

e $5:40 = \dfrac{5}{5}:\dfrac{40}{5} = 1:8$

f $20:20 = \dfrac{20}{20}:\dfrac{20}{20} = 1:1$

3 a $12:16 = \dfrac{12}{4}:\dfrac{16}{4} = 3:4$

b $40:400 = \dfrac{40}{40}:\dfrac{400}{40} = 1:10$

c $25:15 = \dfrac{25}{5}:\dfrac{15}{5} = 5:3$

d $30:5 = \dfrac{30}{5}:\dfrac{5}{5} = 6:1$

e $100:10\,000 = \dfrac{100}{100}:\dfrac{10\,000}{100}$
$$= 1:100$$

f $557:557 = \dfrac{557}{557}:\dfrac{557}{557} = 1:1$

4 a $\dfrac{5}{5}:\dfrac{5}{5} = 1:3$

b $1:\dfrac{1}{3} = \dfrac{3}{3}:\dfrac{1}{3} = 3:1$

c $1:\dfrac{4}{7} = \dfrac{7}{7}:\dfrac{4}{7} = 7:4$

d $\dfrac{1}{2}:\dfrac{1}{4} = \dfrac{2}{4}:\dfrac{1}{4} = 2:1$

e $\dfrac{3}{5}:\dfrac{7}{10} = \dfrac{6}{10}:\dfrac{7}{10} = 6:7$

f $2:1\dfrac{1}{2} = \dfrac{4}{2}:\dfrac{3}{2} = 4:3$

5 a $\$1:40c = 100:40 = 5:2$

b $\$2:\$1.50 = 200:150 = 4:3$

c $1\,m:20\,cm = 100:20 = 5:1$

d $2\ \text{minutes}:40\ \text{seconds} =$
$120:40 = 3:1$

e $2\,kg:500\,g = 2000:500 = 4:1$

f $40\,mL:2\,L = 40:2000 = 1:50$

6 a If 8 ÷ 4 = 2, then ? ÷ 4 = 3. This means the missing number is 12.

b If 16 ÷ 4 = 4, then 20 ÷ 4 = 5. This means the missing number is 5.

c If 24 ÷ 8 = 3, then 40 ÷ 8 = 5. This means the missing number is 5.

7 a As 2 + 3 = 5 parts, then
$$\dfrac{2}{5} \times 40 = \dfrac{2}{5} \times \dfrac{40}{1} = 16$$
$$\dfrac{3}{5} \times 40 = \dfrac{3}{5} \times \dfrac{40}{1} = 24$$
$\therefore$ the numbers are 16 and 24.

b As 3 + 5 = 8 parts, then
$$\dfrac{3}{8} \times 64 = \dfrac{3}{8} \times \dfrac{64}{1} = 24$$
$$\dfrac{5}{8} \times 64 = \dfrac{5}{8} \times \dfrac{64}{1} = 40$$
$\therefore$ \$24 and \$40

c The ratio for Pam and Jen is $2:5$
As 2 + 5 = 7 parts, then
$$\dfrac{2}{7} \times 350 = \dfrac{2}{7} \times \dfrac{350}{1} = 100$$
$$\dfrac{5}{7} \times 350 = \dfrac{5}{7} \times \dfrac{350}{1} = 250$$
$\therefore$ Pam gets \$100 and Jen gets \$250

8 As 3 + 7 = 10 parts, and children is mentioned second, then
$$\dfrac{7}{10} \times 540 = \dfrac{7}{10} \times \dfrac{540}{1} = 378$$
$\therefore$ there were 378 children

9 As 3 + 5 = 8 parts, and the longest piece is 5 parts, then
$$\dfrac{5}{8} \times 2400 = \dfrac{5}{8} \times \dfrac{2400}{1} = 1500$$
$\therefore$ the longer piece is 1500 mm or 1.5 m

RATIOS
INTERMEDIATE TEST PAGE 31

1 $25:35 = 5:7$ **B** ✓ (1 mark)

2 $3:\dfrac{2}{3} = \dfrac{9}{3}:\dfrac{2}{3}$
$$= 9:2 \quad [\text{mult. by 3}] \quad \textbf{C} ✓$$
(1 mark)

3 4 km : 200 m = 4000 : 200
$$= 20:1 \quad \textbf{C} \; \checkmark$$
(1 mark)

4 4 times 3 gives 12. As 9 times 3 gives 27, the missing number is 9. **C** ✓ (1 mark)

5 4 : 6 = 2 : 3 **D** ✓ (1 mark)

6 Try each alternative:
Not A, as 18 not divisible by 4.
Not B, as 2 not divisible by 4.
Not D, as 28 not divisible by 11.
∴ correct answer is 35, as it is divisible by 7 **C** ✓ (1 mark)

7 a 240c : 600c = 24 : 60
$$= 2:5 \; \checkmark$$

b $\dfrac{2}{3} : \dfrac{1}{6} = \dfrac{4}{6} : \dfrac{1}{6}$
$$= 4:1 \; \checkmark$$

c 2 hours : 20 min = 120 : 20
$$= 6:1 \; \checkmark$$
(3 marks)

8 As 60 − 24 = 36,
then ratio is 24 : 36 = 2 : 3 ✓ (1 mark)

9 Total = 140 + 180
$$= 320 \; \checkmark$$
Ratio = 140 : 320
$$= 14:32$$
$$= 7:16 \; \checkmark$$
(2 marks)

10 Remainder = 28 − (4 + 8)
$$= 28 - 12$$
$$= 16 \; \checkmark$$
There are 16 brown-eyed students.
Ratio = 16 : 8
$$= 2:1 \; \checkmark$$
(2 marks)

11 a Total parts = 3 + 1 = 4 ✓
$$\dfrac{3}{4} \times 20 = 15$$
$$\dfrac{1}{4} \times 20 = 5$$
∴ 15 m and 5 m ✓

b Total parts = 3 + 4 = 7 ✓
$$\dfrac{3}{7} \times 560 = 240$$
$$\dfrac{4}{7} \times 560 = 320$$
∴ $240 and $320 ✓
(4 marks)

12 Students present = $\dfrac{9}{10} \times 30$ ✓
$$= 27$$
∴ 27 students present ✓
(2 marks)

13 a No. of oranges = $\dfrac{3}{5} \times 10$ ✓
$$= 6$$
∴ 6 oranges in bowl ✓

b As 6 oranges, then 4 apples.
After 2 pieces taken then ratio is 5 : 3 ✓ (3 marks)

RATIOS
ADVANCED TEST   PAGE 32

1 a 0.7 : 0.007 = 0.700 : 0.007
$$= 700:7$$
$$= 100:1 \; \checkmark$$

b 3.2 : 0.004 = 3.200 : 0.004
$$= 3200:4$$
$$= 800:1 \; \checkmark$$

c $\dfrac{21}{25} : \dfrac{47}{50} = \dfrac{42}{50} : \dfrac{47}{50}$
$$= 42:47 \; \checkmark$$

d $1\dfrac{2}{3} : \dfrac{7}{12} = \dfrac{5}{3} : \dfrac{7}{12}$
$$= \dfrac{20}{12} : \dfrac{7}{12}$$
$$= 20:7 \; \checkmark$$

e $1 : 1\dfrac{5}{9} = \dfrac{9}{9} : \dfrac{14}{9}$
$$= 9:14 \; \checkmark$$

f $\dfrac{2}{3} : \dfrac{8}{27} = \dfrac{18}{27} : \dfrac{8}{27}$
$$= 18:8$$
$$= 9:4 \; \checkmark$$

g $\dfrac{3}{4} : \dfrac{4}{5} : \dfrac{5}{6} = \dfrac{45}{60} : \dfrac{48}{60} : \dfrac{50}{60}$
$$= 45:48:50 \; \checkmark$$

h $0.6 : \dfrac{6}{25} = 0.6 : 0.24$
$$= 0.60:0.24$$
$$= 60:24$$
$$= 15:6$$
$$= 5:2 \; \checkmark$$
(8 marks)

2 a 25c : $25.25 = 25 : 2525
$$= 1:101 \; \checkmark$$

b 120 cm : 1 m = 120 : 100
$$= 6:5 \; \checkmark$$

c 3 days : 6 hours = 72 : 6
$$= 12:1 \; \checkmark$$

d 20 centuries : 10 millennia
$$= 2000:10000$$
$$= 2:10$$
$$= 1:5 \; \checkmark$$

e 10 mm : 1 km = 10 : 1000000
$$= 1:100000 \; \checkmark$$

f 1 cm² : 1 m² = 1 cm² : 100 000 cm²
$$= 1:100000 \; \checkmark$$

g 1 year : 1 leap year = 365 : 366 ✓

h 1 mL : 1 ML
$$= 1\text{ mL} : 1000000000\text{ mL}$$
$$= 1:1000000000 \; \checkmark \text{ (8 marks)}$$

3 a 4 : 8 = 1 : 2 ✓

b Areas (in m²) are 4² and 8²
$$4^2 : 8^2 = 16:64$$
$$= 1:4 \; \checkmark$$

c Volumes (in m³) are 4³ and 8³
$$4^3 : 8^3 = 64:512$$
$$= 1:8 \; \checkmark \text{ (3 marks)}$$

4 Profit = $40000
  a 40000 : 100000 = 2 : 5 ✓
  b 60000 : 100000 : 40000
$$= 3:5:2 \; \checkmark \text{ (2 marks)}$$

5 After rent, James has 75%, or $\dfrac{3}{4}$ remaining.
Fraction saved = $\dfrac{1}{3} \times \dfrac{3}{4}$
$$= \dfrac{1}{4} \; \checkmark$$
Ratio = $\dfrac{1}{4} : \dfrac{1}{4}$
$$= 1:1 \; \checkmark \text{ (2 marks)}$$

6 Increase = $720 − $640
$$= \$80 \checkmark$$
Ratio = 80 : 640
$$= 1:8 \; \checkmark \text{ (2 marks)}$$

7 Total parts = 12 ✓
$$\text{Vans} = \dfrac{2}{{}_1\cancel{12}} \times \dfrac{\cancel{240}^{20}}{1}$$
$$= 40$$
∴ there were 40 vans ✓ (2 marks)

8 a 5 : **3**
   4 : 1
Now, 5 : 3 = 20 : 12 [mult. by 4]
and 4 : 1 = 12 : 3 [mult. by 3].
✓
∴ Aust : Euro : African = 20 : 12 : 3
∴ ratio is 20 : 3 ✓

b Total parts = 20 + 12 + 3

$= 35$ ✓

Australian stamps

$= \dfrac{^4\cancel{20}}{_1\cancel{35}} \times \dfrac{\cancel{210}^{30}}{1}$

$= 120$

∴ there are 120 Australian stamps ✓ **(4 marks)**

9 Perimeter = 56

∴ Sum of length and width = 28

Total parts = 5 + 2

$= 7$

Length $= \dfrac{5}{7} \times 28$

$= 20$ ✓

∴ length is 20 cm (and width is 8 cm)

Area $= 20 \times 8$

$= 160$

∴ area is 160 cm² ✓ **(2 marks)**

10 a 2 : 3

5 : 4

Now, 2 : 3 = 10 : 15 [mult. by 5]

and 5 : 4 = 15 : 12 [mult. by 3]. ✓

∴ A : B : C = 10 : 15 : 12

∴ ratio is 10 : 15 : 12 ✓

b Total parts = 10 + 15 + 12

$= 37$ ✓

Length $= \dfrac{12}{_1\cancel{37}} \times \dfrac{\cancel{74}^{0.2}}{1}$

$= 2.4$

∴ piece C is 2.4 metres long ✓

c Shortest length is piece A.

Length $= \dfrac{10}{_1\cancel{37}} \times \dfrac{\cancel{74}^{0.2}}{1}$ ✓

$= 2$

∴ shortest piece is 2 metres long ✓ **(6 marks)**

11 Total parts = 3 + 5

$= 8$

No. of 20c coins $= \dfrac{3}{_1\cancel{8}} \times \dfrac{\cancel{160}^{20}}{1}$

$= 60$ ✓

∴ 60 twenty-cent coins and 100 fifty-cent coins

$\$0.20 \times 60 + \$0.50 \times 100 = \$62$

∴ \$62 worth of coins ✓ **(2 marks)**

---

12 a If red : blue = 2 : 1, then

blue : red = 1 : 2

1 : **2**

3 : 1

Now, 1 : 2 = 3 : 6 [mult. by 3]

and 3 : 1 = 6 : 2 [mult. by 2]. ✓

∴ blue : red : white = 3 : 6 : 2 ✓

b Total parts = 3 + 6 + 2

$= 11$ ✓

No. of white balls $= \dfrac{2}{_1\cancel{11}} \times \dfrac{\cancel{55}^5}{1}$

$= 10$

∴ there are 10 white balls ✓

c The smallest possible number of red balls is 6. ✓ **(5 marks)**

13 a Suppose there is 1 black jelly bean. This means there are 2 red jelly beans and 4 pink jelly beans.

black : red : pink = 1 : 2 : 4 ✓

b Total parts = 1 + 2 + 4

$= 7$ ✓

No. of black jelly beans

$= \dfrac{1}{_1\cancel{7}} \times \dfrac{\cancel{28}^4}{1}$

$= 4$

∴ there are 4 black jelly beans ✓ **(3 marks)**

14 Total parts = 3 + 4 + 5

$= 12$

Amounts in each jug:

300 mL, 400 mL, 500 mL ✓

As 300 + 400 = 700, then second jug contains 700 mL.

As 700 – 500 = 200, then the second jug has 200 mL more than the third jug. ✓ **(2 marks)**

DISCOUNTS AND BEST BUYS

SKILLS CHECK PAGE 34

1 a New price = \$120 – \$45

$= \$75$

b New price = \$165 – \$55

$= \$110$

c New price = \$89 – \$11.50

$= \$77.50$

2 Original price = \$18 500 + \$1500

$= \$20 000$

3

	Original price	Discount	New price
a	\$540	\$54	**\$486**
b	\$19.90	**\$4.30**	\$15.60
c	**\$17.70**	\$6	\$11.70

4 a Discount = 0.1 × 80

$= 8$

New price = 80 – 8

$= 72$

∴ the new price is \$72

b Discount = 0.15 × 80

$= 12$

New price = 80 – 12

$= 68$

∴ the new price is \$68

c Discount = 0.3 × 80

$= 24$

New price = 80 – 24

$= 56$

∴ the new price is \$56

5 a Discount = 0.2 × 60

$= 12$

New price = 60 – 12

$= 48$

∴ the new price is \$48

b Discount = 0.25 × 60

$= 15$

New price = 60 – 15

$= 45$

∴ the new price is \$45

c Discount = 0.4 × 60

$= 24$

New price = 60 – 24

$= 36$

∴ the new price is \$36

6 a Discount = 0.25 × 300

$= 75$

New price = 300 – 75

$= 225$

∴ the new price is \$225

b Discount = 0.25 × 50

$= 12.5$

New price = 50 – 12.5

$= 37.5$

∴ the new price is \$37.50

7 a Discount = \$4 – \$3

$= \$1$

Percentage $= \dfrac{1}{_1\cancel{4}} \times \dfrac{\cancel{100}^{25}}{1}$

$= 25\%$

WORKED SOLUTIONS

CHECK YOUR SOLUTIONS

b Discount = $15 – $12
= $3

Percentage = $\frac{^1\cancel{3}}{_5\cancel{15}} \times \frac{100}{1} = \frac{1}{_1\cancel{5}} \times \frac{\cancel{100}^{20}}{1}$
= 20%

c Discount = $120 – $84
= $36

Percentage = $\frac{^3\cancel{36}}{_{10}\cancel{120}} \times \frac{100}{1} = \frac{3}{_1\cancel{10}} \times \frac{\cancel{100}^{10}}{1}$
= 30%

8 Cost = 89 + 0.5 × 89
= 133.5 ∴ Toby pays $133.50

9 Cost = 4.50 × 4
= 18 ∴ Kylie pays $18

10 a A 2.40 ÷ 3 = 0.8 per 100 mL
B 4.20 ÷ 5 = 0.84 per 100 mL
∴ A (300 mL) is the better buy
b A 1.80 ÷ 2 = 0.9 per 100 g
B 5.60 ÷ 7 = 0.8 per 100 g
∴ B (700 g) is the better buy.

DISCOUNTS AND BEST BUYS
INTERMEDIATE TEST PAGE 35

1 New price = $32 – $4.50
= $27.50 **B** ✓ (1 mark)

2 Original price = $389 + $35
= $424 **A** ✓ (1 mark)

3 Discount = 20% of $80
= 0.2 × 80
= 16
New price = $80 – $16
= $64 **B** ✓ (1 mark)

4 100 g: $3.10 $3.10 per 100 g
200 g: $6.30 ÷ 2 $3.15 per 100 g
300 g: $9.60 ÷ 3 $3.20 per 100 g
400 g: $12.20 ÷ 4 $3.05 per 100 g
∴ best buy is 400 g jar **D** ✓ (1 mark)

5 Discount = $1000 – $800
= $200
Percentage discount = $\frac{200}{1000} \times 100$
= 20% **B** ✓ (1 mark)

6 '$50 off' $50
'$60 voucher' $60
'you pay $320' $40
'10% saving' $36
∴ greatest discount is '$60 voucher' **B** ✓ (1 mark)

7

Original price	Percentage discount	Discount amount
$10	20%	**$2** ✓
$20	10%	**$2** ✓
$80	**25%** ✓	$20
$50	**30%** ✓	$15

(4 marks)

8 Discount = 25% of $40
= $\frac{1}{4} \times 40$
= 10
New cost = $40 – $10
= $30 ✓
Total cost = $30 + $37 + $35.40
= $102.40 ✓ (2 marks)

9 6 rolls: $4.55 ÷ 6 = $0.76 per roll
8 rolls: $6.20 ÷ 8 = $0.775 per roll
12 rolls: $9.60 ÷ 12 = $4.80 ÷ 6
= $0.80 per roll
16 rolls: $11.84 ÷ 16 = $5.92 ÷ 8
= $0.74 ✓
∴ best value is the 16 rolls ✓ (2 marks)

10 Total = $12 × 3 + $16 × 4
= $100
Discount = 10% of $100
= 0.1 × 100
= 10 ✓
∴ new price = $100 – $10
= $90 ✓ (2 marks)

11 Discount = $1200 – $900
= $300 ✓
Percentage discount = $\frac{300}{1200} \times 100$
= 25%
∴ the discount was 25% ✓ (2 marks)

DISCOUNTS AND BEST BUYS
ADVANCED TEST PAGE 36

1 a Discount = 15% of 1200
= 0.15 × 1200
= 180 ✓
New price = 1200 – 180
= 1020
∴ new price is $1020 ✓
b Discount = 15% of 800
= 0.15 × 800
= 120 ✓
New price = 800 – 120
= 680
∴ new price is $680 ✓ (4 marks)

Excel SMARTSTUDY **YEAR 7 MATHEMATICS** **121**

WORKED SOLUTIONS

2 Discount = $5 ✓

$\%\ \text{Discount} = \dfrac{{}^{1}\cancel{5}}{{}_{2}\cancel{840}} \times \dfrac{\cancel{100}^{25}}{1}\ \%$

$= 12.5\%$ ✓

(2 marks)

3 **a** Discount = $7 ✓

$\%\ \text{Discount} = \dfrac{{}^{1}\cancel{7}}{{}_{10}\cancel{70}} \times \dfrac{\cancel{100}}{1}\ \%$

$= 10\%$

∴ store-wide discount of 10% ✓

b Discount = 10% of 560

$= 0.1 \times 560$

$= 56$

∴ the discount is $56 ✓

c Discount = 10% of 68

$= 0.1 \times 68$

$= 6.8$

∴ the discount is $6.80 ✓

d Discount = 10% of 36

$= 0.1 \times 36$

$= 3.6$ ✓

New price = 36 − 3.6

$= 32.4$

∴ new price is $32.40 ✓

e Discount = 10% of 1340

$= 0.1 \times 1340$

$= 134$ ✓

New price = 1340 − 134

$= 1206$

∴ new price is $1206 ✓

(8 marks)

4 Normal Price = $12 × 2 = $24

Voucher 1: Discount = 20% of 24

$= 0.2 \times 24$

$= 4.8$

∴ saving is $4.80 ✓

Voucher 2: $\dfrac{1}{2}$ of $12 = $6

∴ saving is $6

∴ using voucher 2 saves more money ✓ **(2 marks)**

5 Discount 1 = 20% of 80

$= 0.2 \times 80$

$= 16$

New price = 80 − 16

$= 64$

∴ new price is $64 ✓

Discount 2 = 10% of 64

$= 0.1 \times 64$

$= 6.4$

Total discounts = 16 + 6.4

$= 22.4$

∴ Keith saved $22.40 ✓

(2 marks)

6 **a** Discount = 20% of 15

$= 0.2 \times 15$

$= 3$ ✓

New price = 15 − 3

$= 12$

∴ Wednesday's price is $12 ✓

b Discount = 20% of 12

$= 0.2 \times 12$

$= 2.4$ ✓

New price = 12 − 2.4

$= 9.6$

∴ Thursday's price is $9.60 ✓

(4 marks)

7 200g jar: 100g for $2.40

300g jar: 100g for $2.50

400g jar: 100g for $2.375

500g jar: 100g for $2.30

∴ 500g jar is the best buy ✓✓

(2 marks)

8 Discount = $650 − $520

$= 130 ✓

$\%\ \text{Discount} = \dfrac{{}^{1}\cancel{130}}{{}_{5}\cancel{650}} \times \dfrac{\cancel{100}^{20}}{1}\ \%$

$= 20\%$

∴ discount of 20% ✓ **(2 marks)**

9 **a** 20% of old price = 16 ✓

100% of old price = 16 × 5

$= 80$

∴ old price was $80 ✓

b Discounted price = $80 − $16

$= 64

∴ discounted price is $64 ✓

(3 marks)

10 **a** School Discount = 15% of 100

$= 0.15 \times 100$

$= 15$

Discounted price = 100 − 15

$= 85$

∴ new price is $85 ✓

Daughter discount = 10% of 85

$= 0.1 \times 8.5$

$= 8.5$

Final price = 85 − 8.5

$= 76.5$

∴ final price is $76.50 ✓

b Total discount = $100 − $76.50

$= 23.50 ✓

As original price was $100, then the percentage discount is 23.5% ✓ **(4 marks)**

11 Normal Price = $14 × 2 = $28 ✓

Tuesday: Discount = 25% of 28

$= \dfrac{1}{4} \times 28$

$= 7$

∴ saving is $7

Wednesday: $4 × 2 = $8

∴ saving is $8

Thursday: $\dfrac{1}{2} \times $14 = 7

∴ saving is $7

∴ on Wednesday they pay the least ✓ **(2 marks)**

12 **a** 100 − 10 = 90

90% of original price = 18

10% of original price = 18 ÷ 9

$= 2$ ✓

100% of original price = 2 × 10

$= 20$

∴ the original price was $20 ✓

b Discount = $20 − $18

$= 2

∴ the discount was $2 ✓

(3 marks)

13 **a** Tuesday increase = 20% of 100

$= 20$

Tuesday's price = 100 + 20

$= 120$ ✓

Sunday discount = 25% of 120

$= \dfrac{1}{4} \times 120$

$= 30$

Sunday's price = 120 − 30

$= 90$

∴ the new price is $90 ✓

b From $100, the price drops to $90.

This means a discount of 10%. ✓ (3 marks)

14 Price drop = $4.50 − $4.00

= $0.50 ✓

Savings = $\dfrac{^{1}\cancel{50}}{_{9}\cancel{450}} \times \dfrac{100}{1}$ %

= $\dfrac{100}{9}$ %

= $11\dfrac{1}{9}$ %, which is not 10% ✓ (2 marks)

15 a Store price = $16 + $64

= $80

% Profit = $\dfrac{^{4}\cancel{64}}{_{1}\cancel{16}} \times \dfrac{100}{1}$ % ✓

= 400%

∴ the profit is 400% ✓

b Discount = 40% of 80

= 0.4 × 80

= 32

∴ the discount is $32

New price = 80 − 32

= 48

Profit = 48 − 16

= 32 ✓

% Profit = $\dfrac{^{2}\cancel{32}}{_{1}\cancel{16}} \times \dfrac{100}{1}$ %

= 200%

∴ the profit is 200% ✓

c Discount = 50% of 48

= 24

∴ the discount is $24

New price = 24

Profit = 24 − 16

= 8 ✓

% Profit = $\dfrac{^{1}\cancel{8}}{_{12}\cancel{16}} \times \dfrac{\cancel{100}^{50}}{1}$ %

= 50%

∴ the profit is 50% ✓ (6 marks)

BASIC ALGEBRA CONCEPTS
SKILLS CHECK   PAGE 38

1 a $3 \times a \times b = 3ab$

b $2 \times y \times y = 2y^2$

c $1x^1 = x$

d $2 \times 3 \times b \times a = 6ab$

e $a \times a \times a = a^3$

f $2a \times a \times b \times b − 2a^2b^2$

2 a $5ab = 5 \times a \times b$

b $3x^2 = 3 \times x \times x$

c $7x^3y^2 = 7 \times x \times x \times x \times y \times y$

3 a $a \times 3 = 3a$

b $x + y + 8$

c $\dfrac{a + 2b + c}{3}$

d $k + 5$

e $a − b$

f $5 \times (x + 4) = 5(x + 4)$

4 a $x + 1$

b $y + 2, y + 4$

5 a $y = 3x + 1$

b $b = 2a − 4$

6 a $ab + c = 4 \times 3 + 2$

= 12 + 2

= 14

b $(2b)^2 − 2b^2 = (2 \times 3)^2 − 2 \times 3^2$

= $6^2 − 2 \times 9$

= 36 − 18

= 18

c $\dfrac{ab}{c} = \dfrac{4 \times 3}{2}$

= $\dfrac{12}{2}$

= 6

d $cb − a = 2 \times 3 − 4$

= 6 − 4

= 2

e $\dfrac{a − b}{c − 1} = \dfrac{4 − 3}{2 − 1}$

= $\dfrac{1}{1}$

= 1

f $(a − c)^2 = (4 − 2)^2$

= 2^2

= 4

7 a $x + y = −3 + (−4)$

= −3 − 4

= −7

b $x − y = −3 − (−4)$

= −3 + 4

= 1

c $y − x = −4 − (−3)$

= −4 + 3

= −1

d $6 + y = 6 + (−4)$

= 6 − 4

= 2

e $5 − (y + x) = 5 − (−4 +(−3))$

= 5 − (−4 − 3)

= 5 − (−7)

= 5 + 7

= 12

f $x − (3 − y) = −3 − (3 − (−4))$

= −3 − (3 + 4)

= −3 − 7

= −10

8 a $A = l \times b$

= 18 × 11

= 198

b $A = l \times b$

= 4.2 × 0.8

= 3.36

BASIC ALGEBRA CONCEPTS
INTERMEDIATE TEST   PAGE 39

1 $T = 3 \times p + 2 \times c$

= $3p + 2c$ **A** ✓ (1 mark)

2 Try each alternative.

i.e. try $y = x^2 + 1$

$x = 2, y = 5;$ $x = 3, y = 10$

and so on. **A** ✓ (1 mark)

3 Try a numerical scenario.

'If 6 is an even number, then the next consecutive even number is 8 (i.e. 6 + 2)'

∴ we are adding 2 to the starting number

∴ $a + 2$ **D** ✓ (1 mark)

4 Try a numerical scenario.

'If, for example, 3 metres, then the answer would be $100 \times 3 = 300$ (i.e. 300 cm)'

∴ multiplying original value by 100

∴ $100 \times p = 100p$ **C** ✓ (1 mark)

5 $\dfrac{a − b}{2} = \dfrac{−4 − (−6)}{2}$

= $\dfrac{−4 + 6}{2}$

= $\dfrac{2}{2}$

= 1 **D** ✓ (1 mark)

WORKED SOLUTIONS

CHECK YOUR SOLUTIONS

6 a

o	1	2	3	4
m	8	15	22	29

✓✓

b $m = 7o + 1$ ✓

c If there are 20 octagons then ✓
$$m = 7 \times 20 + 1$$
$$= 140 + 1$$
$$= 141$$
∴ 141 matches required ✓

(5 marks)

7 a $6a - 3b = 6 \times 0.3 - 3 \times 0.5$ ✓
$$= 1.8 - 1.5$$
$$= 0.3 ✓$$

b $\dfrac{10a}{b} = \dfrac{10 \times 0.3}{0.5}$ ✓
$$= \dfrac{3}{0.5}$$
$$= \dfrac{30}{5}$$
$$= 6 ✓$$

c $a^2b = (0.3)^2 \times 0.5$ ✓
$$= 0.09 \times 0.5$$
$$= 0.045 ✓$$

d $2a^2 = 2 \times (0.3)^2$ ✓
$$= 2 \times 0.3 \times 0.3$$
$$= 0.18 ✓$$

e $3b - a = 3 \times 0.5 - 0.3$ ✓
$$= 1.5 - 0.3$$
$$= 1.2 ✓$$

f $(0.2 - ab)^2 = (0.2 - 0.3 \times 0.5)^2$ ✓
$$= (0.2 - 0.15)^2$$
$$= 0.05^2$$
$$= 0.05 \times 0.05$$
$$= 0.0025 ✓$$

(12 marks)

BASIC ALGEBRA CONCEPTS
ADVANCED TEST   PAGE 40

1 a $y = 3x - 2$ ✓

b $y = 3 - 2x$ ✓

c $y = \dfrac{x}{4}$ ✓

d $y = x^2 - 2x$ ✓

e $y = 4 - 3x^2$ ✓   (5 marks)

2 a

f	1	2	3	4
s	1	3	6	10

✓

b The sequence is 1, 3, 6, 10, 15, 21, …
The 6th term is 21.
∴ 21 squares are used in figure 6 ✓

c Substitute $f = 12$ in s:
$$s = \dfrac{12^2 + 12}{2} ✓$$
$$= \dfrac{156}{2}$$
$$= 78$$
∴ 78 squares are used in figure 12 ✓   (4 marks)

3 a Sequence is 40, 50, 60, 70, 80, …
∴ Margot charges \$80 for 6 hours ✓

b 8 hours ✓✓

c $c = 10n + 20$ ✓

d Substitute $n = 9$:
$$c = 10 \times 9 + 20$$
$$= 110$$
∴ Margot earns \$110 ✓   (5 marks)

4 a $\dfrac{ab - 1}{c} = \dfrac{3 \times 5 - 1}{2}$ ✓
$$= \dfrac{14}{2}$$
$$= 7 ✓$$

b $(b - c)(a + c) = (5 - 2)(3 + 2)$ ✓
$$= 3 \times 5$$
$$= 15 ✓ \text{(4 marks)}$$

5 $c = 80n + 210$ ✓   (1 mark)

6 $A = 75t + 100$ ✓   (1 mark)

7 a $T = p^2 - qr$
$$= 3^2 - 4 \times 2 ✓$$
$$= 9 - 8$$
$$= 1 ✓$$

b $T = (-4)^2 - 2 \times (-3)$ ✓
$$= 16 + 6$$
$$= 22 ✓$$ (4 marks)

8 a $x + 3 < 16$ ✓

b The numbers are x and $x + 1$
∴ $x(x + 1) = 20$ ✓

c The numbers are x and $x + 2$
∴ $7x - x(x + 2) = 6$ ✓   (3 marks)

9 If the width is x, then the length is $(x + 5)$.

a $P = 2(x + x + 5)$
$$= 2(2x + 5) ✓$$

b $A = x(x + 5)$ ✓   (2 marks)

10 Write $x\%$ as $\dfrac{x}{100}$
$$P = 700 + \dfrac{x}{100} \times 700$$
$$= 700 + 7x ✓$$ (1 mark)

11 a

x	-2	-1	0	1	2
y	4	3	2	1	0

✓

b $y = 2 - x$ ✓   (2 marks)

USING ALGEBRA
SKILLS CHECK   PAGE 42

1 a $4a, 7a, 3b, ab$
∴ $4a$ and $7a$

b $xy, 4y, 3xy, x^2y^2, -yx$
∴ $xy, 3xy$ and $-yx$

2 a $4x + 7x + 2x + x = 14x$

b $a + a + a + a = 4a$

c $4xy + yx + 3xy = 8xy$

d $4x^2 + 2x^2 = 6x^2$

e $-6y + 3y + y = -2y$

f $-a^3 + a^3 = 0$

g $-2x^3 + 2x^3 + 2x^3 = 2x^3$

h $ab + 2ab + 3ab = 6ab$

i $-4g + g = -3g$

3 a $3a - 2a = a$

b $7b - b = 6b$

c $15a^2b - 20ab = 15a^2b - 20ab$

d $-12y^2 - 2y^2 = -14y^2$

e $8ab - 9ab = -ab$

f $4r - 3r - 2r - r = -2r$

g $7a - 8b = 7a - 8b$

h $-7k - 2k = -9k$

i $2aa - a^2 = 2a^2 - a^2 = a^2$

4 a $4z - 3x + 2z - 5z = -3x + z$

b $12a - 4ab + a - ab = 13a - 5ab$

c $3 - 2a + 7 + a = 10 - a$

d $2y^2 + 3y - 6y + y^2 = 3y^2 - 3y$

e $-4s - 5st + s + ts = -3s - 4st$

f $7a^2 - 3a + 8a - a^2 = 6a^2 + 5a$

g $6y + 2a - 3a - 5y = y - a$

h $12a - a^2 + a - 12a^2 = 13a - 13a^2$

i $32 - 5w + 3w - 30 = 2 - 2w$

5 a $a \times a \times a \times a = a^4$

b $b \times c \times b \times c = b^2c^2$

c $4 \times y \times y \times y \times y = 4y^4$

6 **a** $a^3 = a \times a \times a$

    b $b^6 = b \times b \times b \times b \times b \times b$

    c $5x^2y^3 = 5 \times x \times x \times y \times y \times y$

7 **a** $8x \div 4 = 2x$

    b $3y \div y = 3$

    c $15a \div 5a = 3$

    d $90cd \div 10c = 9d$

    e $16x^2 \div 4x = 4x$

    f $12abd \div 3ad = 4b$

    g $\dfrac{18d}{9d} = 2$

    h $\dfrac{6x^2}{3x} = 2x$

    i $\dfrac{24bg^2}{6g} = 4bg$

8 **a** $3 \times 6y - 5y \times 2 = 18y - 10y$
                          $= 8y$

    b $3a \times 5b - 10ab = 15ab - 10ab$
                           $= 5ab$

    c $20d \div 4d + 3 = 5 + 3$
                       $= 8$

    d $12x - (14x - 2x) = 12x - 12x$
                          $= 0$

    e $32a \div 16 \times 2 = 4a$

    f $(4a)^2 - 4a^2 = 16a^2 - 4a^2$
                      $= 12a^2$

9 **a** $10a - 4a = 6a$ $\therefore\ 4a$

    b $3y \times 7x = 21xy$ $\therefore\ 7x$

    c $12z \div 4z = 3$ $\therefore\ 12z$

    d $-g + 4g = 3g$ $\therefore\ -g$

    e $8ab \div 2ab = 4$ $\therefore\ 2ab$

    f $6w \times 5w = 30w^2$ $\therefore\ 6w$

USING ALGEBRA

INTERMEDIATE TEST   PAGE 43

1 Try each of the alternatives.
    $m \times m \times m = m^3$
           $\neq 3m$ **B** ✓   (1 mark)

2 $5a - 4 + 3a - 2 = 8a - 6$ **A** ✓
                                (1 mark)

3 $-m^2, mm, 5m^2 = -m^2, m^2, 5m^2$
        D ✓   (1 mark)

4 $4b + 6 \times 2b = 4b + 12b$
               $= 16b$ **A** ✓
                                (1 mark)

5 $(3a)^2 - 3a^2 = 3a \times 3a - 3a^2$
                  $= 9a^2 - 3a^2$
                  $= 6a^2$ **C** ✓
                              (1 mark)

6

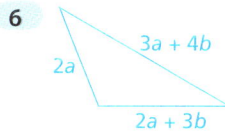

    Perimeter = sum of all sides
                $= 2a + 2a + 3b + 3a + 4b$ ✓
                $= 7a + 7b$
    $\therefore$ perimeter is $(7a + 7b)$ units ✓
                              (2 marks)

7 The numbers will be $x,\ x + 1$
    and $x + 2$.
    Average $= \dfrac{x + x + 1 + x + 2}{3}$ ✓
               $= \dfrac{3x + 3}{3}$
    $\therefore$ average is $\dfrac{3x + 3}{3}$ ✓

    [This can be written as $x + 1$]
                              (2 marks)

8 **a**

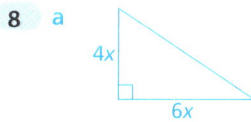

    Area $= \dfrac{1}{2} \times 6x \times 4x$ ✓
           $= 3x \times 4x$
           $= 12x^2$
    $\therefore$ area is $12x^2$ units^2 ✓

    b

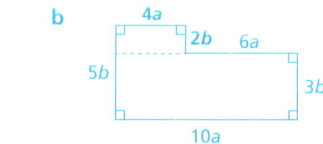

    Area $= 10a \times 3b + 4a \times 2b$ ✓
           $= 30ab + 8ab$
           $= 38ab$
    $\therefore$ area is $38ab$ units^2 ✓
                              (5 marks)

9 **a** $3a - 2b - 5a + 6b = -2a + 4b$ ✓

    b $8x - 3xy + x = 9x - 3xy$ ✓
                            (2 marks)

10 Biscuits $= 3 \times m + 2 \times m$ ✓
              $= 3m + 2m$
               $= 5m$
    $\therefore$ they have $5m$ biscuits ✓
                            (2 marks)

11 **a** $40y \div 10 + 3 \times 2y = 4y + 6y$ ✓
                            $= 10y$ ✓

    b $\dfrac{12x}{6} + 3x = 2x + 3x$ ✓
                $= 5x$ ✓   (4 marks)

---

12 Pay $= 2 \times 5 \times p$ ✓
         $= 10p$
    $\therefore$ Darren is paid \$$10p$ ✓
                        (2 marks)

USING ALGEBRA

ADVANCED TEST   PAGE 44

1 **a** $3x - 2y - 4x + 5y = -x + 3y$ ✓

    b $4a - 3 - 9 - 7a = -3a - 12$ ✓

    c $2x^2 - 2xy - 6x^2 - yx$
        $= -4x^2 - 3xy$ ✓

    d $-2w - q - w + q = -3w$ ✓
                            (4 marks)

2 **a** $3^x \times 3^y = 3^{x+y}$ ✓

    b $3^x \div 3^y = 3^{x-y}$ ✓

    c $(3^x)^y = 3^{xy}$ ✓   (3 marks)

3 **a** $5y \times (-3y) = -15y^2$ ✓

    b $(-4a)^2 = 16a^2$ ✓

    c $16d^2 \div 4d = 4d$ ✓

    d $\dfrac{16g}{4g^2} = \dfrac{4}{g}$ ✓

    e $\dfrac{-20w^2}{5w} = -4w$ ✓   (5 marks)

4 n tomato seedlings
    $2n$ lettuces
    $(2n - 6)$ pumpkins ✓
    Total $= n + 2n + 2n - 6$
           $= 5n - 6$ ✓   (2 marks)

5 Perimeter $= 7y \times 3$
              $= 21y$
    $\therefore$ $21y$ cm ✓   (1 mark)

6 Length of each side $= 5x$ ✓
           Perimeter $= 5x \times 4$
                   $= 20x$
    $\therefore$ perimeter is $20x$ cm ✓
                            (2 marks)

7 **a** $12y \div 4 - 2 \times 5y = 3y - 10y$ ✓
                        $= -7y$

    b $(10a - 6a \times 3)^2 = (10a - 18a)^2$ ✓
                         $= (-8a)^2$
                         $= 64a^2$ ✓

    c $\dfrac{3a - 4a \times 2}{5a} = \dfrac{3a - 8a}{5a}$ ✓
                   $= \dfrac{-5a}{5a}$
                   $= -1$ ✓

d $r(3 - 4 \times 2) - 3r$
$= r(3 - 8) - 3r$ ✔
$= -5r - 3r$
$= -8r$ ✔

e $(2a - 7a)(6b - 8b)$
$= (-5a)(-2b)$ ✔
$= 10ab$ ✔ (10 marks)

8 a The numbers are $n, n + 2, n + 4, n + 6$
Sum $= n + n + 2 + n + 4 + n + 6$
$= 4n + 12$ ✔

b $n + 6 - n = 6$ ✔

c Average $= \dfrac{4n + 12}{4}$ (this can be simplified to $n + 3$)
✔ (3 marks)

9 a Length $= 4x - 3$ ∴ $(4x - 3)$ cm ✔

b Perimeter $= 2(4x - 3 + x)$
$= 2(5x - 3)$ ∴ $2(5x - 3)$ cm ✔

c Area $= x(4x - 3)$ ∴ $x(4x - 3)$ cm^2 ✔ (3 marks)

10 a $x + 12 = 40$ ✔

b $x - 6 = 40$ ✔

c $5x = 30$ ✔

d $\dfrac{x}{4} = 7$ ✔ (4 marks)

11 Toni earns $\$(p + 40)$ and Simon $\$(p - 80)$. ✔
Total $= p + p + 40 + p - 80$
$= 3p - 40$
∴ the total amount is $\$(3p - 40)$ ✔ (2 marks)

12 The laps are $b, 2b, 4b, 8b, 16b$ ✔
Total $= b + 2b + 4b + 8b + 16b$
$= 31b$
∴ Adrianna will swim a total of $31b$ laps. ✔ (2 marks)

13 a $2, 4c, 8c^2,$ _____
The rule is multiplying by $2c$:
$8c^2 \times 2c = 16c^3$
∴ the next term is $16c^3$ ✔

b $27p, -9p, 3p,$ _____
The rule is dividing by -3:
$3p \div -3 = -p$
∴ the next term is $-p$ ✔

c $3x + 7y, 5x + 4y, 7x + y,$ _____
The rule is adding $2x$ and subtracting $3y$:
$7x + y + 2x - 3y = 9x - 2y$
∴ the next term is $9x - 2y$ ✔

d $4a - 3b, 3a - 2b, 2a - b,$ _____
The rule is subtracting a and adding b:
$2a - b - a + b = a$
∴ the next term is a ✔

e $125x^3, 25x^2, 5x,$ _____
The rule is dividing by $5x$:
$\dfrac{5x}{5x} = 1$
∴ the next term is 1 ✔

f $3x - y, -6x + 2y, 12x - 4y,$ _____
The rule is multiplying both terms by $y -2$:
As $12x \times -2 = -24x$ and $-4y \times -2 = 8y$, then $-24x + 8y$
∴ the next term is $-24x + 8y$ ✔ (6 marks)

14 Consider the answer to the question, 'what exceeds 6 by 3?' To find the answer we can add. This means
$3x - 7y + 2x + 3y = 5x - 4y$ ✔ (1 mark)

15 Cameron is y, Emilie is $y - 6$ and Jack is $3y$. Jack's father is $3y + 28$. ✔
Difference $= 3y + 28 - (y - 6)$
$= 3y + 28 - y + 6$
$= 2y + 34$
∴ the difference is $(2y + 34)$ years ✔ (2 marks)

16 a $x(x + 4) = 28$ ✔

b $5x + 7 = 22$ ✔

c $3x - 8 = 34$ ✔

d $\dfrac{x}{3} + 11 = 17$ ✔

e $40 - 8x = 16$ ✔ (5 marks)

17 The numbers are x and $x + 6$. ✔
$x + x + 6 = 27$
$2x + 6 = 27$ ✔ (2 marks)

SIMPLE EQUATIONS AND GRAPHS
SKILLS CHECK   PAGE 46

1 a $y = x + 3$

x	0	1	2	3
y	3	4	5	6

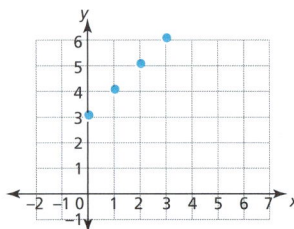

WORKED SOLUTIONS

b $y = 2x + 1$

x	0	1	2	3
y	**1**	**3**	**5**	**7**

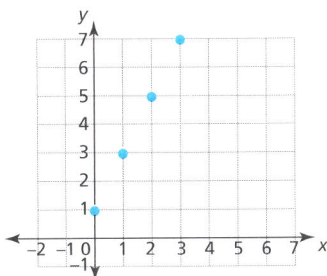

c $y = 3 - x$

x	0	1	2	3
y	**3**	**2**	**1**	**0**

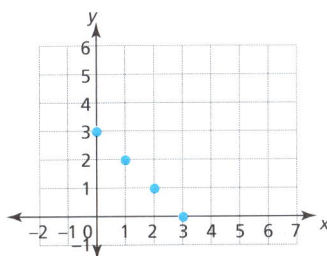

2 a $x + 4 = 7$
$x + 4 - 4 = 7 - 4$
$x = 3$

b $a + 3 = 2$
$a + 3 - 3 = 2 - 3$
$a = -1$

c $k + 6 = -1$
$k + 6 - 6 = -1 - 6$
$k = -7$

3 a $r - 3 = 2$
$r - 3 + 3 = 2 + 3$
$r = 5$

b $s - 7 = 10$
$s - 7 + 7 = 10 + 7$
$s = 17$

c $w - 4 = -2$
$w - 4 + 4 = -2 + 4$
$w = 2$

4 a $4y = 12$
$\dfrac{4y}{4} = \dfrac{12}{4}$
$y = 3$

b $3w = 18$
$\dfrac{3w}{3} = \dfrac{18}{3}$
$w = 6$

c $2a = 11$
$\dfrac{2a}{2} = \dfrac{11}{2}$
$a = 5.5$

5 a $\dfrac{x}{2} = 5$
$2 \times \dfrac{x}{2} = 5 \times 2$
$x = 10$

b $\dfrac{a}{3} = 2$
$3 \times \dfrac{a}{3} = 2 \times 3$
$a = 6$

c $\dfrac{x}{5} = 4$
$5 \times \dfrac{x}{5} = 4 \times 5$
$x = 20$

6 a $2a - 3 = 5$
$2a - 3 + 3 = 5 + 3$
$\dfrac{2a}{2} = \dfrac{8}{2}$
$a = 4$

b $1 + 2y = 3$
$1 - 1 + 2y = 3 - 1$
$\dfrac{2y}{2} = \dfrac{2}{2}$
$y = 1$

c $\dfrac{t - 1}{4} = 2$
$4 \times \dfrac{t - 1}{4} = 2 \times 4$
$t - 1 = 8$
$t - 1 + 1 = 8 + 1$
$t = 9$

7 a $x + 5 = 7$
$2 + 5 = 7?$ yes
$\therefore$ true

b $4x + 1 = 9$
$4 \times 2 + 1 = 9?$ yes
$\therefore$ true

c $3 - x = 5$
$3 - 2 = 5?$ no
$\therefore$ false

8 a 2 horizontal intervals
on graph
$\therefore$ 2 rest stops

b At 11 am: 70 km
At noon: 40 km
$\therefore$ distance = 70 − 40
$= 30$
$\therefore$ travelled 30 km

c Distance = 70 + 70
$= 140$
$\therefore$ travelled 140 km

d Steepest part of graph
= fastest speed
$\therefore$ between 1 pm and 2 pm
{Note:
1–2 p.m.: 40 km/h,
8–10 am: 35 km/h,
11–noon: 30 km/h}

SIMPLE EQUATIONS AND GRAPHS
INTERMEDIATE TEST   PAGE 47

1 Substitute
$x = 2$ in $y = 2x + 1$
$y = 2 \times 2 + 1$
$= 4 + 1$
$= 5$ **C** ✓   (1 mark)

2 'what number' $+ 3 = 5$
'what number' $= 5 - 3$
$= 2$
$\therefore x = 2$
Or: $x + 3 = 5$
$x = 5 - 3$
$= 2$ **B** ✓   (1 mark)

3 A: $2 - 2 = 8$ no
B: $2 \times 2 = 6$ no
C: $4 - 2 = 2$ yes   **C** ✓ (1 mark)

4 A: $-1 - 3 = -4$ yes
B: $2 - (-1) = 3$ yes
C: $-1 + 2 = 1$ yes
D: $3 \times -1 = 3$ no   **D** ✓
(1 mark)

5 a $2x - 1 = 9$
$2x - 1 + 1 = 9 + 1$
$\dfrac{2x}{2} = \dfrac{10}{2}$ ✓
$x = 5$ ✓

b $\dfrac{t - 1}{4} = 3$
$4 \times \dfrac{t - 1}{4} = 3 \times 4$
$t - 1 = 12$ ✓
$t - 1 + 1 = 12 + 1$
$t = 13$ ✓

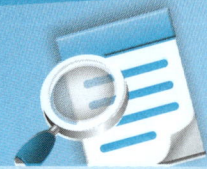

c $2 + 3a = 4$
$2 + 3a - 2 = 4 - 2$
$3a = 2$ ✓
$\frac{3a}{3} = \frac{2}{3}$
$a = \frac{2}{3}$ ✓ (6 marks)

6 $y = 3x - 1$

x	0	1	2
y	–1	2	**5**

✓

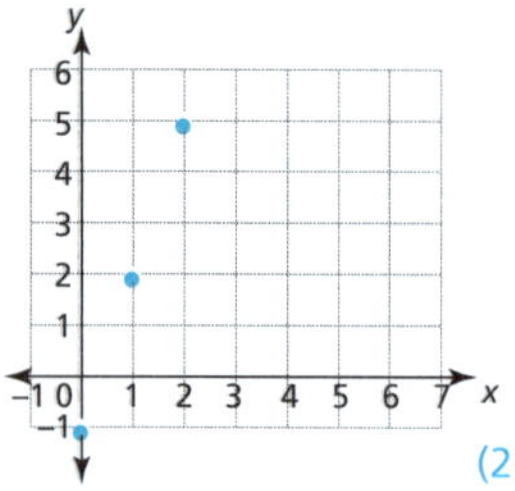

✓ (2 marks)

7 Draw up a table to help find the rule:

x	0	1	2	3	4
y	6	5	4	3	2

The rule is $y = 6 - x$ or $x + y = 6$. ✓✓ (2 marks)

8 **a** $1\frac{1}{2} + \frac{1}{2} = 2$ h ✓
b 60 km/h ✓
c 60 + 60 = 120 km ✓
d 40 km in half hour is 80 km/h ✓ (4 marks)

SIMPLE EQUATIONS AND GRAPHS ADVANCED TEST PAGE 48

1 **a** $3x - 2 = 2x + 1$
$3x - 2x = 1 + 2$ ✓
$x = 3$ ✓

b $4t - 3 = t - 9$
$4t - t = -9 + 3$
$3t = -6$ ✓
$\frac{3t}{3} = \frac{-6}{3}$
$t = -2$ ✓

c $8p = 28 - 6p$
$8p + 6p = 28$
$14p = 28$ ✓
$\frac{14p}{14} = \frac{28}{14}$
$p = 2$ ✓

d $\frac{2t - 1}{5} = 5$
$3 \times \frac{2t - 1}{5} = 3 \times 5$
$2t - 1 = 15$ ✓
$2t = 15 + 1$
$2t = 16$
$\frac{2t}{2} = \frac{16}{2}$
$t = 8$ ✓ (8 marks)

2 **a** $x + x + 3 = 21$ ✓
$2x + 3 = 21$
$2x = 21 - 3$
$2x = 18$
$\frac{2x}{2} = \frac{18}{2}$
$x = 9$
∴ the number is 9 ✓

b $4x - 6 = 14$ ✓
$4x = 14 + 6$
$4x = 20$
$\frac{4x}{4} = \frac{20}{4}$
$x = 5$
∴ the number is 5 ✓

c $20 + 6x = 32$ ✓
$6x = 32 - 20$
$6x = 12$
$\frac{6x}{6} = \frac{12}{6}$
$x = 2$
∴ the number is 2 ✓

d $\frac{x + 3}{2} = 7$ ✓
$2 \times \frac{x + 3}{2} = 2 \times 7$
$x + 3 = 14$
$x = 14 - 3$
$x = 11$
∴ the number is 11 ✓ (8 marks)

3 **a** Total $= x + 12$ ✓
b $x + 12 = 54$ ✓
c $x + 12 = 54$
$x = 54 - 12$ ✓
$x = 42$
∴ Nicole had 42 teapots before her birthday ✓ (4 marks)

4 Let the width $= x$
∴ length $= x + 4$
$x + 4 + x + 4 + x + x = 40$ ✓
$4x + 8 = 40$
$4x = 40 - 8$
$4x = 32$
$\frac{4x}{4} = \frac{32}{4}$
$x = 8$
∴ length is $x + 4 = 12$
∴ the dimensions are 12 cm and 8 cm ✓ (2 marks)

5 A pentagon has 5 sides.
As 45 ÷ 5 = 9, then each side is 9 cm long.
∴ $x + 2 = 9$ ✓
$x = 9 - 2$
$x = 7$ ✓ (2 marks)

6 Let the numbers be $p, p + 2, p + 4$.
$p + p + 2 + p + 4 = 27$ ✓
$3p + 6 = 27$
$3p = 27 - 6$
$3p = 21$
$\frac{3p}{3} = \frac{21}{3}$
$p = 7$
∴ the numbers are 7, 9, 11 ✓ (2 marks)

7 Let Phoebe's age $= x$
∴ Penelope's age $= x - 2$ and Ingrid's age $= x + 3$
$x + x - 2 + x + 3 = 49$ ✓
$3x + 1 = 49$
$3x = 49 - 1$
$3x = 48$
$\frac{3x}{3} = \frac{48}{3}$
$x = 16$
∴ Phoebe is 16, Penelope is 14, Ingrid is 19 ✓ (2 marks)

8 $2x + 6 = 16$ ✓
$2x = 16 - 6$
$2x = 10$
$\frac{2x}{2} = \frac{10}{2}$
$x = 5$
∴ Ava is 5 years old ✓ (2 marks)

9 Let number of hours = n

$80 + 70n = 290$ ✓

$70n = 290 - 80$

$70n = 210$

$\dfrac{70n}{70} = \dfrac{210}{70}$

$n = 3$

∴ it took 3 hours to repair the machine ✓ **(2 marks)**

10 Let cost price = x

$2x + 10 = 96$ ✓

$2x = 96 - 10$

$2x = 86$

$\dfrac{2x}{2} = \dfrac{86}{2}$

$x = 43$

∴ the ornament cost $43 ✓ **(2 marks)**

11 Let lowest mark = x

Highest mark = $2x + 6$

$2x + 6 + x = 120$ ✓

$3x + 6 = 120$

$3x = 120 - 6$

$3x = 114$

$\dfrac{3x}{3} = \dfrac{114}{3}$

$x = 38$

As $2 \times 38 + 6 = 82$, the highest mark was 82. ✓ **(2 marks)**

12 Let the number of males = x

Number of females = $3x + 40$

$3x + 40 + x = 760$ ✓

$4x + 40 = 760$

$4x = 760 - 40$

$4x = 720$

$\dfrac{4x}{4} = \dfrac{720}{4}$

$x = 180$

∴ there were 180 men at the concert ✓ **(2 marks)**

13 Let John's earnings = x

Gai's earnings = $3x - 80$

$x + 3x - 80 = 2100$ ✓

$4x - 80 = 2100$

$4x = 2100 + 80$

$4x = 2180$

$\dfrac{4x}{4} = \dfrac{2180}{4}$

$x = 545$

As $545 \times 3 - 80 = 1555$, then Gai earns $1555 ✓ **(2 marks)**

14 Let cost of the shoes = x

Cost of the skirt = $2x - 22$

$x + 2x - 22 = 158$ ✓

$3x - 22 = 158$

$3x = 158 + 22$

$x = 180$

$\dfrac{3x}{3} = \dfrac{180}{3}$

$x = 60$

As $2 \times 60 - 22 = 98$, then Emily spent $98 on the skirt. ✓

(2 marks)

15 Let the amount for first person = x

Amount for second person = $x - 50$

Amount for third person = $x + 10$

$x + x - 50 + x + 10 = 170$ ✓

$3x - 40 = 170$

$3x = 170 + 40$

$3x = 210$

$\dfrac{3x}{3} = \dfrac{210}{3}$

$x = 70$

∴ the people receive $70, $20, $80 ✓ **(2 marks)**

16 Let the number of children = x

Number of women = $4x$

Number of men = $2x + 20$

$x + 4x + 2x + 20 = 384$ ✓

$7x + 20 = 384$

$7x = 384 - 20$

$7x = 364$

$\dfrac{7x}{7} = \dfrac{364}{7}$

$x = 52$

As $52 \times 4 = 208$ and $52 \times 2 + 20 = 124$, then 208 women, 124 men and 52 children. ✓ **(2 marks)**

AREA AND VOLUME
SKILLS CHECK
PAGE 50

1 a Area $= 12 \times 12$

$= 144$

∴ the area of the square is 144 cm²

b Area $= 8.2 \times 5$

$= 41.0$

∴ the area of the rectangle is 41 cm²

c Area $= 6 \times 4$

$= 24$

∴ the area of the parallelogram is 24 cm²

d Area $= 11 \times 5$

$= 55$

∴ the area of the parallelogram is 55 cm²

2 a Area $= \dfrac{1}{2}bh$

$= \dfrac{1}{2} \times 12 \times 7$

$= 42$

∴ the area of the triangle is 42 cm²

b Area $= \dfrac{1}{2}bh$

$= \dfrac{1}{2} \times 14 \times 8$

$= 56$

∴ the area of the triangle is 56 cm²

c Area $= \dfrac{1}{2}bh$

$= \dfrac{1}{2} \times 9 \times 5$

$= 22\dfrac{1}{2}$

∴ the area of the triangle is 22.5 cm²

d Area $= \dfrac{1}{2}bh$

$= \dfrac{1}{2} \times 4\dfrac{1}{2} \times 2\dfrac{2}{3}$

$= \dfrac{1}{\cancel{2}_{1}} \times \dfrac{\cancel{9}^{3}}{\cancel{2}_{1}} \times \dfrac{\cancel{8}^{2}}{\cancel{3}_{1}}$

∴ the area of the triangle is 6 cm²

3 a

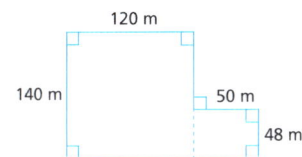

Shape is rectangle + rectangle

∴ $A = 140 \times 120 + 50 \times 48$

$= 16\,800 + 2400$

$= 19\,200$

∴ the area of the shape is 19 200 m²

b

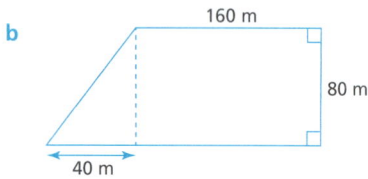

Shape is rectangle + triangle

$\therefore A = 160 \times 80 + \dfrac{1}{2} \times 40 \times 80$

$= 12\,800 + 1600$

$= 14\,400$

$\therefore$ the area of the shape is $14\,400$ m^2

4 Area $= 140 \times 80$

$= 11\,200$

Cost $= 11\,200 \times 0.04$

$= 448$

$\therefore$ the cost of fertiliser is $448

5 a Volume $=$ area of rect. $\times$ perp. height

$V = lbh$

$= 19 \times 5 \times 6$

$= 570$　　　$\therefore$ 570 cm^3

b Volume $=$ area of rect. $\times$ perp. height

$V = lbh$

$= 8 \times 12 \times 8$

$= 768$　　　$\therefore$ 768 cm^3

AREA AND VOLUME
INTERMEDIATE TEST　PAGE 51

1 Area of triangle $= \dfrac{1}{2} \times 8 \times 5$

$= 20$

Rectangle is 10 cm by 2 cm which has also an area of 20 cm^2　**D** ✓　　　　(1 mark)

2 As 12 cm length　$\therefore$ 6 squares

As 8 cm length　$\therefore$ 4 squares

Number of squares $= 6 \times 4$

$= 24$

$\therefore$ 24 squares　**B** ✓　　　(1 mark)

3 Perimeter $= 20$ cm

$\therefore$ length + breadth $= 10$

i.e. $6 +$ breadth $= 10$

breadth $= 4$

Area $= 6 \times 4$

$= 24$

$\therefore$ area is 24 cm^2　**A**　✓　　(1 mark)

4 Area $=$ base $\times$ perpendicular height

$72 = 18 \times$ perpendicular height

Perpendicular height $= 72 \div 18$

$= 36 \div 9$

$= 4$

$\therefore$ perpendicular height is 4 cm　**A**　✓　(1 mark)

5 $V = l \times b \times h$

$= 8 \times 6 \times 4$

$= 192$

$\therefore$ volume is 192 cm^3　**D** ✓　　(1 mark)

6 $V = s^3$

$64 = s^3$

$s = \sqrt[3]{64}$

$s = 4$

$\therefore$ side is 4 cm　**A** ✓　　(1 mark)

7 The diagram represents the net of a rectangular prism measuring 4 cm × 3 cm × 2 cm

Volume $= 4 \times 3 \times 2$

$= 24$ cm^3　**A** ✓　　(1 mark)

8 a

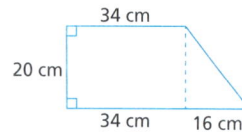

Area $= 34 \times 20 + \dfrac{1}{2} \times 16 \times 20$ ✓

$= 680 + 160$

$= 840$

$\therefore$ area is 840 cm^2 ✓

b

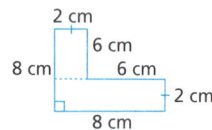

Area $= 8 \times 2 + 6 \times 2$ ✓

$= 16 + 12$

$= 28$

$\therefore$ area is 28 cm^2 ✓　　(4 marks)

9 a Area $= 12 \times 7 - 5 \times 2$ ✓

$= 84 - 10$ ✓

$= 74$

$\therefore$ area is 74 cm^2 ✓

b Area $= 20 \times 10 - 16 \times 6$ ✓

$= 200 - 96$ ✓

$= 104$

$\therefore$ area is 104 m^2 ✓　　(6 marks)

10 a Area $= 8 \times 6$

$= 48$

$\therefore$ area is 48 m^2 ✓

b 8 m ÷ 0.4 m $= 80 \div 4$

$= 20$ ✓

i.e. rolls $= 20 \times 3$

$= 60$

$\therefore$ 60 rolls required ✓

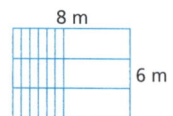

c Cost $= \$3.60 \times 60$ ✓

$= \$216$

$\therefore$ cost of rolls is $216 ✓

d Time $= 60 \div 2$
$\quad\quad\quad = 30$
$\quad \therefore$ Jo takes 30 minutes to lay
$\quad\quad$ rolls ✓ $\quad\quad\quad$ **(6 marks)**

AREA AND VOLUME
ADVANCED TEST $\quad$ PAGE 52

1 a Area $= 16 \times 9$
$\quad\quad\quad = 144$
$\quad \therefore$ area is 144 cm^2 ✓

b Area $= 3.4 \times 0.8$
$\quad\quad\quad = 2.72$
$\quad \therefore$ area is 2.72 cm^2 ✓

c Area $= 2\dfrac{3}{4} \times \dfrac{4}{5}$
$\quad\quad = \dfrac{11}{1\cancel{4}} \times \dfrac{\cancel{4}^1}{5}$ ✓
$\quad\quad = \dfrac{11}{5}$
$\quad\quad = 2\dfrac{1}{5}$
$\quad \therefore$ area is $2\dfrac{1}{5}$ cm^2 ✓
$\quad\quad\quad\quad\quad$ **(4 marks)**

2 a Area $= 30 \times 30$
$\quad\quad\quad = 900$
$\quad \therefore$ area is 900 cm^2 ✓

b Area $= 0.07 \times 0.07$
$\quad\quad\quad = 0.0049$
$\quad \therefore$ area is 0.0049 cm^2 ✓

c Area $= 1\dfrac{2}{3} \times 1\dfrac{2}{3}$
$\quad\quad = \dfrac{5}{3} \times \dfrac{5}{3}$ ✓
$\quad\quad = \dfrac{25}{9}$
$\quad\quad = 2\dfrac{7}{9}$
$\quad \therefore$ area is $2\dfrac{7}{9}$ cm^2 ✓ **(4 marks)**

3 a Area $= 15 \times 12$
$\quad\quad\quad = 180$
$\quad \therefore$ area is 180 cm^2 ✓

b Area $= 4.8 \times 3$
$\quad\quad\quad = 14.4$
$\quad \therefore$ area is 14.4 cm^2 ✓

c Area $= 2\dfrac{1}{2} \times 1\dfrac{1}{5}$
$\quad\quad = \dfrac{\cancel{5}^1}{\cancel{2}_1} \times \dfrac{\cancel{6}^3}{\cancel{5}_1}$ ✓
$\quad\quad = 3$
$\quad \therefore$ area is 3 cm^2 ✓ **(4 marks)**

4 a Area $= \dfrac{1}{2} \times 20 \times 11.4$
$\quad\quad = 10 \times 11.4$ ✓
$\quad\quad = 114$
$\quad \therefore$ area is 114 cm^2 ✓

b Area $= \dfrac{1}{2} \times 6.4 \times 8$
$\quad\quad = 3.2 \times 8$ ✓
$\quad\quad = 25.6$
$\quad \therefore$ area is 25.6 cm^2 ✓

c Area $= \dfrac{1}{2} \times 1\dfrac{3}{5} \times \dfrac{5}{8}$
$\quad\quad = \dfrac{1}{2} \times \dfrac{\cancel{8}^1}{\cancel{5}_1} \times \dfrac{\cancel{5}^1}{\cancel{8}_1}$ ✓
$\quad\quad = \dfrac{1}{2}$
$\quad \therefore$ area is $\dfrac{1}{2}$ cm^2 ✓ **(6 marks)**

5 a length $= 12.09 \div 3$ ✓
$\quad\quad\quad = 4.03$
$\quad \therefore$ length is 4.03 cm ✓

b length $= \sqrt{12\dfrac{1}{4}}$ ✓
$\quad\quad = \sqrt{\dfrac{49}{4}}$
$\quad\quad = \dfrac{7}{2}$
$\quad\quad = 3\dfrac{1}{2}$
$\quad \therefore$ length is $3\dfrac{1}{2}$ cm ✓

c height $= 1\dfrac{3}{4} \div \dfrac{3}{8}$ ✓
$\quad\quad = \dfrac{7}{1\cancel{4}} \times \dfrac{\cancel{8}^2}{3}$
$\quad\quad = \dfrac{14}{3}$
$\quad\quad = 4\dfrac{2}{3}$
$\quad \therefore$ height is $4\dfrac{2}{3}$ cm ✓

d Area $= \dfrac{1}{2} \times$ base $\times$ height
$\quad 16.5 = \dfrac{1}{2} \times$ base $\times 3$
$\quad 16.5 = 1.5 \times$ base
$\quad$ base $= 16.5 \div 1.5$ ✓
$\quad\quad\quad = 33 \div 3$
$\quad\quad\quad = 11$
$\quad \therefore$ base is 11 cm ✓ **(8 marks)**

6 Area $= 8 \times 5$
$\quad\quad\quad = 40$ ✓
$\quad$ Cost $= 35 \times 40$
$\quad\quad\quad = 1400$
$\quad \therefore$ the cost will be $1400 ✓
$\quad\quad\quad\quad\quad$ **(2 marks)**

7 Area $= 25.6 \times 10$
$\quad\quad\quad = 256$
$\quad$ Number of bottles $= 256 \div 64$
$\quad\quad\quad\quad\quad\quad = 32 \div 8$
$\quad\quad\quad\quad\quad\quad = 4$ ✓
$\quad\quad$ Cost $= 4.8 \times 4$
$\quad\quad\quad\quad = 19.2$
$\quad \therefore$ Jason will need 4 bottles at a
$\quad\quad$ cost of $19.20 ✓ $\quad$ **(2 marks)**

8 First, 8 m $= 800$ cm, 5 m $= 500$ cm
$\quad$ Also, $800 \div 50 = 16$ and
$\quad 500 \div 50 = 10$.
$\quad$ As $16 \times 10 = 160$, Simone will
$\quad$ need 160 tiles. ✓
$\quad$ Cost $= 160 \times 4$
$\quad\quad\quad = 640$
$\quad \therefore$ the tiles will cost $640 ✓
$\quad\quad\quad\quad\quad$ **(2 marks)**

9 Perimeter $= 400 \div 5$
$\quad\quad\quad\quad = 80$
$\quad$ The length of fencing is 80 m. ✓
$\quad$ The largest area formed is a
$\quad$ square with side length 20 m.
$\quad$ Area $= 20 \times 20$
$\quad\quad\quad = 400$
$\quad \therefore$ the largest area is 400 m^2 ✓
$\quad\quad\quad\quad\quad$ **(2 marks)**

10 Volume of cereal $= \dfrac{2}{3} \times 24 \times 7 \times 30$
$\quad\quad\quad\quad\quad\quad\quad$ ✓
$\quad\quad\quad\quad = 48 \times 7 \times 10$
$\quad\quad\quad\quad = 3360$
$\quad \therefore$ the volume of cereal is
$\quad\quad$ 3360 cm^3 ✓ $\quad$ **(2 marks)**

11 First, $16 \div 2 = 8$, and
$\quad 12 \div 0.4 = 120 \div 4$
$\quad\quad\quad\quad\quad = 30$
$\quad$ As $30 \times 8 = 240$, then need 240
$\quad$ rolls. ✓
$\quad$ Cost $= 240 \times 5$
$\quad\quad\quad = 1200$
$\quad \therefore$ the cost of the turf is $1200 ✓
$\quad\quad\quad\quad\quad$ **(2 marks)**

WORKED SOLUTIONS

12   Area = 36 × 5
     = 180 ✓
Amount = 180 × 0.1
       = 18
∴   need 18 kilograms ✓
                    (2 marks)

13   As 30 + 8 = 38 and 22 + 8 = 30, the
cardboard is 38 cm by 30 cm ✓
Border Area = 38 × 30 − 30 × 22
          = 1140 − 660
          = 480
∴   area of border is 480 cm² ✓
                    (2 marks)

14   Area = 400
Length = $\sqrt{400}$
       = 20
The cube has side length of
20 cm. ✓
Volume = 20 × 20 × 20
       = 8000
The volume is 8000 cm³
As 1000 cm³ = 1000 mL = 1 L,
the capacity is 8 L. ✓   (2 marks)

15   Vol. above water = 16 × 4 × 0.08
              = 64 × 0.08
              = 5.12 ✓
The volume is 5.12 km³
As 5.12 × 9 = 46.08, the total
volume of ice is 46.08 km³. ✓
                    (2 marks)

SOLIDS, TRANSFORMATIONS AND SYMMETRY
SKILLS CHECK   PAGE 54

1 a   Net of a cube
    b   Trapezoidal prism
    c   Cylinder

2 a
    b
    c

3 a
    b
    c

4

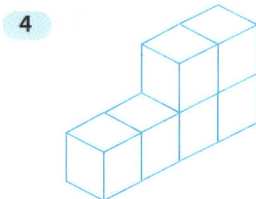

5 a   8

    b   1

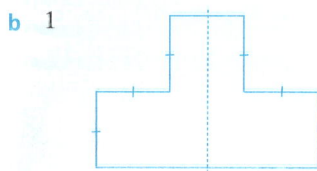

    c   infinite number

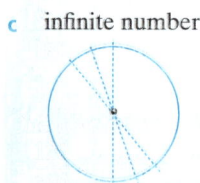

6 a   2, with centre of symmetry X
    b   2, with centre of symmetry X
    c   3, with centre of symmetry X

7 a   a rotation of 90° will repeat
       the shape
       ∴   order of rotation 4

    b   a rotation of 180° will repeat
       the shape
       ∴   order of rotation 2
    c   a rotation of 90° will repeat
       the shape
       ∴   order of rotation 4

SOLIDS, TRANSFORMATIONS AND SYMMETRY
INTERMEDIATE TEST   PAGE 55

1   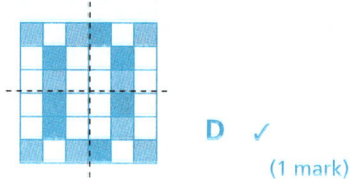 ∴ triangular
         prism **A** ✓
                    (1 mark)

2   A rectangle has line symmetry
and an order of rotational
symmetry of 2.   **D** ✓
                    (1 mark)

3   A rotation of 120° will place the
image over the original.
This means an order
of 3. **C** ✓   (1 mark)

4   A kite. [Parallelogram has 0,
equilateral triangle has 3 and
scalene triangle has 0.] **B** ✓
                    (1 mark)

5   Need 7 more squares shaded.

         D ✓
                    (1 mark)

6 a   ✓

    b   ✓

    c   ✓

                    (3 marks)

WORKED SOLUTIONS

7 ✓✓

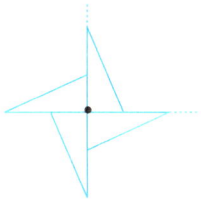

(2 marks)

8 ✓✓

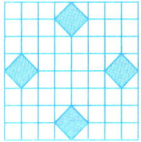

(2 marks)

9 ✓✓

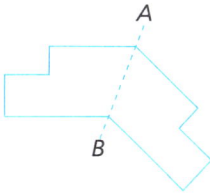

A

B

(2 marks)

SOLIDS, TRANSFORMATIONS AND SYMMETRY
ADVANCED TEST   PAGE 56

1
a square: 4 ✓
b rectangle: 2 ✓
c parallelogram: 2 ✓
d rhombus: 2 ✓
e trapezium: no (or 1) ✓
f circle: infinite ✓
g ellipse: 2 ✓
h scalene triangle: no (or 1) ✓
i isosceles triangle: no (or 1) ✓
j equilateral triangle: 3 ✓
k regular pentagon: 5 ✓
l regular hexagon: 6 ✓
m regular octagon: 8 ✓   (13 marks)

2 8 ✓✓

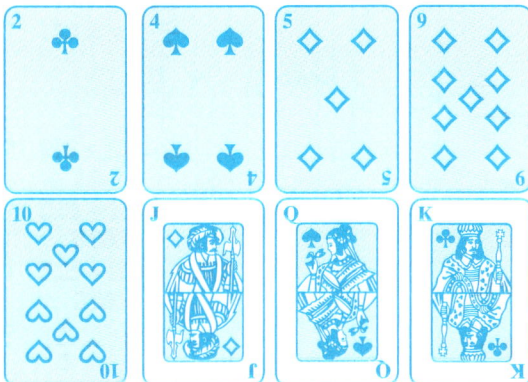

(2 marks)

3
a 10 ✓   b 5 ✓
c 4 ✓   d 4 ✓
e 6 ✓   f 7 ✓   (6 marks)

4
a
Front   Top   Right ✓✓✓

b
Front   Top   Right ✓✓✓

c
Front   Top   Right ✓✓✓

d
Front   Top   Right ✓✓✓

e
Front   Top   Right ✓✓✓

f
Front   Top   Right ✓✓✓

(18 marks)

5
Front   Top   Right ✓✓✓

(3 marks)

6 a

✓✓

b

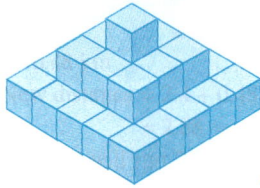

✓✓   (4 marks)

7 a

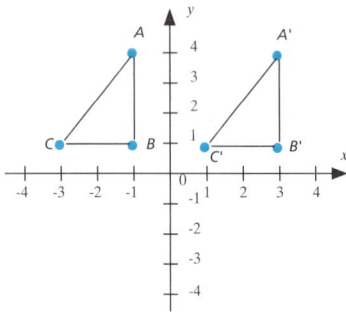

B' (3, 1) ✓

b

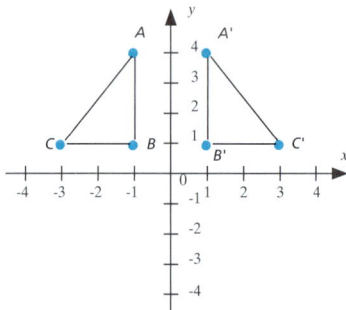

A' (1, 4) ✓

c

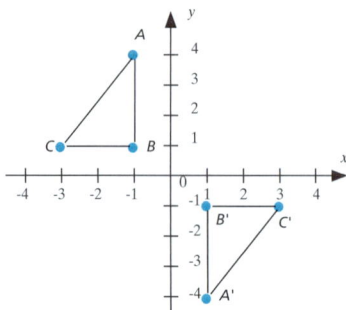

C' (3, –1) ✓   (3 marks)

ANGLES AND LINES
SKILLS CHECK   PAGE 59

1 a ∠ABC or ∠CBA or ∠B
　　b ∠FEG or ∠GEF

2 a 62°, acute
　　b 355°, reflex
　　c 151°, obtuse

3 a ∠ADB or ∠BEC, others
　　b ∠DAB, ∠BAC, others
　　c ∠DAB and ∠BAC, ∠DBA and ∠ABC, others

4 a As 90 − 72 = 18
　　　∴ complement is 18°
　　b As 180 − 100 = 80
　　　∴ supplement is 80°
　　c As 90 minus $x = 90 − x$
　　　∴ complement is $(90 − x)°$
　　d As 180 minus $y = 180 − y$
　　　∴ supplement is $(180 − y)°$

5 a $x = 180 − 68$　(straight angle is 180°)
　　　　$= 112$
　　　∴ $x = 112$
　　b $y = 90 − 35$　(right angle is 90°)
　　　　$= 55$
　　　∴ $y = 55$
　　c $a = 360 − (140 + 160)$　(revolution is 360°)
　　　　$= 360 − 300$
　　　　$= 60$
　　　∴ $a = 60$

6 a Using 'corresponding angles in parallel lines equal'
　　　　$x = 58$
　　　Using 'vertically opposite angles equal'
　　　　$y = 58$
　　　∴ $x = 58, y = 58$
　　b Using 'alternate angles in parallel lines equal'
　　　　$x = 76$
　　　Using 'straight angle is 180°'
　　　　$y = 180 − 76$
　　　　　$= 104$
　　　∴ $x = 76, y = 104$
　　c Using 'corresponding angles in parallel lines equal'
　　　　$x = 70$
　　　Using 'straight angle is 180°'
　　　　$y = 180 − (70 + 60)$
　　　　　$= 180 − 130$
　　　　　$= 50$
　　　∴ $x = 70, y = 50$

7　**a**　$x = 180 - 135$　(straight angle)
　　　　$= 45$

　b　$x = 360 - (90 + 140)$　(revolution)
　　　　$= 360 - 230$
　　　　$= 130$

　c　$x = 125$　(corresponding angles, parallel lines)
　　　　or (corr. $\angle$s, ‖ lines)

ANGLES AND LINES
INTERMEDIATE TEST　PAGE 60

1

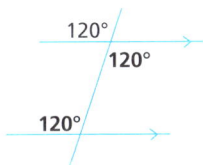

$x = 120$　(vert. opp $\angle$s)
$y = 120$　(corresp. $\angle$s equal, ‖ lines)
$\therefore x = 120,\ y = 120$　**B**　✓　(1 mark)

2　Complementary $\angle$s add up to $90°$
As $75 + 15 = 90$,
then the complement is $15°$　**B**　✓　(1 mark)

3　Supplementary $\angle$s add up to $180°$
As $\angle ACB$ and $\angle DCB$ form a straight line
($180°$), they are supplementary.　**C**　✓　(1 mark)

4　Try each of the alternatives.
$x = 105$　(co-interior $\angle$s, $AB \parallel CD$)　**D**　✓　(1 mark)

5

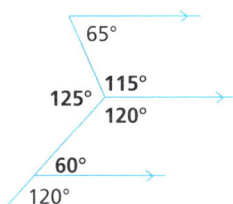

Try each of the alternatives.
$a = 115$　(co-interior $\angle$s, ‖ lines)
$b = 60$　($\angle$s in a straight line)
$c = 120$　(corresp. $\angle$s, ‖ lines)
$d = 360 - (115 + 120)$　($\angle$s in a revolution)
　$= 360 - 235$
　$= 125$
　$\neq 135$　**D**　✓　(1 mark)

6　**a**

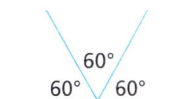

$x + x + x = 180$　($\angle$s in a straight line)　✓
　　$3x = 180$
　　$x = 60$　✓

b

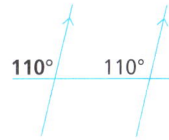

$2x = 110$　(corresp. $\angle$s, ‖ lines)　✓
$x = 55$　✓

c

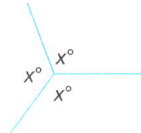

$x + x + x = 360$　($\angle$s in a revolution)　✓
　　$3x = 360$
　　$x = 120$　✓　(6 marks)

7

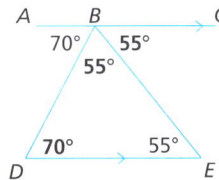

$\angle BDE = 70°$　(alt. $\angle$s, $AC \parallel DE$)　✓✓
$\angle CBE = 55°$　(alt. $\angle$s, $AC \parallel DE$)　✓✓
$\angle DBE = 55°$　($\angle$s in a straight line)　✓✓　(6 marks)

ANGLES AND LINES
ADVANCED TEST　PAGE 61

1　**a**　$x = 43$
　　　　$y = 137$　✓
　b　$x = 360 - (150 + 80)$
　　　　$= 360 - 230$
　　　　$= 130$　✓
　c　$2x + 90 = 360$
　　　　$2x = 360 - 90$
　　　　$2x = 270$
　　　　$x = 135$　✓　(3 marks)

2　**a**　$2x + 10 + 50 = 180$　✓
　　　　$2x + 60 = 180$
　　　　$2x = 180 - 60$
　　　　$2x = 120$
　　　　$x = 60$　✓
　b　$2x + 10 = x + 40$　✓
　　　　$2x - x = 40 - 10$
　　　　$x = 30$　✓
　c　$2x + 10 + 3x + 2x = 360$　✓
　　　　$7x + 10 = 360$
　　　　$7x = 360 - 10$
　　　　$7x = 350$
　　　　$x = 50$　✓　(6 marks)

3 $(90 - y)°$ ✓ (1 mark)

4 $(180 - p)°$ ✓ (1 mark)

5 a $x = 180 - 78$
$= 102$ ✓

b $x + 70 + 160 = 360$
$x + 230 = 360$
$x = 360 - 230$
$x = 130$ ✓

c $x = 130$ ✓ (3 marks)

6 a

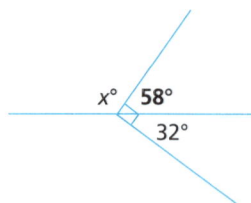

$x = 180 - 58$
$= 122$ ✓

b $x + 35 + 280 = 360$
$x + 315 = 360$
$x = 360 - 315$
$= 45$ ✓

c $x + 90 + 41 = 180$
$x + 131 = 180$
$x = 180 - 131$
$= 49$ ✓

d $y = 180 - (40 + 60)$
$= 180 - 100$
$= 80$ ✓
$\therefore x = 80$ ✓
$\therefore z = 180 - 80$
$= 100$ ✓

e $2x + 70 = 180$
$2x = 180 - 70$
$2x = 110$
$x = 55$ ✓

f $2x + 20 = 90$
$2x = 90 - 20$
$2x = 70$
$x = 35$ ✓ (8 marks)

7 a $2x + 140 + 90 = 360$ ✓
$2x + 230 = 360$
$2x = 360 - 230$
$2x = 130$
$x = 65$ ✓

b $2y + 30 + y = 90$ ✓
$3y + 30 = 90$
$3y = 90 - 30$
$3y = 60$
$y = 20$ ✓

c $x + 50 = 120$ ✓
$x + 50 = 120$
$x = 120 - 50$
$x = 70$ ✓

d $4x + 20 + x + 10 = 180$ ✓
$5x + 30 = 180$
$5x = 180 - 30$
$5x = 150$
$x = 30$ ✓

e $2y + y + 10 + y - 10 = 180$ ✓
$4y = 180$
$y = 45$ ✓

f $3x + 2x + 140 + 90 = 360$ ✓
$5x + 230 = 360$
$5x = 360 - 230$
$5x = 130$
$x = 26$ ✓ (12 marks)

8 $2x + 20 + x + 10 = 90$ ✓
$3x + 30 = 90$
$3x = 90 - 30$
$3x = 60$
$x = 20$ ✓ (2 marks)

9 $4x + 20 = 2x + 60$ ✓
$4x - 2x = 60 - 20$
$2x = 40$
$x = 20$ ✓ (2 marks)

10 $2x + x + 40 + 20 = 180$ ✓
$3x + 60 = 180$
$3x = 180 - 60$
$3x = 120$
$x = 40$ ✓ (2 marks)

11 a $x = 80$ [alt ∠ s, ‖ lines] ✓
$z = 70$ [alt ∠ s, ‖ lines] ✓
$y = 30$ [straight line] ✓

b $360 - 245 = 115$, then
$x = 180 - 115$ [co-int ∠ s, ‖ lines]
$= 65$ ✓

c $180 - 70 = 110$, then
$x + 40 = 110$
$x = 110 - 40$
$= 70$ ✓
$z = 180 - (70 + 70)$
$= 180 - 140$
$= 40$ ✓
$y = 180 - 40$
$= 140$ ✓

d

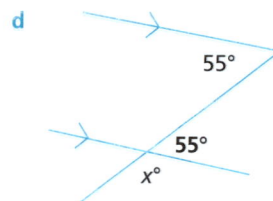

$x = 180 - 55$
$= 125$ ✓

e

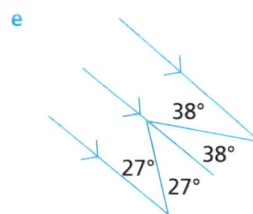

$x = 27 + 38$
$= 65$ ✓

f $x = 50$ [alt ∠ s, ‖ lines] ✓
$60 + 50 + y + 35 = 180$
$y + 145 = 180$
$y = 180 - 145$
$= 35$ ✓ (11 marks)

12 a $3x + 10 = 2x + 40$ ✓
$3x - 2x = 40 - 10$
$x = 30$ ✓

b $6x - 10 = 4x + 30$ ✓
$6x - 4x = 30 + 10$
$2x = 40$
$x = 20$ ✓

c $3x + 40 + x + 20 = 180$ ✓
$4x + 60 = 180$
$4x = 180 - 60$
$4x = 120$
$x = 30$ ✓ (6 marks)

1 **a** $x = 180 - (80 + 55)$ ($\angle$ sum of Δ)
   $= 180 - 135$
   $= 45$

   b $b = 180 - (70 + 70)$ (isos. Δ and $\angle$ sum of Δ)
   $= 180 - 140$
   $= 40$

   c $a = 360 - (110 + 80 + 70)$ ($\angle$ sum of quad.)
   $= 360 - 260$
   $= 100$

   d $x = 180 - 120$ (straight $\angle$)
   $= 60$
   $\therefore y = 120 - 40$ (ext. $\angle$ of Δ equals sum of
            2 int. opp. $\angle$s)
   $= 80$

   e $t = 180 - 60$ (straight $\angle$)
   $= 120$

   f $q = 360 - (90 + 80 + 80)$ ($\angle$ sum of quad.)
   $= 360 - 250$
   $= 110$

2 **a** $2x = 360 - (160 + 100 + 40)$
   $= 360 - 300$
   $\dfrac{2x}{2} = \dfrac{60}{2}$
   $x = 30$

   b $x = 360 - (90 + 40 + 200)$
   $= 30$

   c $2a + 30 + 110 + 3a + 60 + 50 = 360$
   $5a + 250 = 360$
   $\dfrac{5a}{5} = \dfrac{110}{5}$
   $a = 22$

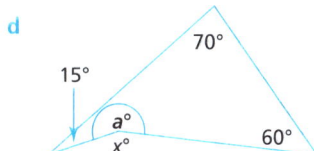

   d
   First find a:
   $70 + 60 + 15 + a = 360$
   $a + 145 = 360$
   $a = 360 - 145$
   $a = 215$
   $\therefore x = 360 - 215 = 145$

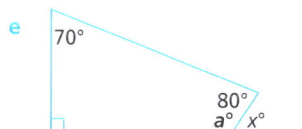

e
First find a: $a = 360 - (90 + 70 + 80)$
            $= 360 - 240 = 120$
$\therefore x = 180 - 120 = 60$

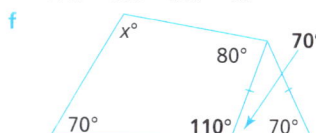

f
$x = 360 - (70 + 110 + 80)$
   $= 360 - 260 = 100$

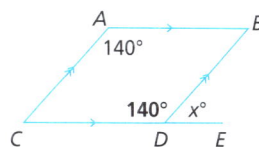

3 **a**
$\angle BDC = 140$ (opp. $\angle$s of ||ogram equal)
   $x = 40$ (straight $\angle$)

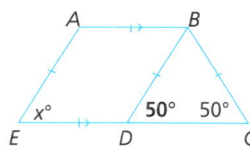

   b
$\angle BDC = 50°$ (base $\angle$s of isos. Δ)
$ABED$ is a rhombus   (opp. sides parallel,
            adjacent sides equal)
$x = 50$ (corr. $\angle$s, $AE \parallel BD$)

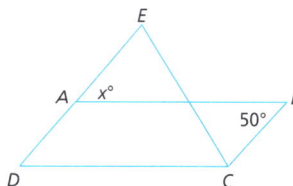

4 **a**
$\angle ADC = 50°$ (opp. $\angle$s of ||ogram equal)
   $x = 50$ (corr. $\angle$s, $AB \parallel DC$)

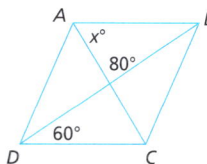

   b
$\angle ABD = 60°$ (alt. $\angle$s, $AB \parallel DC$)
   $x = 40$ ($\angle$ sum of Δ)

WORKED SOLUTIONS

1   Angle sum is 360°.   **C** ✓   (1 mark)

2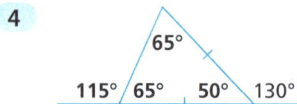

$c = 40$ (∠s in a straight line)
Isosceles Δ therefore both other ∠s equal.
$2d = 180 - 40$ (∠ sum of Δ)
$2d = 140$
$d = 70$
∴ $c = 40, d = 70$ **D** ✓   (1 mark)

3   Let the missing angle be x.
$40 + 57 + x = 180$ (∠ sum of Δ)
$x + 97 = 180$
$x = 83$
∴ missing angle is 83
i.e. triangle is scalene as all angles are different
in size, and acute (40°, 57° and 83°)   **D** ✓   (1 mark)

4

$x = 115°$ **B** ✓   (1 mark)

5   Quadrilateral cannot be a trapezium.   **D** ✓ (1 mark)

6   The quadrilateral is a kite.   **A** ✓   (1 mark)

7   **a** $x = 180 - (90 + 72)$ (∠ sum of Δ)
    $= 180 - 162$
    $= 18$
    $y = 90 + 72$ (ext. ∠ of Δ equals sum
            of 2 int. opp. ∠s)
    $= 162$
∴ $x = 18, y = 162$ ✓✓
b $x = 70$ (base ∠s of isos. Δ)
    $70 + y = 110$ (co-int. ∠s, ‖ lines)
    $y = 40$
∴ $x = 70, y = 40$ ✓✓
c $x = 360 - (90 + 90 + 130)$ (∠ sum of quad.)
    $= 360 - 310$
    $= 50$
    $y = 180 - 50$ (∠s in a straight line)
    $= 130$
∴ $x = 50, y = 130$ ✓✓   (6 marks)

8   **a** $x = 180 - (70 + 55)$ (∠ sum of Δ)
    $= 180 - 125$
    $= 55$ ✓✓
b $x = 65$ (base ∠s of isos. Δ) ✓✓

c $x = 360 - (110 + 100 + 60)$ (∠ sum of quad.)
    $= 360 - 270$
    $= 90$ ✓✓   (6 marks)

9   **a**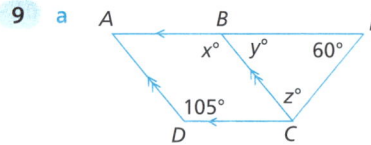

$x = 105$ (opp. ∠s of paralleogram equal)   ✓
$y = 75$ (∠s in a straight line)   ✓
$z = 45$ (∠ sum of Δ)   ✓

b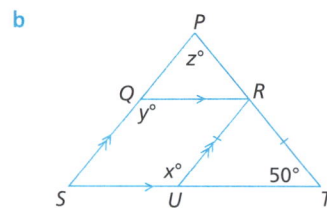

∠$RUT = 50$ (base ∠s of isos. Δ equal)
∴ $x = 130$ (∠s in a straight line) ✓
$y = 130$ (opp. ∠s of parallelogram equal) ✓
Also, ∠$PST = 50$ (corr. ∠s equal, $SP ‖ UR$)
$z = 80$ (∠ sum of Δ PST) ✓   (6 marks)

1   **a** $x = 180 - (90 + 42)$
    $= 180 - 32$
    $= 48$ ✓
b   As $180 - 150 = 30, 180 - 155 = 25$, then
    $x + 30 + 25 = 180$
    $x + 55 = 180$
    $x = 180 - 55$
    $= 125$ ✓
c $z = 180 - (80 + 30)$
    $= 180 - 110$
    $= 70$ ✓
    $y = 180 - 80$
    $= 100$ ✓
    $x = 180 - (70 + 100)$
    $= 180 - 170$
    $= 10$ ✓
d $x = 180 - (70 + 55)$
    $= 180 - 125$
    $= 55$ ✓

WORKED SOLUTIONS

e $x = 180 - (90 + 50)$
$= 180 - 140$
$= 40$ ✓
As $40 + 20 = 60$, then
$y = 180 - (90 + 60)$
$= 180 - 150$
$= 30$ ✓

f $x = 180 - (90 + 55)$
$= 180 - 145$
$= 35$ ✓
∴ $y = 35$ ✓
$z = 180 - (90 + 35)$
$= 180 - 125$
$= 55$ ✓ (11 marks)

2 a $2x + 80 + 80 = 180$ ✓
$2x + 160 = 180$
$2x = 180 - 160$
$2x = 20$
$x = 10$ ✓

b $y + 75 + 75 = 180$ ✓
$y + 150 = 180$
$y = 180 - 150$
$y = 30$
∴ $x = 75$ [alt. ∠ s, ‖ lines] ✓

c $x + x + 40 = 180$
$2x + 40 = 180$
$2x = 180 - 40$
$2x = 140$
$x = 70$ ✓
∴ $y = 40$ [alt. ∠ s, ‖ lines] ✓ (6 marks)

3 a $x + 35 + 40 + 55 = 180$ ✓
$x + 130 = 180$
$x = 180 - 130$
$x = 50$ ✓

b $z = 90 - 50$
$= 40$ ✓
$y = 90 - 40$
$= 50$ ✓
$x = 180 - (50 + 90)$
$= 180 - 140$
$= 40$ ✓

c

∴ $x = 90 - 45$ ✓
$= 45$ ✓ (7 marks)

4 a $4x + 3x + 2x = 180$ ✓
$9x = 180$
$x = 20$ ✓

b $x + 10 + x + 20 + 120 = 180$ ✓
$2x + 150 = 180$
$2x = 180 - 150$
$2x = 30$
$x = 15$ ✓

c $2x + 20 + x + 10 + 60 = 180$ ✓
$3x + 90 = 180$
$3x = 180 - 90$
$3x = 90$
$x = 30$ ✓ (6 marks)

5 a $2x = 63 + 55$ ✓
$2x = 118$
$x = 59$ ✓

b $2x + 20 = 90 + 24$ ✓
$2x + 20 = 114$
$2x = 114 - 20$
$2x = 94$
$x = 47$ ✓

c As $180 - 130 = 50$, then
$50 + 50 + 2x = 180$ ✓
$2x + 100 = 180$
$2x = 180 - 80$
$2x = 80$
$x = 40$ ✓

d $2x + 30 = x + 40$ ✓
$2x - x = 40 - 30$
$x = 10$ ✓

e $2x + 20 = 120$ ✓
$2x = 120 - 20$
$2x = 100$
$x = 50$ ✓

f

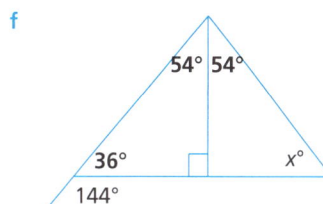

∴ $x = 90 - 54$ ✓
$= 36$ ✓ (12 marks)

6 a $x = 360 - (90 + 90 + 135)$
$= 360 - 315$
$= 45$ ✓

b $x = 360 - (20 + 240 + 30)$
$= 360 - 290$
$= 70$ ✓

c $x = 360 - (60 + 125 + 135)$
$= 360 - 320$
$= 40$ ✓

d $x = 360 - [360 - (90 + 55 + 130)]$
$= 90 + 55 + 130$
$= 275$ ✓

e As $360 - 140 = 220$, then
$2a + a + a + 220 = 360$ ✓
$4a + 220 = 360$
$4a = 360 - 220$
$4a = 140$
$a = 35$ ✓

f $2y - 60 + 80 + 3y + 40 + y = 360$ ✓
$6y + 60 = 360$
$6y = 360 - 60$
$6y = 300$
$y = 50$ ✓ (8 marks)

PROBABILITY
SKILLS CHECK PAGE 69

1 a $Pr(3) = \dfrac{\text{no. favourable outcomes}}{\text{no. possible outcomes}} = \dfrac{1}{9}$

b There are 4 even-numbered balls, so $Pr(\text{even}) = \dfrac{4}{9}$

c There are 5 odd-numbered balls, so $Pr(\text{odd}) = \dfrac{5}{9}$

d $Pr(\text{not odd}) = 1 - Pr(\text{odd}) = 1 - \dfrac{5}{9} = \dfrac{4}{9}$

e Four of the balls have composite numbers (4, 6, 8 and 9: note that 1 is neither prime nor composite), so $Pr(\text{composite}) = \dfrac{4}{9}$

f Four of the balls have prime numbers (2, 3, 5 and 7), so $Pr(\text{prime}) = \dfrac{4}{9}$

g Balls 3, 6 and 9 are divisible by 3, so $Pr(\text{divisible by 3}) = \dfrac{3}{9} = \dfrac{1}{3}$

h The numbers 1, 3 and 5 are factors of 15, so $Pr(\text{factor of 15}) = \dfrac{3}{9} = \dfrac{1}{3}$

i There are 6 numbers less than 7, so $Pr(\text{less than 7}) = \dfrac{6}{9} = \dfrac{2}{3}$

j There are 5 numbers greater than 4, so $Pr(\text{greater than 4}) = \dfrac{5}{9}$

k $Pr(\text{3 or 5}) = \dfrac{2}{9}$

l All of the numbers must be either even or odd, so $Pr(\text{even or odd}) = 1$

2 a $Pr(6) = \dfrac{1}{6}$

b $Pr(\text{less than 4}) = \dfrac{3}{6} = \dfrac{1}{2}$

c $Pr(\text{not 3}) = 1 - \dfrac{1}{6} = \dfrac{5}{6}$

d $Pr(\text{not an odd number}) = 1 - \dfrac{3}{6} = \dfrac{1}{2}$

e $Pr(\text{square number}) = \dfrac{2}{6} = \dfrac{1}{3}$

f $Pr(\text{seven}) = 0$

3 a $Pr(\text{red}) = \dfrac{4}{10} = \dfrac{2}{5}$

b $Pr(\text{white}) = \dfrac{3}{10}$

c $Pr(\text{white or green}) = \dfrac{5}{10} = \dfrac{1}{2}$

d $Pr(\text{not blue}) = 1 - \dfrac{1}{10} = \dfrac{9}{10}$

e $Pr(\text{black}) = 0$

f $Pr(\text{red, white or blue}) = \dfrac{8}{10} = \dfrac{4}{5}$

4 $Pr(\text{red jelly bean}) = \dfrac{4}{7}$

5 a There are 3 red sectors and 8 sectors in total, so $Pr(\text{red}) = \dfrac{3}{8}$

b $Pr(\text{green}) = \dfrac{1}{8}$

c $Pr(\text{not blue}) = 1 - Pr(\text{blue})$
$= 1 - \dfrac{4}{8} = \dfrac{1}{2}$

6 If 5 red jelly babies remain, then a red was chosen (and eaten)
$\therefore Pr(\text{red chosen}) = \dfrac{6}{12} = \dfrac{1}{2}$

7 a $Pr(\text{male}) = 1 - Pr(\text{female})$
$= 1 - 0.53$
$= 0.47$
$\therefore$ probability of male is 0.47

b Number $= 0.53 \times 1200$
$= 636$
$\therefore$ 636 females likely to be born

8 a $Pr(\text{watch TV}) = \dfrac{80}{360} = \dfrac{2}{9}$

b tidy room $= 360° - (120° + 80° + 90°)$
$= 360° - 290°$
$= 70°$
$\therefore Pr(\text{not tidy}) = 1 - Pr(\text{tidy})$
$= 1 - \dfrac{70}{360}$
$= \dfrac{29}{36}$

WORKED SOLUTIONS

PROBABILITY
INTERMEDIATE TEST   PAGE 70

1   10 cards in total; 4 cards are blue.

$$\therefore\ Pr(\text{blue}) = \frac{4}{10}$$
$$= \frac{2}{5}\quad \textbf{B}\ \checkmark$$

(1 mark)

2 $Pr(\text{throwing a three}) = \dfrac{1}{6}$

$$\therefore\ Pr(\text{not a three}) = 1 - \frac{1}{6}$$
$$= \frac{5}{6}\quad \textbf{D}\ \checkmark$$

(1 mark)

3   11 cards in total; two cards have a 'B'.

$$\therefore\ Pr(\text{B}) = \frac{2}{11}\quad \textbf{C}\ \checkmark$$

(1 mark)

4   52 cards; two are red 7s (the 7 of hearts and the 7 of diamonds).

$$\therefore\ Pr(\text{red 7}) = \frac{2}{52}$$
$$= \frac{1}{26}\quad \textbf{A}\ \checkmark$$

(1 mark)

5   Peter predicts either 41, 42, 43, 44 or 45.

$$\therefore\ Pr(\text{Peter correct}) = \frac{5}{45}$$
$$= \frac{1}{9}\quad \textbf{A}\ \checkmark$$

(1 mark)

6   **a**   Total of eight balls.

$$\therefore\ Pr(\text{red}) = \frac{4}{8} = \frac{1}{2}\quad \checkmark$$

b $Pr(\text{white}) = \dfrac{2}{8}$

$$= \frac{1}{4}\quad \checkmark$$

c $Pr(\text{green}) = \dfrac{1}{4}$

$$\therefore\ Pr(\text{not green}) = 1 - \frac{1}{4}$$
$$= \frac{3}{4}\quad \checkmark$$

(3 marks)

7   **a** $Pr(\text{winning first prize}) = \dfrac{10}{100\,000}$

$$= \frac{1}{10\,000}\quad \checkmark$$

b   After first prize is drawn, 99 999 tickets remain—Sharon has 10. $\checkmark$

$$\therefore\ Pr(\text{winning second prize}) = \frac{10}{99\,999}\quad \checkmark$$

(3 marks)

8   There are four faces with either a 2 or 3.

$$\therefore\ Pr(\text{2 or 3}) = \frac{4}{6}\quad \checkmark$$
$$= \frac{2}{3}\quad \checkmark$$

(2 marks)

9   **a** $Pr(\text{Mitchell wins}) = \dfrac{1}{100}\quad \checkmark$

b   There are two numbers that are one off Mitchell's ticket number.   i.e. 13 and 15

$$\therefore\ Pr(\text{13 or 15}) = \frac{2}{100}$$
$$= \frac{1}{50}\quad \checkmark$$

(2 marks)

10   **a**   There is one '$50' on screen.

$$\therefore\ Pr(\$50) = \frac{1}{9}\quad \checkmark$$

b   There are three '$0's on screen.

$$\therefore\ Pr(\$0) = \frac{3}{9}$$
$$= \frac{1}{3}\quad \checkmark$$

c   Could win $50, $80 or $75.

$$\therefore\ Pr(\text{at least }\$50) = \frac{3}{9}$$
$$= \frac{1}{3}\quad \checkmark$$

(3 marks)

PROBABILITY
ADVANCED TEST   PAGE 71

1   **a** $Pr(\text{A}) = \dfrac{1}{6}\quad \checkmark$

b $Pr(\text{C}) = \dfrac{2}{6} = \dfrac{1}{3}\quad \checkmark$

c $Pr(\text{vowel}) = \dfrac{2}{6} = \dfrac{1}{3}\quad \checkmark$

d $Pr(\text{consonant}) = \dfrac{4}{6} = \dfrac{2}{3}\quad \checkmark$

e $Pr(\text{not a consonant}) = 1 - \dfrac{2}{3} = \dfrac{1}{3}\quad \checkmark$ (5 marks)

2   **a**

	1	2	3	4	5	6
1	2	3	4	5	6	7
2	3	4	5	6	7	8
3	4	5	6	7	8	9
4	5	6	7	8	9	10
5	6	7	8	9	10	11
6	7	8	9	10	11	12 $\checkmark\checkmark$

b   7 $\checkmark$

WORKED SOLUTIONS

c **i** $Pr(\text{odd}) = \dfrac{18}{36} = \dfrac{1}{2}$ ✓

ii $Pr(< 7) = \dfrac{15}{36} = \dfrac{5}{12}$ ✓

iii $Pr(\text{square}) = \dfrac{7}{36}$ ✓

iv $Pr(\text{prime}) = \dfrac{15}{36} = \dfrac{5}{12}$ ✓

v $Pr(\text{divisible by 3}) = \dfrac{12}{36} = \dfrac{1}{3}$ ✓

vi $Pr(\text{multiple of 4}) = \dfrac{9}{36} = \dfrac{1}{4}$ ✓

vii $Pr(\text{factor of 12}) = \dfrac{12}{36} = \dfrac{1}{3}$ ✓   (10 marks)

3 **a** $1 - \left(\dfrac{1}{2} + \dfrac{1}{3}\right) = 1 - \dfrac{3+2}{6}$

$= 1 - \dfrac{5}{6}$

$= \dfrac{1}{6}$

Probabilities are $\dfrac{1}{2}, \dfrac{1}{3}, \dfrac{1}{6}$ ✓

∴ smallest number of balls is 6 ✓

b **i** $Pr(1) = \dfrac{1}{6}$ ✓

ii $Pr(\text{less than 3}) = 1 - Pr(3)$

$= 1 - \dfrac{1}{3}$

$= \dfrac{2}{3}$ ✓

iii $Pr(\text{odd}) = Pr(1 \text{ or } 3)$

$= \dfrac{1}{6} + \dfrac{1}{3}$

$= \dfrac{1+2}{6}$

$= \dfrac{3}{6} = \dfrac{1}{2}$ ✓   (5 marks)

4 Sample space: 1, 2, 2, 4, 5, 6

a $Pr(2) = \dfrac{2}{6} = \dfrac{1}{3}$ ✓

b $Pr(\text{even}) = \dfrac{4}{6} = \dfrac{2}{3}$ ✓

c $Pr(< 3) = \dfrac{3}{6} = \dfrac{1}{2}$ ✓   (3 marks)

5 **a** $Pr(\text{red}) = 1 - (0.25 + 0.3 + 0.1)$

$= 1 - 0.65$

$= 0.35$ ✓

b blue: $0.25 \times 40 = 10$

green: $0.3 \times 40 = 12$

red: $0.35 \times 40 = 14$

yellow: $0.1 \times 40 = 4$

∴ 10 blue, 12 green, 14 red and 4 yellow ✓

c $0.25 \times 10 = 2.5$. As it is impossible to have 2.5 balls, there cannot be 10 balls in the bag. ✓

d The smallest number of balls is 20, which means 5 blue, 6 green, 7 red and 2 yellow ✓   (4 marks)

6 **a**

	1	2	3	4	5	6
1	1	2	3	4	5	6
2	2	4	6	8	10	12
3	3	6	9	12	15	18
4	4	8	12	16	20	24
5	5	10	15	20	25	30
6	6	12	18	24	30	36

✓✓

b 6 and 12 ✓

c **i** $Pr(\text{even}) = \dfrac{27}{36} = \dfrac{3}{4}$ ✓

ii $Pr(\text{composite}) = \dfrac{29}{36}$ ✓

iii $Pr(\text{multiple of 4}) = \dfrac{15}{36} = \dfrac{5}{12}$ ✓

iv $Pr(\text{factor of 36}) = \dfrac{20}{36} = \dfrac{5}{9}$ ✓

v $Pr(\text{prime and odd}) = \dfrac{4}{36} = \dfrac{1}{9}$ ✓

vi $Pr(\text{prime or odd}) = \dfrac{11}{36}$ ✓   (9 marks)

7 **a** Let there be 1 green ball.

This means 3 pink balls, 2 red balls and 6 orange balls.

This means in a bag of 12 balls, there are 6 orange, 3 pink, 2 red and 1 green.

∴ $Pr(\text{orange}) = \dfrac{6}{12} = \dfrac{1}{2}$

$Pr(\text{pink}) = \dfrac{3}{12} = \dfrac{1}{4}$

$Pr(\text{red}) = \dfrac{2}{12} = \dfrac{1}{6}$

$Pr(\text{green}) = \dfrac{1}{12}$ ✓✓

b The smallest possible number is 10. ✓

c As $\dfrac{1}{6} \times 72 = 12$, then there will be 12 red balls in the bag. ✓

d From part **a** there are now 3 pink balls, 6 orange balls and a green ball.

$Pr(\text{orange or green}) = \dfrac{7}{10}$ ✓   (5 marks)

WORKED SOLUTIONS

DATA REPRESENTATION
SKILLS CHECK   PAGE 73

1

2

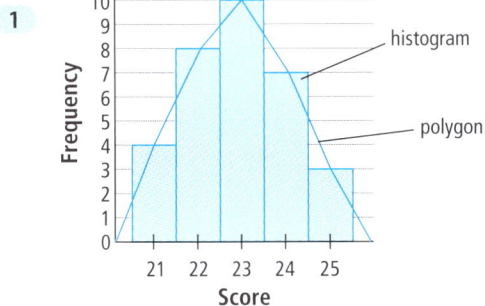

Class interval (kg)	Class centre (kg)	Tally	Frequency
46–50	48	||||	4
51–55	53	⊦⊦⊦ |||	8
56–60	58	||||	4
61–65	63	⊦⊦⊦ ⊦⊦⊦	10
66–70	68	|||	3
71–75	73	|	1

3

Score	Frequency
71	3
72	5
73	7
74	6
75	1

4

Stem	Leaf
5	1 3 7 8
6	0 1 3 7 8 9 9
7	0 1 1 3 3 6 7 8 8 8 9 9
8	0 1 2 4 4 5 9
9	0 1

5

Class interval	Class centre	Frequency
20–29	24.5	5
30–39	34.5	7
40–49	44.5	7
50–59	54.5	5
60–69	64.5	6

DATA REPRESENTATION
INTERMEDIATE TEST   PAGE 74

1 a

Score	Frequency
1	4
2	7
3	7
4	11
5	4
6	2

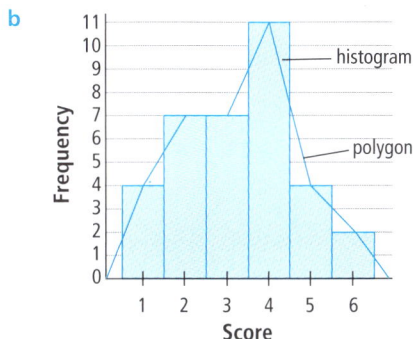

✓✓✓

b

✓✓✓

c From table: 4 + 7 = 11 ✓   (7 marks)

2 a

Colour	Angle	Frequency
blonde	135°	27
brown	100°	20
black	90°	18
red	35°	7

✓✓

b

Student hair colour

✓✓✓ (5 marks)

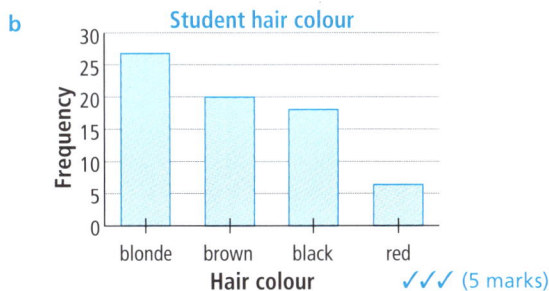

3 a The outlier is 12. ✓

b

Shoe size	Frequency
6	2
7	4
8	3
9	6
10	3
11	0
12	1

✓✓

c size 9 ✓

d 12 − 6 = 6 ✓   (5 marks)

4   a   18 boys ✓

b   9.5 ✓

c

Class interval	Class centre	Frequency
4.0–4.9	4.45	3
5.0–5.9	5.45	9
6.0–6.9	6.45	6
7.0–7.9	7.45	5
8.0–8.9	8.45	6
9.0–9.9	9.45	2

✓✓✓

d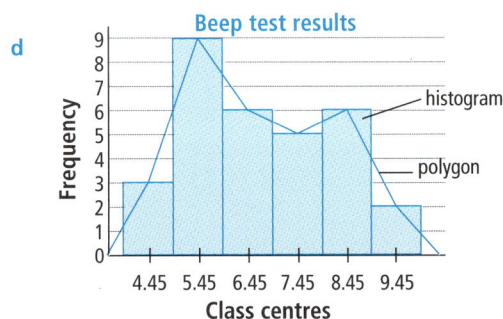

✓✓✓✓   (9 marks)

DATA REPRESENTATION
ADVANCED TEST   PAGE 75

1   a   i   Food amount $= \dfrac{2}{8} \times 1200$

$= \dfrac{1}{4} \times 1200$

$= 300$

∴ \$300 spent on food ✓

ii   rent amount $= \dfrac{3}{{}_{1}8} \times \dfrac{1200^{150}}{1}$

$= 450$

∴ \$450 spent on rent ✓

b   i   three-eighths $= 360$

one-eighth $= 360 \div 3$

$= 120$

∴ \$120 saved ✓

ii   five-eighths $= 120 \times 5$

$= 600$

∴ \$600 spent on other activities ✓ (4 marks)

2

red	blue		green

✓✓ (2 marks)

3

Marks	Students
60–69	3
70–79	5
80–89	4
90–99	4

✓ (1 mark)

4   a

dogs	rabbits	cats	birds

✓

b   Use the fact that there are 2 birds:

1 part = 2

3 parts = 6

∴ 6 rabbits ✓

c $\dfrac{4}{10} \times \dfrac{360}{1} = 144$

∴ an angle of 144° ✓ (3 marks)

5   a   i $\dfrac{5}{10} \times \dfrac{100}{1} = 50$

∴ 50% of the time ✓

ii $\dfrac{3}{10} \times \dfrac{100}{1} = 30$

∴ 30% of the time ✓

b   i $\dfrac{2}{10} \times \dfrac{60}{1} = 12$

∴ 12 minutes on bike ✓

ii $\dfrac{5}{10} \times \dfrac{60}{1} = 30$

∴ 30 minutes on treadmill ✓

c   i   2 parts = 15

1 part = 7.5

5 parts = 7.5 × 2

$= 37.5$

∴ 37.5 minutes on treadmill ✓

ii   3 parts = 7.5 × 3

$= 22.5$

∴ 22.5 minutes on weights ✓ (6 marks)

6   a

NSW	SA		Victoria

✓✓

b   i $\dfrac{1}{4} \times 36 = 9$

∴ 9 people born in NSW ✓

WORKED SOLUTIONS

ii Angle for Victoria = 240°

$$\frac{24\cancel{0}}{36\cancel{0}} \times \frac{36}{1} = 24$$

∴ 24 students born in Victoria ✓

c i One-quarter = 18

Four-quarters = 18 × 4

= 72

∴ 72 students were involved in the survey ✓

ii $\dfrac{^{1}6\cancel{0}}{_{16}36\cancel{0}} \times \dfrac{72^{12}}{1} = 12$

∴ 12 students born in South Australia ✓

iii $\dfrac{^{2}24\cancel{0}}{_{17}36\cancel{0}} \times \dfrac{72^{24}}{1} = 48$

∴ 48 students born in Victoria ✓ (7 marks)

7

Girls		Boys
9	3	
9 6 5 2 0	4	2 2 6 6 7 9
3 3 1	5	8 9
	6	1

✓✓

(2 marks)

DATA ANALYSIS
SKILLS CHECK PAGE 77

1 a census **b** sample
 c census **d** census

2 a No change = 34 + 26 = 60 students

$$= \frac{60}{100} \times \frac{100}{1}\%$$

$$= 60\%$$

b 40 students (20 + 20) want to change

% female $= \dfrac{20}{40} \times \dfrac{100}{1}\% = 50\%$

3 a $\dfrac{4 + 7 + 8 + 4 + 2}{5} = \dfrac{25}{5} = 5$

b $\dfrac{3 + 11 + 14 + 7 + 6 + 7}{6} = \dfrac{48}{6} = 8$

c $\dfrac{0.4 + 2.56 + 3.84 + 4}{4} = \dfrac{10.8}{4} = 2.7$

d $\dfrac{-4 + 7 + 6 + 8 + (-2)}{5} = \dfrac{15}{5} = 3$

4 a Sum of eight scores = 8 × 6 = 48

2 + 5 + 6 + 10 + 15 + 3 + x + 5 = 48

x + 46 = 48

∴ x = 2

b Sum of eight scores = 48

3 + y + 6 + 9 + 2 + (−1) + 4 + 8 = 48

y + 31 = 48

∴ y = 17

5 Placing calculator in STAT mode:

a $\bar{x} = 5.13$ (2 decimal places)

b $\bar{x} = 14.64$ (2 decimal places)

6 Sum of five scores = 5 × 10 = 50

Sum of six scores = 6 × 12 = 72

∴ sixth score = 72 − 50

= 22

∴ the new score is 22

7 a 6, 11, 14, 25, 35

∴ median is 14

b 2, 41, 43, 44, 44, 56, 56, 58, 76, 98

∴ median is middle of 44 and 56

∴ median is 50

8 a Mode = 3

b Mode = 9 and 12

9 a Range = 12 − 2 ∴ 10

b Range = 11 − (−15)

= 11 + 15 ∴ 26

10 Group 1: 5, 5, 6, 7, 6, 7, 5, 7, 6, 6

Using calculator in STAT mode, $\bar{x} = 6$

∴ mean = 6

To find median: 5, 5, 5, 6, 6, 6, 6, 7, 7

Both middle scores are 6

∴ median = 6

The number 6 occurs most often (4 times)

∴ mode = 6

Range = 7 − 5

∴ range = 2

Group 2: 3, 9, 8, 7, 2, 4, 7, 5, 8, 7, 3

Using calculator in STAT mode, $\bar{x} = 6$

∴ mean = 6

To find median: 2, 3, 4, 5, 7, 7, 7, 8, 8, 9

Both middle scores are 7

∴ median = 7

The number 7 occurs most often (3 times)

∴ mode = 7

Range = 9 − 2

∴ range = 7

Therefore:

a The mean of both groups is the same
($\bar{x} = 6$)

b The median of Group 1 (6) is less than the median of Group 2 (7).

c The mode of Group 1 (6) is less than the mode of Group 2 (7).

d The range of Group 1 (2) is less than the range of Group 2 (7).

11 a Range = 9 − 2 = 7

∴ scores are 2, 3, 5, 7, 8, 8, 9

The median is the same as the range

∴ x = 7

b Median = $\dfrac{2 + 4}{2}$ = 3

Range = 3

$5 - x = 3$

$x = 2$

DATA ANALYSIS
INTERMEDIATE TEST   PAGE 78

1 Mean = $\dfrac{4 + 7 + 2 + 8 + 6 + 4 + 3 + 0 + 1 + 5}{10}$

= $\dfrac{40}{10}$

= 4

[use STAT mode on calculator] **B** ✓   (1 mark)

2 For the median to be 6, the scores in order must be
2, 4, x, 10.

Now, the median (6) is middle of 4 and x.

∴ $x = 8$ because the middle of 4 and 8 is 6 **C** ✓
(1 mark)

3 Mode is the most common score.

i.e. the mode is 4 **C** ✓   (1 mark)

4 As the range is 10 and the lowest score is –1,
the highest score is 9.

∴ $y = 9$ **C** ✓   (1 mark)

5 Try each of the alternatives.

Mode of English marks = 68

Mode of science marks = 79

∴ mode of English marks is less than mode of
science marks **D** ✓   (1 mark)

6 **a** Mean = $\dfrac{9 + 6 + 5 + 5 + 2 + 3 + 3}{7}$

= $\dfrac{35}{7}$

= 5 ✓

[use STAT mode on calculator]

b Scores: 2, 3, 5, 5, 5, 6, 9

Median is 5 ✓

c Mode = 5 ✓

d Range = 9 – 2

= 7 ✓   (4 marks)

7 **a** Mean = $\dfrac{4 + 0 + 3 + 5 + 11 + (-3) + 6 + 3 + 5 + 9}{10}$

= $\dfrac{43}{10}$

= 4.3 ✓

[use STAT mode on calculator]

b Scores: –3, 0, 3, 3, 4, 5, 5, 6, 9, 11

Median is the middle of 4 and 5.

∴ median is 4.5 ✓

c Mode = 3 and 5 ✓

d Range = 11 – (–3)

= 14 ✓   (4 marks)

8 Average of 4 tests = 76

Sum of 4 tests = 76 × 4

= 304

Sum of 5 tests = 80 × 5

= 400 ✓

Difference = 400 – 304

= 96

∴ Jo must score 96 in her next test ✓   (2 marks)

9 Mean age = $\dfrac{42 + 42 + 14 + 11 + 6}{5}$

= $\dfrac{115}{5}$

= 23

[use STAT mode on calculator]

∴ mean age is 23 years ✓

Mean height = $\dfrac{176 + 172 + 165 + 158 + 145}{5}$

= $\dfrac{816}{5}$ = 163.2

[use STAT mode on calculator]

∴ mean height is 163.2 cm ✓   (2 marks)

10 **Location:** the mean of the Tigers (166 cm) is lower
than the Eagles' mean (167 cm). The median of the
Tigers (165.5) is lower than the median for the Eagles
(167 cm). The mode of the Tigers (163 cm) is lower
than the mode of the Eagles (164 cm). ✓✓✓

Spread: the range of the Tigers (12 cm) is less than
the range of the Eagles (14 cm). ✓   (4 marks)

DATA ANALYSIS
ADVANCED TEST   PAGE 79

1 Total mass = 52 × 3

= 156 ✓

Len's mass = 156 – (48 + 50)

= 156 – 98

= 58

∴ Len has a mass of 58 kg ✓   (2 marks)

2 Total for 6 months

= 120 000 × 4 + 150 000 + 180 000

= 480 000 + 330 000

= 810 000 ✓

Mean = 810 000 ÷ 6

= 135 000

∴ the mean was $135 000 ✓   (2 marks)

3 The numbers could be 3, 4, 8, 9;
or 3, 5, 7, 9 ✓   (1 mark)

4 The scores are 4, 6, 7, 7 ✓   (1 mark)

WORKED SOLUTIONS

5 **a** 4, 6, 6, **6**, 8, 8, 12

∴ the new score was 6 ✓

b 4, **5**, 6, 6, 8, 8, 12

∴ the new score was 5 ✓

c 4, 6, 6, **7**, 8, 8, 12

∴ the new score was 7 ✓

d **0**, 4, 6, 6, 8, 8, 12

OR: 4, 6, 6, 8, 8, 12, **16**

∴ the new score was 0 or 16 ✓ **(4 marks)**

6 Sum of 5 scores = 9 × 5

= 45 ✓

Sum of 5 scores after change = 11 × 5

= 55

As 55 − 45 = 10, then the score increased by 10 ✓ **(2 marks)**

7 0, 2, 2, 2, 4, 4

a mode unchanged ✓

b median unchanged ✓

c range increases ✓

d mean decreases ✓ **(4 marks)**

8 **a** 4, 6, 6, 9, 10 ✓

b 1, 2, 6, 6, 10 ✓ **(2 marks)**

9 Total in 4 games = 3 × 4

= 12

Total in 5 games = 4 × 5

= 20 ✓

Increase = 20 − 12

= 8

The score in the fifth game was 8:3. ✓ **(2 marks)**

10 **a** **i** Mean = $\dfrac{0.4 + 0.04 + 0.4 + 0.04 + 4 + 0.4}{6}$

= $\dfrac{5.28}{6}$

= 0.88 ✓

ii mode = 0.4 ✓

iii 0.04, 0.04, 0.4, 0.4, 0.4, 4

∴ median is 0.4 ✓

iv range = 4 − 0.04

= 3.96 ✓

b **i** Mean = $(\dfrac{1}{4} + \dfrac{1}{2} + \dfrac{3}{4} + \dfrac{1}{3} + \dfrac{1}{4}) \div 5$

= $\dfrac{3 + 6 + 9 + 4 + 3}{12} \div 5$

= $\dfrac{\overset{5}{25}}{12} \times \dfrac{1}{\underset{1}{5}}$

= $\dfrac{5}{12}$ ✓

ii mode = $\dfrac{1}{4}$ ✓

iii $\dfrac{1}{4}, \dfrac{1}{4}, \dfrac{1}{3}, \dfrac{1}{2}, \dfrac{3}{4}$

∴ median is $\dfrac{1}{3}$ ✓

iv range = $\dfrac{3}{4} - \dfrac{1}{4}$

= $\dfrac{2}{4}$

= $\dfrac{1}{2}$ ✓

c **i** Mean = $\dfrac{4 - 3 + 2 - 1 - 1 + 1 - 2}{7}$

= 0 ✓

ii mode = −1 ✓

iii −3, −2, −1, −1, 1, 2, 4

∴ median is −1 ✓

iv range = 4 − −3

= 7 ✓ **(12 marks)**

11 Mean of 4 scores = 8

Total of 4 scores = 8 × 4

= 32 ✓

Let the new score = x

Mean of 6 scores = 12

Total of 6 scores = 12 × 6

= 72

∴ 32 + 12 + x = 72

x + 44 = 72

x = 72 − 44

= 28

∴ the other new score is 28 ✓ **(2 marks)**

12 One new score is less then the median and the other is more than the median. This means the median remains at 6. ✓ **(1 mark)**

13 Mean of 10 scores = 4

Total of 10 scores = 4 × 10

= 40 ✓

Mean of 12 scores = 8

Total of 12 scores = 8 × 12

= 96

Sum of 2 new scores = 96 − 40

= 56

Mean of 2 new scores = 56 ÷ 2

= 28

∴ the mean of the two scores is 28 ✓ **(2 marks)**

14 If the mean did not change then the mean height of Joshua and Mia is 140.

Total of Joshua and Mia = 140 × 2

= 280 ✓

Height of Mia = 280 − 143

= 137

∴ Mia has a height of 137 cm ✓ **(2 marks)**

WORKED SOLUTIONS

15   Mean of 4 tests $= 70$
Total for 4 tests $= 70 \times 4$
$\qquad\qquad\qquad = 280$ ✓
Mean of 5 tests $= 75$
Total of 5 tests $= 75 \times 5$
$\qquad\qquad\qquad = 375$
Result in 5th test $= 375 - 280$
$\qquad\qquad\qquad\quad = 95$
∴ Sheridan needs to score 95% ✓   **(2 marks)**

16 a   Mean of 6 scores $= 5$
$\qquad$Total of scores $= 6 \times 5$
$\qquad\qquad\qquad\qquad = 30$ ✓
∴ $1 + 3 + 4 + x + 8 + 8 = 30$
$\qquad\qquad\qquad x + 24 = 30$
$\qquad\qquad\qquad\qquad x = 30 - 24$
$\qquad\qquad\qquad\qquad x = 6$ ✓

   b median is 6:
     ∴ middle of 4 and x is 6.
     ∴ $x = 8$ ✓   **(3 marks)**

17 Mean temp. of 5 mornings $= -3$
    Sum temp. of 5 mornings $= -3 \times 5$
$\qquad\qquad\qquad\qquad\qquad = -15$ ✓
    Mean temp. of 6 mornings $= -2$
    Sum temp. of 6 mornings $= -2 \times 6$
$\qquad\qquad\qquad\qquad\qquad = -12$
$\qquad\qquad$Difference $= -12 - {-15}$
$\qquad\qquad\qquad\qquad = -12 + 15$
$\qquad\qquad\qquad\qquad = 3$
∴ the temperature on sixth morning was 3° ✓
               (2 marks)

18 If median is 3 then scores are $x, 3, 4$.
    If range is 3 then scores are $1, 3, 4$. ✓
    This means the missing scores are 1 and 3. ✓ **(2 marks)**

19   Mean age of boys $= 10$
     Total age of boys $= 12 \times 4$
$\qquad\qquad\qquad\qquad = 48$
     Mean age of girls $= 6$
     Total age of girls $= 6 \times 2$
$\qquad\qquad\qquad\qquad = 12$ ✓
    Total age of children $= 60$
    Mean age of children $= 60 \div 6$
$\qquad\qquad\qquad\qquad\qquad = 10$
∴ the mean age is 10 ✓   **(2 marks)**

INTERPRETING DATA
FROM GRAPHS
SKILLS CHECK   PAGE 81

1 **a** Maths quiz results

Score (x)	Frequency (f)	fx
13	1	13
14	1	14
15	2	30
16	5	80
17	7	119
18	6	108
19	5	95
Totals	$\Sigma f = 27$	$\Sigma fx = 459$

  b **i** Mean $= \dfrac{459}{27}$ ∴ 17

     ii Median $= 14$th score ∴ 17
    iii Mode $= 17$
    iv Range $= 19 - 13$ ∴ 6

  c There are $(5 + 2 + 1 + 1)$ results less than 17.
    $\dfrac{9}{27} = \dfrac{1}{3}$ ∴ $\dfrac{1}{3}$ of results are less than 17

  d There are $(6 + 5)$ results greater than 17.
    ∴ probability is $\dfrac{11}{27}$

2 **a**

Score (x)	Frequency (f)	fx
3	7	**21**
5	**7**	35
7	12	**84**
10	**4**	**40**
Totals	$\Sigma f = 30$	$\Sigma fx = 180$

  b **i** Mean $= \dfrac{180}{30}$ ∴ 6

     ii Median $=$ average of 15th and 16th scores. The
        15th and 16th scores are both 7. ∴ 7
    iii Mode $= 7$
    iv Range $= 10 - 3$ ∴ 7

  c There are $(7 + 7)$ scores less than 7. ∴ 14
  d Mean is 6. There are $(12 + 4)$ scores greater than 6.
    Probability $= \dfrac{16}{30} = \dfrac{8}{15}$

    ∴ probability is $\dfrac{8}{15}$

WORKED SOLUTIONS

3 a i Mean = $\dfrac{\text{number of cars}}{\text{number of families}}$

$= \dfrac{(1 \times 4) + (2 \times 7) + (3 \times 5) + (4 \times 3) + (5 \times 1)}{4 + 7 + 5 + 3 + 1}$

$= \dfrac{50}{20} = 2.5$ ∴ mean is 2.5

ii There are 20 scores, so the median will be the average of the 10th and 11th scores. The 10th and 11th scores are both 2. ∴ median = 2

iii Mode = 2

iv Range = 5 – 1 ∴ range is 4

b 5 families own 3 cars and there are 20 families in total, so $= \dfrac{5}{20} = \dfrac{1}{4}$

∴ probability is $\dfrac{1}{4}$

4 a i Mean = $\dfrac{\begin{array}{c}(148 \times 2) + (149 \times 4) + (150 \times 6) \\ + (151 \times 5) + (152 \times 3)\end{array}}{2 + 4 + 6 + 5 + 3}$

$= \dfrac{3003}{20} = 150.15$ ∴ mean is 150.15

ii There are 20 scores, so the median will be the average of the 10th and 11th scores. The 10th and 11th scores are both 150.

∴ median = 150

iii Mode = 150

iv Range = 152 – 148 ∴ range is 4

b 6 packets contain less than 150,

so $= \dfrac{6}{20} \times \dfrac{100}{1}\% = 30\%$

∴ 30% of packets

5 a i Mean = 70.4 [using STAT mode on calculator]

ii Median = 8th score ∴ median = 72

iii Mode = 78

iv Range = 89 – 50 ∴ range is 39

b Mean is 70.4, so seven scores are less than the mean. There are 15 scores in total.

so $= \dfrac{7}{15} \times \dfrac{100}{1}\% = 46.666666\%$

∴ 46.7%

INTERPRETING DATA FROM GRAPHS
INTERMEDIATE TEST   PAGE 82

1 Median, the middle score, is 33.
As range is 33 and the lowest score is 12, then highest score = 33 + 12 = 45
∴ missing digit is 5   **A** ✓   (1 mark)

2

Score (x)	Frequency (f)	fx
2	5	**10**
4	**8**	32
5	**9**	**45**
7	3	**21**
Totals	$\Sigma f = 25$	$\Sigma fx = 108$

By completing the table, the value of y is 45.   **D** ✓
(1 mark)

3

Score	Frequency
x	5
y	8

The median is 6 so y = 6.
As range is 4, then x = 2   **B** ✓   (1 mark)

4

Score (x)	Frequency (f)	fx
21	3	63
22	5	110
23	7	161
24	6	144
25	4	100
Totals	$\Sigma f = 25$	$\Sigma fx = 578$

a Mean $= \dfrac{\Sigma fx}{\Sigma f}$ ✓

$= \dfrac{578}{25}$

$= 23.12$ ✓

b Mode = 23 ✓

c Median: as there are 25 scores we look for the 13th score ($\dfrac{25 + 1}{2}$th score)

i.e. 13th score is 23
∴ median is 23 ✓

d Range = 25 – 21
$= 4$ ✓   (5 marks)

5

Score (x)	Frequency (f)	fx
1	3	3
2	4	8
3	2	6
4	4	16
5	2	10
Totals	$\Sigma f = 15$	$\Sigma fx = 43$

a **i** Mean $= \dfrac{\Sigma fx}{\Sigma f}$ ✓

$= \dfrac{43}{15}$

$= 2.8\dot{6}$

∴ mean = 2.9 ✓

ii Median: as there are 15 scores, the median is the $\dfrac{15+1}{2}$th score—i.e. the 8th score.

Working down the frequency column, the 8th score is 3.

∴ median is 3 ✓

iii Mode = 2 and 4 ✓
[2 and 4 occur most frequently]

iv Range = 5 − 1 = 4
∴ range is 4 ✓

b As there are 3 families with one mobile phone,

Pr(one phone) $= \dfrac{3}{15} = \dfrac{1}{5}$

∴ Probability $= \dfrac{1}{5}$ ✓   (6 marks)

INTERPRETING DATA FROM GRAPHS
ADVANCED TEST   PAGE 83

1 Mode = 70 ✓
range = 91 − 50
= 41 ✓
median = 70 ✓   (3 marks)

2 Mode = 10 ✓
range = 10 − 6
= 4 ✓
median = 9 ✓   (3 marks)

3 Mode = 6 ✓
range = 8 − 2
= 6 ✓
median = 6 ✓

mean
$= \dfrac{2 \times 3 + 3 + 4 + 5 + 6 \times 4 + 7 + 8 \times 2}{13}$

$= \dfrac{65}{13}$

$= 5$ ✓   (4 marks)

4 **a** Mode = 154 ✓
range = 165 − 143
= 22 ✓
median = 152 ✓

b Mode = 150 ✓
range = 161 − 133
= 28 ✓
median = 149 ✓

c Mode = 150 and 154 ✓
range = 165 − 133
= 32 ✓
median = 150 ✓

d Pr(150 cm) $= \dfrac{4}{25}$ ✓   (10 marks)

5 **a** $x < 3$ ✓
b $x > 5$ ✓
c If mean is 4.7, then the frequency of 5 would be less than 5. Try $x = 3$:

Score	Frequency	Score × Freq
4	5	**20**
5	**3**	**15**
6	2	**12**
Total	**10**	**47**

∴ mean = 47 ÷ 10
= 4.7
∴ $x = 3$ ✓   (3 marks)

6 **a** As 69 − 37 = 32, then the value of a is 2. ✓
b Median of 50.5 is halfway between unknown and 52. This means the unknown must be 49.
∴ the value of b is 9. ✓   (2 marks)

7 **a** Total students = 3 + 5 + 5 + 5 + 6 + 3
= 27 ✓
b Total girls = 2 + 3 + 2 + 3 + 2 + 1
= 13 ✓
c 2 boys have 5 mobiles in their homes ✓
d Total mobiles
= 3 × 0 + 5 × 1 + 5 × 2 + 5 × 3 + 6 × 4 + 3 × 5 ✓
= 0 + 5 + 10 + 15 + 24 + 15
= 69 ✓
e **i** 4 ✓
ii 1 and 3 ✓

f **i** For the group:

x	f	fx
0	3	0
1	5	5
2	5	10
3	5	15
4	6	24
5	3	15
Total	**27**	**69**

median is 3 ✓

ii For the girls:

x	f	fx
0	2	0
1	3	3
2	2	4
3	3	9
4	2	8
5	1	5
Total	**13**	**29**

median is 2 ✓

g **i** Mean for group $= \dfrac{69}{27}$

$$= 2\tfrac{5}{9} \checkmark$$

ii Mean for girls $= \dfrac{29}{13}$

$$= 2\tfrac{3}{13} \checkmark \qquad \text{(11 marks)}$$

SAMPLE EXAM PAPER 1
Part A: Multiple Choice **PAGE 85**

1 Multiples of 6: 6, 12, 18, 24, …
Multiples of 8: 8, 16, 24, …
∴ LCM is 24 **C** ✓ (1 mark)

2 $12 - 4 \times 3 = 12 - 12$
$= 0$ **A** ✓ (1 mark)

3 Try each alternative.
$\dfrac{3}{4} = \dfrac{5 \times 3}{5 \times 4}$ **C** ✓ (1 mark)

4 $\dfrac{12}{16} = \dfrac{3}{4}$
∴ the missing value is 3 **C** ✓ (1 mark)

5 $\dfrac{3}{5} - \dfrac{1}{10} = \dfrac{6-1}{10}$
$= \dfrac{5}{10}$
$= \dfrac{1}{2}$ **C** ✓ (1 mark)

6 $\dfrac{3}{4} \times \dfrac{2}{3} = \dfrac{1}{2}$ **A** ✓ (1 mark)

7 $1.76 - 0.40 = 1.36$ **B** ✓ (1 mark)

8 1 line of symmetry **A** ✓ (1 mark)

9 Percentage $= \dfrac{6}{20} \times \dfrac{100}{1}$
$= 30\%$ **D** ✓ (1 mark)

10 Arrange in ascending order:
1, 2, 3, 5, 6, 8, 12
The median is 5 **A** ✓ (1 mark)

SAMPLE EXAM PAPER 1
Part B: Short Answer **PAGE 86**

11 The mode (most common score) is 3. ✓ (1 mark)

12 As 90 − 72 = 18, then the complement is 18°. ✓ (1 mark)

13 360 820 ✓ (1 mark)

14 $12 \div 4 \times 2 = 6$ ✓ (1 mark)

15 As $2\tfrac{1}{2} = \dfrac{5}{2}$, the reciprocal is $\dfrac{2}{5}$ ✓ (1 mark)

16 4 out of 16 shaded
i.e. $\dfrac{4}{16} = \dfrac{1}{4}$ ✓ (1 mark)

17 $2 - 1\tfrac{3}{5} = 1 - \dfrac{3}{5}$
$= \dfrac{2}{5}$ ✓ (1 mark)

18 $\dfrac{1}{2} + \dfrac{1}{4} + \dfrac{1}{8} = \dfrac{4+2+1}{8}$
$= \dfrac{7}{8}$ ✓ (1 mark)

19 $4 + 0.7 + 0.002 + 0.00005 = 4.70205$ ✓ (1 mark)

20 ![number line with X at 2.47 between 2 and 3] ✓ (1 mark)

21 $3.200 - 1.047 = 2.153$ ✓ (1 mark)

22 $4.8 \div 0.006 = 4800 \div 6$
$= 800$ ✓ (1 mark)

23 $(-4) - 2 + 6 = 0$ ✓ (1 mark)

24 6, 3, 0, −1, −12 ✓ (1 mark)

25 $7 \times a \times a \times b \times b \times b$ ✓ (1 mark)

26 $y = x - 1$ ✓ (1 mark)

27 $4x - 3x + 2x = 3x$ ✓ (1 mark)

28 $4:14 = 2:7$ ✓ (1 mark)

29 $-2 - (-3) = -2 + 3$
$\qquad = 1$ ✓ (1 mark)

30 $2x - 1 = 7$
i.e. 2 times a number minus 1 equals 7
∴ the number is 4
∴ $x = 4$ ✓ (1 mark)

31 Perimeter $= 12.2 \times 6$
$\qquad = 73.2$
∴ perimeter is 73.2 cm ✓ (1 mark)

32 Range $= 11 - 2$
$\qquad = 9$ ✓ (1 mark)

33 $-1 - 4 = -5$
∴ -5 is 4 units to the left of -1. ✓ (1 mark)

34 Area $= 1.2 \times 0.7$
$\qquad = 0.84$
∴ area is 0.84 cm^2 ✓ (1 mark)

35 1 m = 100 cm,
Area $= 100 \times 45$
$\qquad = 4500$
∴ area is 4500 cm^2 ✓ (1 mark)

36 Area $= \frac{1}{2} \times 16 \times 8$
$\qquad = 64$
∴ area is 64 cm^2 ✓ (1 mark)

37 Total $= 600 \times 24$
$\qquad = 14\,400$
∴ 14 400 mL   i.e. 14.4 L ✓ (1 mark)

38 $x = 180 - 21$
$\qquad = 59$ ✓ (1 mark)

39 Size $= 360 - (120 + 40 + 70)$
$\qquad = 360 - 230$
$\qquad = 130$
∴ the angle is 130°. ✓ (1 mark)

40 Number not played centre = 2
Percentage $= \frac{2}{8} \times \frac{100}{1}$
$\qquad = 25\%$
∴ 25% of the team have not played centre. ✓ (1 mark)

SAMPLE EXAM PAPER 1
Part C PAGE 87

41 84 ✓   ∴ $84 = 2 \times 2 \times 3 \times 7$ ✓ (2 marks)
7   12
4   3
2   2

42 Peter: 4, 8, 12, …
Paul: 6, 12, … ✓
As LCM is 12, they hiccup again after 12 s ✓ (2 marks)

43 $15 \div 5 + 3 \times 7 = 3 + 21$ ✓
$\qquad = 24$ ✓ (2 marks)

44 Total parts $= 2 + 3$
$\qquad = 5$ ✓
Shorter length $= \frac{2}{5} \times \frac{100}{1} = 4$
∴ the shorter length is 4 metres ✓ (2 marks)

45 $\frac{12}{15} = \frac{x}{10}$
As $\frac{12}{15} = \frac{4}{5} = \frac{8}{10}$ ✓   ∴ $x = 8$ ✓ (2 marks)

46 Rewriting in cents:
$\frac{360}{1000} = \frac{9}{25}$ ✓✓ (2 marks)

47 $2\frac{1}{2} + 3\frac{1}{3} = 5 + \frac{3+2}{6}$ ✓
$\qquad = 5\frac{5}{6}$ ✓ (2 marks)

48 $\frac{4}{5} + \frac{2}{3} \times \frac{3}{5} = \frac{4}{5} + \frac{2}{5}$ ✓
$\qquad = \frac{6}{5}$
$\qquad = 1\frac{1}{5}$ ✓ (2 marks)

49 $2\frac{1}{2} \times 2\frac{1}{2} = \frac{5}{2} \times \frac{5}{2}$ ✓
$\qquad = \frac{25}{4}$
$\qquad = 6\frac{1}{4}$ ✓ (2 marks)

50 Cost $= 14 \times 3\frac{1}{2}$ ✓
$\qquad = 7 \times 7$ [shortcut]
$\qquad = 49$
∴ cost is $49 ✓ (2 marks)

51 $9)\overline{7.000\,00\ldots}$ $0.777\,77\ldots$ ∴ $0.\dot{7}$ ✓✓ (2 marks)

52 $0.4 + 1.6 \div 4 = 0.4 + 0.4$
$\qquad = 0.8$ ✓✓ (2 marks)

53 Average = $\dfrac{7.5 + 8 + 6.5 + 7.5 + 8}{5}$ ✓

   $= \dfrac{37.5}{5}$

   $= 7.5$

   ∴ Rhonda's average was 7.5 per judge ✓   (2 marks)

54 Area = 4.5×2.5 ✓

   $= 11.25$

   ∴ area is 11.25 m² ✓   (2 marks)

55 **a** Number = $15 - (4 + 3)$

   $= 15 - 7$

   $= 8$ ✓

   b Probability = $\dfrac{8}{15}$ ✓   (2 marks)

56 $0.16 \times 40 = 6.40$ ✓

   ∴ $6.40 ✓   (2 marks)

57 $x = 75$ ✓

   and $y = 75$ ✓   (2 marks)

58 **a**

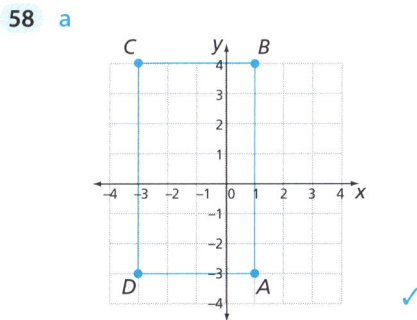

   ✓

   b rectangle ✓   (2 marks)

59 $4a \times 3 - 18a \div 6 = 12a - 3a$ ✓

   $= 9a$ ✓   (2 marks)

60 $(14 \div 7) \times 3 + 4 \times 2 = 2 \times 3 + 8$ ✓

   $= 6 + 8$

   $= 14$ ✓   (2 marks)

61 **a** $4x = 24$ ✓

   b $\dfrac{4x}{4} = \dfrac{24}{4}$ ∴ $x = 6$ ✓   (2 marks)

62 **a** Mandarins ✓

   b 3 cm out of 10 cm = 30 students out of 100

   ∴ 30 students ✓   (2 marks)

63 **a** Cost = $55 + $36

   $= $91

   [Note: Jarod was free, 4 years old]

   ∴ admission cost is $91 ✓

   b Cost of 2 adults and 2 children

   $= $55 + $55 + $36 + $36

   $= $182

   Saving = $182 - $165

   $= $17 ✓   (2 marks)

64 $P = 2(15.5 + 10.5)$

   $= 52$ ✓

   Cost = $52 \times $9

   $= $468

   ∴ fencing costs $468 ✓   (2 marks)

65 **a** $26 - 8 = 18$ ✓

   b 15 ✓   (2 marks)

66

Score (x)	Frequency (f)	fx
14	2	**28**
15	3	**45**
16	5	**80**
Totals	$\Sigma f = \mathbf{10}$	$\Sigma fx = \mathbf{153}$

✓✓

   (2 marks)

67 Mean = $\dfrac{153}{10}$ ✓

   $= 15.3$ ✓   (2 marks)

68 New price = $189.00 - $69.50 ✓

   $= $119.50 ✓   (2 marks)

69 $x = 180 - 125$

   $= 55$ ✓

   $y = 180 - 2 \times 55$

   $= 70$ ✓   (2 marks)

70 100 g: $2.20 per 100 g

   200 g: $2.05 per 100 g

   400 g: $2.00 per 100 g ✓

   500 g: $2.04 per 100 g

   ∴ best buy is 400 g packet ✓   (2 marks)

SAMPLE EXAM PAPER 2
Part A: Multiple Choice   PAGE 90

1 Try each alternative.

   $10 + 2 \div 2 = 10 + 1$

   $\ne 6$ **C** ✓   (1 mark)

2 $\dfrac{2}{3} = \dfrac{4}{6}$ **A** ✓ (1 mark)

3 As $5\overline{)3.0}^{\,0.6}$ then $\dfrac{3}{5} = 0.6$ **D** ✓   (1 mark)

4 Try each alternative.

   i.e. $1.674 = 1.67$ (corr. to 2 dec. pl.)   **D** ✓   (1 mark)

5 $1.6 \times 0.04 = 0.064$ **A** ✓   (1 mark)

6 From the table $y = 3x - 1$ **B** ✓   (1 mark)

7 $30a \div 3 + 2 \times 2a = 10a + 4a$

   $= 14a$ **B** ✓   (1 mark)

8 Perimeter = 16 mm
∴ side = 4 mm
Area = 4 × 4
= 16
∴ area is 16 mm² **C** ✓ (1 mark)

9 From diagram:
$a = 75$ (corr. ∠s, ∥ lines)
$b = 75$ (vert. opp. ∠s) **A** ✓ (1 mark)

10 As 180 − 64 = 116,
then the supplement of 64° is 116° **C** ✓ (1 mark)

SAMPLE EXAM PAPER 2
Part B: Short Answer PAGE 91

11 If divisible by 6 then also divisible by 2 and 3; 47 644
is divisible by 2, but as 4 + 7 + 6 + 4 + 4 = 25, which is
not divisible by 3, therefore not divisible by 6.
∴ false ✓ (1 mark)

12 $12 + 5 \le 2 \times 11$ ✓ (1 mark)

13 23 × 47 + 77 × 47 = 47 × (23 + 77)
= 47 × 100
= 4700 ✓ (1 mark)

14 Rewriting in cents:
$\dfrac{40}{240} = \dfrac{1}{6}$ ✓ (1 mark)

15 $\dfrac{56}{70} = \dfrac{14 \times 4}{14 \times 5}$
$= \dfrac{4}{5}$
$= \dfrac{4}{x}$ ∴ x = 5 ✓ (1 mark)

16 $\dfrac{3}{5} \times \dfrac{30}{1} = 18$ ∴ $18 ✓ (1 mark)

17 $8\overline{)1.000}$ ∴ $\dfrac{1}{8} = 0.125$ ✓ (1 mark)
0.125

18 0.02 × y = 8
y = 8 ÷ 0.02
= 800 ÷ 2
= 400 ∴ y = 400 ✓ (1 mark)

19 47.62 × 100 = 4762 ✓ (1 mark)

20 $\sqrt{9} \times \sqrt{36} \times \sqrt{4} = 3 \times 6 \times 2$
= 36 ✓ (1 mark)

21 9 − (−3) = 9 + 3
= 12 ∴ 12° ✓ (1 mark)

22 $3y^2 = 3 \times 4 \times 4$
= 48 ✓ (1 mark)

23 $\dfrac{4p}{q} = \dfrac{4 \times 0.6}{1.2}$
$= \dfrac{2.4}{1.2}$
$= \dfrac{24}{12}$
= 2 ✓ (1 mark)

24 $4a - 2b - 3a + 6b = a + 4b$ ✓ (1 mark)

25 $3a \times 2b - 4ab \times 5 = 6ab - 20ab$
$= -14ab$ ✓ (1 mark)

26 x = 120 − 75
= 45 ✓ (1 mark)

27 $2 : $2.40 = 200 : 240
= 20 : 24
= 5 : 6 ✓ (1 mark)

28 Range = 6 − (−3)
= 6 + 3
= 9 ✓ (1 mark)

29 0.15 × 600 = 90 ∴ 90 cm ✓ (1 mark)

30 Using 2 metres = 200 cm,
Area = 200 × 40
= 8000
∴ 8000 cm² ✓ (1 mark)

31 Mean = $\dfrac{3 + 7 + 4 + 2 + 8 + 12}{6}$
$= \dfrac{36}{6}$
= 6
∴ the mean is 6 ✓ (1 mark)

32 Volume = 4^3 = 64
∴ volume is 64 cm³ ✓ (1 mark)

33 Area = $\dfrac{1}{2} \times 120 \times 40 = 2400$
∴ the area is 2400 cm² ✓ (1 mark)

34 b − a = (−7) − (−2)
= −7 + 2
= −5 ✓ (1 mark)

35 As 2 L = 2000 mL
then 240 ÷ 2000 = 0.12 c/mL ✓
i.e. $2000\overline{)240.00}$ (1 mark)
0.12

36

x = 360 − (60 + 110 + 72)
= 360 − 242
= 118 ✓ (1 mark)

37 As $5 \times 60 = 300$ seconds, then

percentage $= \dfrac{30}{300} \times 100$

$= \dfrac{1}{10} \times 100$

$= 10$ ∴ 10% ✓ (1 mark)

38 7 odd numbers out of 12

∴ $Pr(\text{odd number}) = \dfrac{7}{12}$ ✓ (1 mark)

39 0.21, $18\% = 0.18$, $\dfrac{1}{20} = 0.05$, $\dfrac{1}{5} = 0.20$,

$3\% = 0.03$

∴ order is 3%, $\dfrac{1}{20}$, 18%, $\dfrac{1}{5}$, 0.21

∴ middle is 18% ✓ (1 mark)

40 3 lines of symmetry ✓ (1 mark)

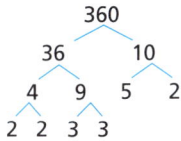

SAMPLE EXAM PAPER 2
Part C PAGE 92

41   360 ✓   ∴ $360 = 2^3 \times 3^2 \times 5$ ✓

36   10   (2 marks)

4 9   5   2

2 2   3   3

42 a 23, 29 ✓

b 46, 48, 49, 50, 51, 52, 54 ✓ (2 marks)

43 $\dfrac{30 \times 4}{4 + 6} = \dfrac{120}{10}$ ✓

$= 12$ ✓ (2 marks)

44 $2x + 1 = 7$

$2x + 1 - 1 = 7 - 1$

$2x = 6$ ✓

$\dfrac{2x}{2} = \dfrac{6}{2}$

$x = 3$ ✓ (2 marks)

45 Profit $= \$800 - \$600$

$= \$200$ ✓

∴ $\dfrac{200}{600} = \dfrac{1}{3}$ ✓ (2 marks)

46 $\dfrac{10 \times 8 \times 6 \times 4}{20 \times 16 \times 3 \times 2} = 1$ ✓✓ (2 marks)

47 $1 - \left(\dfrac{1}{5} + \dfrac{3}{8} + \dfrac{1}{4} \right) = 1 - \dfrac{8 + 15 + 10}{40}$ ✓

$= 1 - \dfrac{33}{40}$

$= \dfrac{7}{40}$

∴ $\dfrac{7}{40}$ of congregation are females aged under 30 ✓

(2 marks)

48 $3\dfrac{2}{3} - 1\dfrac{1}{4} = 2 + \dfrac{8 - 3}{12}$ ✓

$= 2\dfrac{5}{12}$ ✓ (2 marks)

49 $1\dfrac{3}{4} \div \dfrac{9}{10} = \dfrac{7}{4} \times \dfrac{10}{9}$ ✓

$= \dfrac{35}{18}$

$= 1\dfrac{17}{18}$ ✓ (2 marks)

50 Reciprocal of $2\dfrac{1}{4}$ is $\dfrac{4}{9}$.

∴ $2\dfrac{1}{4} \times \dfrac{4}{9} = \dfrac{9}{4} \times \dfrac{4}{9}$ ✓

$= 1$ ✓ (2 marks)

51 Number $= \dfrac{3}{5} \times \dfrac{1}{2} \times \dfrac{30}{1}$ ✓

$= 9$

∴ 9 blond girls in 7P ✓ (2 marks)

52 $11\overline{)4.0000\ldots}^{\,0.3636\ldots}$ ∴ $\dfrac{4}{11} = 0.\dot{3}\dot{6}$ ✓✓ (2 marks)

53 As decimals:

$\dfrac{3}{5} = 0.6$, $0.\dot{6} = 0.6666\ldots$, $\dfrac{29}{50} = 0.58$, $\dfrac{14}{25} = 0.56$ ✓

∴ $\dfrac{14}{25}$, $\dfrac{29}{50}$, $\dfrac{3}{5}$, $0.\dot{6}$ ✓ (2 marks)

54 $(1.2)^2 - (0.5)^2 = 1.2 \times 1.2 - 0.5 \times 0.5$ ✓

$= 1.44 - 0.25$

$= 1.19$ ✓ (2 marks)

55 Number $= 8 \div 1.4$ ✓

$= 80 \div 14$

$= 40 \div 7$ [shortcut]

$= 5\dfrac{5}{7}$ ∴ 5 shirts can be made ✓ (2 marks)

56 Cost $= 1.622 \times 30$ ✓

$= 48.66$

∴ Lisa pays $48.66 ✓ (2 marks)

57 a First 2 hours he drove 60 km, then back 60 km.
From 2 pm to 3 pm he drove 100 km, then after
a rest he drove the last 20 km.
Total $= 60 + 60 + 100 + 20$

$= 240$

∴ 240 km ✓

b Steepest section of graph is between
12 pm and 1 pm. ✓ (2 marks)

58 $2x - k = 5$

If $x = 3$ is a solution we substitute:

$2 \times 3 - k = 5$ ✓

$6 - k = 5$

$k = 1$ ✓ (2 marks)

59 a $b = 2a + 3$ ✓

b $p = 2 \times 10 + 3$
   $= 20 + 3$
   $= 23$ ✓ (2 marks)

60 $15ab \div 5a + 3 \times 4b = 3b + 12b$ ✓
   $= 15b$ ✓ (2 marks)

61

12 cm
10 cm
12 cm   6 cm

Area $= 12 \times 10 + \dfrac{1}{2} \times 6 \times 10$ ✓

   $= 120 + 30$
   $= 150$
∴ 150 cm^2 ✓ (2 marks)

62 D is 5 units to the right of $A(0, -2)$ ✓
   ∴ $D(5, -2)$ ✓ (2 marks)

63 **a** Students $= 2 + 4 + 5 + 3 + 4$
         $= 18$ ✓
   b Range $= 11 - 7$
         $= 4$ ✓ (2 marks)

64 **a** 5 out of $6 = \dfrac{5}{6}$ ✓

   b Prime numbers 2, 3, 5
         3 out of $6 = \dfrac{1}{2}$ ✓ (2 marks)

65 **a** Mode $= 1$ ✓
   b Median $= 1$ ✓ (2 marks)

66 Dimensions of inside rectangle are
   12 m by 4 m.
   Area of shaded region $= 12 \times 4$ ✓
                $= 48$
   ∴ shaded area is 48 m^2 ✓ (2 marks)

67 **a** Pattern is subtracting 3.
         ∴ $2 - 3 = -1$ ✓
   b Pattern is subtracting 0.15
         ∴ $1.10 - 0.15 = 0.95$ ✓ (2 marks)

68

A
70°
70°   40°   140°
B   C   D

$\angle ACB = 40°$ (straight $\angle$) ✓
$\angle CBA = 70°$ (base $\angle$s of isos. $\triangle$) ✓
∴ $x = 70$ (2 marks)

69 As 2 L = 2000 mL,
   Remainder $= 2000 - 300$
         $= 1700$ ✓
   Percentage $= \dfrac{1700}{2000} \times \dfrac{100}{1}$

         $= 85\%$ ✓ (2 marks)

70 **a** Students $= 2 + 4 + 1 + 2$
         $= 9$ ✓
   b Marks were 7, 7, 8, 8, 8, 8, 9, 10, 10
      The median is 8 ✓ (2 marks)

SAMPLE EXAM PAPER 3
Part A: Multiple Choice   PAGE 96

1 Try each of the alternatives.
   As 342 is divisible by 2 and 3, it is divisible
   by 6. i.e. 342 has a factor 6   **C** ✓ (1 mark)

2 $\dfrac{3}{5} \div \dfrac{3}{4} = \dfrac{3}{5} \times \dfrac{4}{3}$

      $= \dfrac{4}{5}$ **B** ✓ (1 mark)

3 Try each of the alternatives.
   Rewrite each with a denominator of 12.
   $\dfrac{1}{2} = \dfrac{6}{12}, \dfrac{2}{3} = \dfrac{8}{12}, \dfrac{3}{4} = \dfrac{9}{12}$ **A** ✓ (1 mark)

4

0        $\frac{1}{2}$ X 1

As X has to be greater than $\dfrac{3}{4}$, check each of the

alternatives. All except $\dfrac{4}{5}$ are smaller.

i.e. $\dfrac{4}{5} = 0.8$ and $\dfrac{3}{4} = 0.75$ **C** ✓ (1 mark)

5 Try each of the alternatives.
   $0.6 \div 2 = 0.3$ **D** ✓ (1 mark)

6 Subtracting 3   i.e. $2 - 3 = -1$ **C** ✓ (1 mark)

7 $-3 - (-1) = -3 + 1$
      $= -2$ **A** ✓ (1 mark)

8 Try each of the alternatives.
   i.e. $ab - 2 = 3 \times 4 - 2$
         $= 12 - 2$
         $= 10$ **D** ✓ (1 mark)

9 Try each of the alternatives.
   $y = 3 - x$
   $b = 3 - (-2)$
      $= 3 + 2$
      $= 5$ **B** ✓ (1 mark)

10

80°
50°   50°   130°

Base angles are each 50°.
∴ $x = 80$ **C** ✓ (1 mark)

WORKED SOLUTIONS

SAMPLE EXAM PAPER 3
Part B: Short Answer   PAGE 97

11 Multiples of 4: ..., 116, 120, 124, ...
Multiples of 5: ..., 115, 120, 125, ...
Multiples of 6: ..., 114, 120, 126, ...
∴ the number is 120 ✓ (1 mark)

12 Volume = $1.2 × 0.8 × 0.4$
$= 0.96 × 0.4$
$= 0.384$
∴ volume is 0.384 cm^3 ✓ (1 mark)

13 $\sqrt[3]{7+9} \neq (9-4)^2$ ✓ (1 mark)

14 $14 - [(2 + 7) ÷ 3 + 4] = 7$ ✓ (1 mark)

15 Halfway is similar to the average.
∴ $\left(\dfrac{1}{3} + \dfrac{1}{2}\right) ÷ 2 = \dfrac{2+3}{6} ÷ \dfrac{2}{1}$
$= \dfrac{5}{6} × \dfrac{1}{2}$
$= \dfrac{5}{12}$ ✓ (1 mark)

16 $\dfrac{4}{5} + \dfrac{3}{4} = \dfrac{16 + 15}{20}$
$= \dfrac{31}{20}$
$= 1\dfrac{11}{20}$ ✓ (1 mark)

17 $\dfrac{4}{5} = 0.8,\ 0.73,\ 0.728,\ \dfrac{2}{3} = 0.\dot{6}$
∴ $\dfrac{2}{3},\ 0.728,\ 0.73,\ \dfrac{4}{5}$ ✓ (1 mark)

18 $\dfrac{4.5 + 1.5}{0.3} = \dfrac{6}{0.3}$
$= \dfrac{60}{3}$
$= 20$ ✓ (1 mark)

19 $(1 - 0.4)^2 = 0.6^2$
$= 0.6 × 0.6$
$= 0.36$ ✓ (1 mark)

20 Let the unknown temperature be x.
As the average temperature is $0\,°C$, then the sum of the three temperatures is also $0\,°C$.
i.e. $-4 + 1 + x = 0$
$-3 + x = 0$
$x = 3$
∴ temperature on Wednesday was $3\,°C$ ✓ (1 mark)

21 $a^2 + b^2 = 4^2 + 3^2$
$= 16 + 9$
$= 25$ ✓ (1 mark)

22 Cost $= p × d$
$= pd$
i.e. cost is $\$pd$
∴ Change $= m - pd$
i.e. change is $\$(m - pd)$ ✓ (1 mark)

23 Area $= \dfrac{1}{2} × 7a × 4a$
$= 14a^2$
∴ area is $14a^2$ cm^2 ✓ (1 mark)

24 $4a^2 - (4a)^2 = 4a^2 - 16a^2$
$= -12a^2$ ✓ (1 mark)

25

∠$BCD = 50°$
Here is the proof:
∠$BDE = 130°$ (opp. ∠s of parallelogram)
∠$BDC = 50°$ (∠s in a straight line)
As $BD = BC$ (given)
∠$BCD = ∠BDC$ (base ∠s of isos. Δ)
∴ ∠$BCD = 50°$ ✓ (1 mark)

26 Let the number be x.
$5(x + 2) = 15$
$5x + 10 = 15$
$5x = 5$
$x = 1$
∴ the number is 1 ✓ (1 mark)

27 Length $= 4 - (-2) = 6$
Breadth $= 3 - (-2) = 5$
Perimeter $= 2(6 + 5)$
$= 22$
∴ perimeter is 22 units ✓ (1 mark)

28 As 1000 mm $= 1$ m and
1000 m $= 1$ km then
$1\,000\,000$ mm $= 1$ km
i.e. in y km, $1\,000\,000 × y = 1\,000\,000y$
∴ y km $= 1\,000\,000y$ mm ✓ (1 mark)

29 Total distance $= 240 + 160$
$= 400$
Amount of petrol $= 400 ÷ 100 × 9$
$= 36$
Cost $= \$1.50 × 36$
$= \$3 × 18$ [shortcut]
$= \$54$ ✓ (1 mark)

30 $(1\text{ min }12\text{ s}) × 10 = 10$ min 120 s
$= 12$ min ✓ (1 mark)

31 Area $= \dfrac{1}{2} × 6 × 3$
$= 9$
∴ area is 9 m^2 ✓ (1 mark)

WORKED SOLUTIONS

32 Volume = 125
Side length = $\sqrt[3]{125}$ = 5
Area of face = 5 × 5 = 25
∴ area of square face is 25 cm^2 ✓ (1 mark)

33 $2x + 90 + 138 = 360$
$2x + 228 = 360$
$2x = 132$
$x = 66$ ✓ (1 mark)

34 A drip every 4 seconds = 15 drips per minute
Loss = 0.25 × 15 × 60
= 225
∴ water loss is 225 mL in an hour ✓ (1 mark)

35 $12 - (-1 - (-4)) = 12 - (-1 + 4)$
$= 12 - 3$
$= 9$ ✓ (1 mark)

36 The missing number is 8 because the 2 middle numbers must be 52 and 58 if the median is 55. ✓ (1 mark)

37 $\angle AGE = 110°$
∴ $\angle BGH = 110°$ (vertically opp. ∠s)
Now $\angle BGH$ and $\angle DHF$ are corresp. ∠s
∴ $\angle BGH = \angle DHF$ if $AB \parallel CD$
∴ $\angle DHF = 110°$ ✓ (1 mark)

38 $\dfrac{4}{x} = 2$
$x \times \dfrac{4}{x} = 2 \times x$
$4 = 2x$
$2x = 4$
$\dfrac{2x}{2} = \dfrac{4}{2}$
$x = 2$ ✓ (1 mark)

39 Area = 20 × 18
= 360
∴ the area is 360 m^2
Cost = 360 ÷ 10 × 0.40
= 36 × 0.4
= 14.4
∴ the cost is $14.40 ✓ (1 mark)

40 Area of small Δ = $\dfrac{1}{2}$ × 2 × 2
= 2
Area of large Δ = $\dfrac{1}{2}$ × 4 × 4
= 8
Percentage = $\dfrac{2}{8}$ × 100%
= 25% ✓ (1 mark)

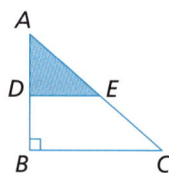

SAMPLE EXAM PAPER 3
Part C PAGE 99

41 784 ✓ $784 = 2 × 2 × 2 × 2 × 7 × 7$
8   98 $= 2^2 × 2^2 × 7^2$
4 2 49 2 ∴ $\sqrt{784} = 4 × 7 = 28$ ✓
2 2   7   7 (2 marks)

42 Mean of 4 scores = 16
Sum of 4 scores = 16 × 4
= 64 ✓
Mean of 5 scores = 18
Sum of 5 scores = 18 × 5
= 90
Added score = 90 − 64
= 26
∴ new score is 26 ✓ (2 marks)

43 $3^2 + 4 × 5 - 3 = 9 + 20 - 3$ ✓
= 26 ✓ (2 marks)

44 Cost price = 6.50 − 1.50
= 5.00 ✓
∴ Fraction = $\dfrac{150}{500}$
= $\dfrac{3}{10}$ ✓ (2 marks)

45 $39\frac{11}{24}$ ✓ ∴ $947 = 39 × 24 + 11$ ✓
24)947
72
227
216
11 (2 marks)

46 Difference in parts = 5 − 3
= 2
2 parts = 8
1 part = 4
8 parts = 32
∴ there is a total of 32 on the tram ✓
Women = $\dfrac{5}{8}$ × 32
= 20
∴ 20 women on the tram ✓ (2 marks)

47 $9300 ÷ 200 = 93 ÷ 2$ ✓
= 46.5 ✓ (2 marks)

48 15 squares unshaded
∴ $\dfrac{2}{3}$ × 15 = 10 ✓
i.e. 10 more squares shaded
Unshaded = 18 − (3 + 10)
= 5
∴ $\dfrac{5}{18}$ is unshaded ✓ (2 marks)

158 *Excel* SMARTSTUDY YEAR 7 MATHEMATICS

WORKED SOLUTIONS

49 $2\frac{1}{4} - 1\frac{3}{5} = 1 + \frac{1}{4} - \frac{3}{5}$

$= 1 + \frac{5 - 12}{20}$

$= 1 + \frac{-7}{20}$ ✓

$= 1 - \frac{7}{20}$

$= \frac{13}{20}$ ✓ (2 marks)

50 Cost/kg $= 15 \div 2\frac{1}{2}$ ✓

$= 30 \div 5$ [shortcut]

$= 6$

∴ cheese costs $6 for one kg ✓ (2 marks)

51 $3\frac{1}{2} \div 2\frac{1}{3} = \frac{7}{2} \div \frac{7}{3}$ ✓

$= \frac{7}{2} \times \frac{3}{7}$

$= 1\frac{1}{2}$ ✓ (2 marks)

52 $\left(\frac{4}{5} + \frac{1}{2}\right) \div \left(\frac{4}{5} - \frac{1}{2}\right) = \frac{8 + 5}{10} \div \frac{8 - 5}{10}$ ✓

$= \frac{13}{10} \div \frac{3}{10}$

$= \frac{13}{10} \times \frac{10}{3}$

$= \frac{13}{3}$

$= 4\frac{1}{3}$ ✓ (2 marks)

53 Three-quarters of height $= 12$

One-quarter of height $= 12 \div 3$

$= 4$ ✓

Four-quarters of height $= 4 \times 4$

$= 16$

∴ final height is 16 m ✓ (2 marks)

54 $99\overline{)26.000\,00\ldots}$ = 0.262\,62\ldots$ ✓ ∴ $\frac{26}{99} = 0.\dot{2}\dot{6}$ ✓ (2 marks)

55 Paint for 7 rooms $= 14.4 \div 4 \times 7$ ✓

$= 3.6 \times 7$

$= 25.2$

∴ 25.2 L of paint required ✓ (2 marks)

56 $(0.21 \div 0.7)^2 = (2.1 \div 7)^2$ ✓

$= 0.3^2$

$= 0.3 \times 0.3$

$= 0.09$ ✓ (2 marks)

57 $(4.85 \times 10^3) \div (0.5 \times 10^2) = 4850 \div 50$

$= 485 \div 5$

$= 97$ ✓✓ (2 marks)

58 $4, 6, x, y$

If range is 8, then $y = 12$

∴ $4, 6, x, 12$

If median is 8, then 8 is in the middle of 6 and x. This means $x = 10$.

∴ $4, 6, 10, 12$ are the scores. ✓

Mean $= \frac{4 + 6 + 10 + 12}{4}$

$= \frac{32}{4}$

$= 8$ ✓ (2 marks)

59 Suppose existing youth group is 20 boys and 30 girls. On the special night, there would be 60 boys and 60 girls.

∴ boys : girls = 1:1 ✓✓ (2 marks)

60 $\frac{5^2 - 2^2 - 1^2}{\sqrt{3^2 + 4^2}} = \frac{25 - 4 - 1}{\sqrt{9 + 16}}$ ✓

$= \frac{20}{\sqrt{25}}$

$= \frac{20}{5}$

$= 4$ ✓ (2 marks)

61 Larry needs to make 2 cuts to make 3 pieces and 5 cuts to make six pieces.

Minutes for 2 cuts $= 6$

Minutes for 1 cut $= 3$

Minutes for 5 cuts $= 15$

∴ 15 minutes for 6 pieces ✓✓ (2 marks)

62 Fraction of children $= 1 - \left(\frac{3}{8} + \frac{1}{3}\right)$

$= 1 - \left(\frac{9 + 8}{24}\right)$

$= 1 - \frac{17}{24}$

$= \frac{7}{24}$ ✓

Number of children $= \frac{7}{24} \times 2400$

$= 700$

∴ 700 children on ship ✓ (2 marks)

63 **a**

People (p)	2	3	4	5	✓
Handshakes (h)	1	3	6	10	

b triangular numbers ✓ (2 marks)

64 **a** The numbers are $x, x + 2, x + 4$

∴ $x + x + 2 + x + 4 = 27$

$3x + 6 = 27$ ✓

b $3x + 6 - 6 = 27 - 6$

$3x = 21$

$x = 7$

∴ $7, 9, 11$ ✓ (2 marks)

65 **a** mathematics ✓

b Average $= \dfrac{60 + 85 + 70 + 65}{4}$

$= \dfrac{280}{4}$

$= 70$

∴ average of the results is 70 ✓ (2 marks)

66 Perimeter $= 2 \times (\text{length} + \text{width})$

$26 = 2 \times (8 + \text{width})$

$13 - 8 = 8 + \text{width} - 8$

$\text{width} = 5$ ✓

Old dimensions were 8 cm by 5 cm.

New dimensions are 16 cm by 10 cm.

New area $= 16 \times 10$

$= 160$

∴ area is 160 cm^2 ✓ (2 marks)

67 Three-eighths cannot swim means five-eighths can swim.

Difference $= \dfrac{5}{8} - \dfrac{3}{8}$

$= \dfrac{2}{8}$

$= \dfrac{1}{4}$ ✓

One-quarter of group $= 8$

Four-quarters of group $= 8 \times 4$

$= 32$

∴ there are 32 students in the group ✓ (2 marks)

68 Use a table to help with your solution:

folder	$1.20	1
ruler	$0.60	2
pencil	$0.30	1

Cost $= \$1.20 + \$0.60 \times 2 + \$0.30$

$= \$2.70$ ✓

Change $= \$10 - \$2.70$

$= \$7.30$

∴ Sam's change is $7.30 ✓ (2 marks)

69 Discount of 40% means Bob is paying only 60% of the usual amount.

60% of cost $= \$720$

10% of cost $= \$720 \div 6$

$= \$120$

100% of cost $= \$120 \times 10$

$= \$1200$

∴ Bob would have to pay $1200 ✓✓ (2 marks)

70 **a** $C = 3t + 40$ ✓

b $115 = 3t + 40$

$3t + 40 = 115$

$3t = 115 - 40$

$3t = 75$

$\dfrac{3t}{3} = \dfrac{75}{3}$

$t = 25$

∴ 25 minutes ✓ (2 marks)

Transfer your **percentage score** that you calculated in the **Your Feedback** box at the end of each **test** and **exam** to the table below. This will help you work out your areas of strength and weakness.

Test Topic	Intermediate Test Score	Advanced Test Score
Number and Algebra: Multiples, Factors and Primes	%	%
Number and Algebra: Numbers and Directed Numbers	%	%
Number and Algebra: Basic Fraction Concepts	%	%
Number and Algebra: Using Fractions	%	%
Number and Algebra: Basic Decimal Concepts	%	%
Number and Algebra: Using Decimals	%	%
Number and Algebra: Basic Percentage Concepts	%	%
Number and Algebra: Ratios	%	%
Number and Algebra: Discounts and Best Buys	%	%
Number and Algebra: Basic Algebra Concepts	%	%
Number and Algebra: Using Algebra	%	%
Number and Algebra: Simple Equations and Graphs	%	%
Measurement and Geometry: Area and Volume	%	%
Measurement and Geometry: Solids, Transformations and Symmetry	%	%
Measurement and Geometry: Angles and Lines	%	%
Measurement and Geometry: Triangles and Quadrilaterals	%	%
Statistics and Probability: Probability	%	%
Statistics and Probability: Data Representation	%	%
Statistics and Probability: Data Analysis	%	%
Statistics and Probability: Interpreting Data from Graphs	%	%
Sample Exam Papers		
Sample Exam Paper 1		%
Sample Exam Paper 2		%
Sample Exam Paper 3		%

Do you want to improve your scores in the Tests and Sample Exams? Check that:

✓ You are ready.

This is a revision workbook designed specifically for the revision of work already done. It is not a replacement for your textbook or class notes. Cover the topic in class or in your own time by reading your textbook or the *Excel Year 7 Mathematics Study Guide*, before using this book for further practice on the topic.

✓ You are revising in the right order.

Maths is a subject that builds on previous knowledge. Often you will need to have a good grasp of an early topic in order to fully understand a later topic.

✓ Your standards are realistic.

You cannot expect to score 100% all the time. Remember that this book has been designed to help you identify your strengths as well as your weaknesses, so it is OK to make mistakes. The key to success is learning from those mistakes.

✓ You are not rushing through the questions.

Many Maths students fail to read questions properly. This accounts for a large number of the mistakes made in tests and exams. Although your time is limited, you must still take enough time to read each question carefully. If necessary, read the question a second (or even third) time. Don't start your answer until you are sure that you understand the question. For the longer questions, take a moment or two to plan your answer.

✓ You are allowing yourself enough time to study.

Preparation for any test or exam requires a sufficient investment of time to be undertaken successfully. This means that you have to plan ahead. Don't wait until a week or so before an exam, for example, to ask yourself the question: How much time will I need to devote to this subject to revise it thoroughly? Don't forget to allow sufficient time for your other subjects—maths isn't the only subject you will have to sit an exam for!

✓ You are OK.

You may be having some problems unrelated to your schoolwork. It is wise to sort out such problems as quickly as possible. Speak to your teacher, a parent or your school counsellor if you think you need help.

INDEX

NOTES

NOTES